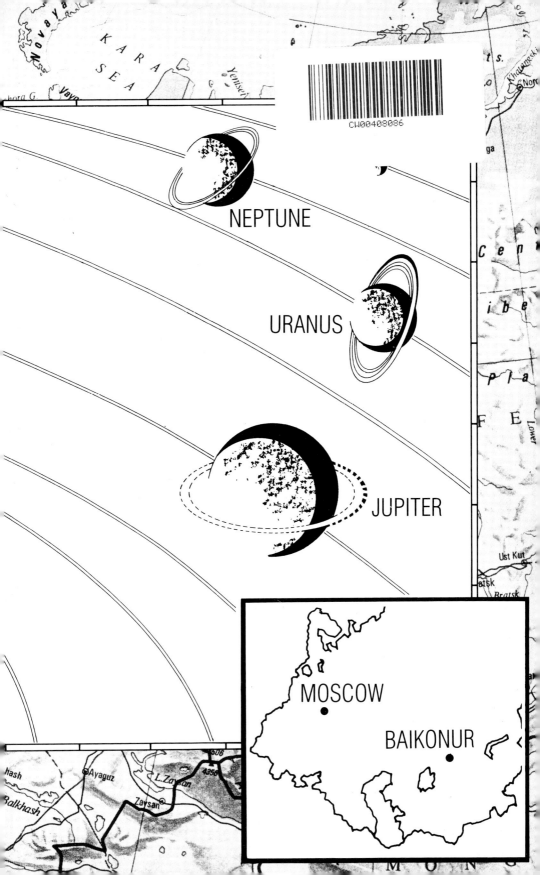

NEPTUNE

URANUS

JUPITER

MOSCOW

BAIKONUR

VALENTINA

First Woman in Space

Valentina Tereshkova meets A. Lothian following a press conference for the Women of the Year Lunch in London, October 1984

VALENTINA

First Woman in Space

CONVERSATIONS
WITH A. LOTHIAN

Karen from Tony,
July 1993

The Pentland Press
Edinburgh · Cambridge · Durham

First published in 1993 by
The Pentland Press
1 Hutton Close
South Church
Bishop Auckland
Durham

ISBN 1 85821 064 X

The author has greatly valued the excellent work of the typesetter.

Typeset by Elite Typesetting Techniques, Southampton.
Printed and bound in Great Britain by BPCC (Wheatons) Ltd.

Conversations with the cosmonaut
Valentina Tereshkova
as West meets East
during ten years which changed the world

Dedicated to new century children

THIS BOOK IS PUBLISHED ON THE OCCASION OF THE THIRTIETH ANNIVERSARY OF THE FLIGHT FROM 16TH TO 19TH JUNE 1963 OF VALENTINA TERESHKOVA, FIRST WOMAN IN SPACE

Acknowledgements

I owe an immense debt of gratitude to the following for their
assistance and advice without which this
commemorative publication could not have been completed

Barry Banfield
Carol Banfield
Ann Barr
Carole Blake
Dr Heather Couper
Karen Cunningham
Mikki Doyle
Hanno Fry
Renee Goddard
Professor Margaret Gowing
Magnus Linklater
Peter Lothian
Ian McColl
Elizabeth McLeish
Dr Davidson Nicol
Susan Raven
Daniel Russell
Professor Gordon Smith
Liz Spicer
Frances Tulloch

I also thank the translators Meg Luckins and Elizabeth Zolina

ABOVE ALL I THANK VALENTINA TERESHKOVA FOR HER
INSPIRATION AND CO-OPERATION.

Contents

Part I – Journey with a Cosmonaut

Illustrations

Introduction – Ten years which changed the world, 1983–1993. The road from misunderstanding to understanding away from nuclear war.

THE FIRST MILESTONE – *Meeting Valentina Tereshkova*

UK Women of the Year invite Valentina Tereshkova to be their international guest of honour, 1983 – Valentina Tereshkova and A. Lothian meet in London, 1984 – Valentina addresses Women of the Year Lunch, October 1984

THE SECOND MILESTONE – *The World Congress of Women*

A. Lothian, delegate to the World Congress of Women in Moscow , 1987 – At the congress Mikhail Gorbachev explains Perestroika – Valentina, a member of the Soviet delegation to Britain, 1988

THE THIRD MILESTONE – *The Millennium of the Russian Orthodox Church*

Millennium of the Russian Orthodox Church, 1988 – A. Lothian attends celebrations and ceremonies – The Church Assembly in Zagorsk – Festive concert in the Bolshoi Theatre at the invitation of Patriarch Pimen –

Pilgrimage to Vladimir and Suzdal – The Soviet Prime Minister's official reception; Gromyko answers delegates' questions – A message for Margaret Thatcher from an Orthodox Church leader

THE FOURTH MILESTONE – *In Star City*

1988, the Twenty-Fifth Anniversary of Valentina's Space Flight; Celebration in Star City, the Soviet space research centre – A. Lothian learns of Soviet achievements in cosmonautics past, present and future including plans for exploration of Mars

THE FIFTH MILESTONE – *The Russian Road to Democracy*

1990, the CSCE conference in Moscow, attended by delegates from twenty nations – The choices for Russia's new democratic voters – Guests of Valentina Tereshkova visit Moscow to study Russian art and culture, June 1990

THE SIXTH MILESTONE – *Honorary Doctorate, Edinburgh University*

Valentina's work for Disarmament honoured by an Honorary Doctorate from Edinburgh University – The Degree Ceremony, November 1990 – Valentina in Scotland – Guest of the GB-USSR Association – Visit to Abbotsford, home of Sir Walter Scott

THE SEVENTH MILESTONE – *The United Nations Alliance*

The USA and USSR become allies within the United Nations during the Gulf War, 1991 – The August Coup, Moscow 1991 – The end of the Soviet Union – Valentina works with space explorers to protect the planet – November, 1991, A. Lothian in Moscow to record twelve Conversations in which Valentina describes the most significant stages of her life story – Together they visit Yaroslavl to see Valentina's homeland – February, 1992, Conversations completed in Moscow – April, 1992, Valentina addresses the International Science Festival in Edinburgh for the United Nations Year of Space – Future plans for a conference in Moscow on Global Morality to mark the fiftieth anniversary of the founding of the United Nations

Part II – Conversations with a Cosmonaut

Prologue – 'We were sitting by the log fire'

VALENTINA SPEAKS

THE FIRST CONVERSATION – *Childhood in the Soviet Union*

THE SECOND CONVERSATION – *Youth, School and Work*

THE THIRD CONVERSATION – *Space Training and the Flight*

THE FOURTH CONVERSATION – *Meeting World Leaders as a World Heroine*

THE FIFTH CONVERSATION – *Personal Life, Interests and Friends*

THE SIXTH CONVERSATION – *Women and Work*

Illustrations

Frontispiece: Valentina Tereshkova meets A. Lothian following a press conference for the Women of the Year Lunch in London, October 1984. *Courtesy of the Press Association*

Part I: Journey with a Cosmonaut

between pages 102 and 103

A. Lothian, October 1984

Valentina Tereshkova. Lecture at the Royal Aeronautical Society, London, October 1984

Mikhail Gorbachev addresses the World Congress of Women in the Kremlin Palace of Congresses, Moscow, June 1987. A. Lothian third left, middle row

World Congress of Women, June 1987. A Lothian and Mikki Doyle, Women's Editor of the *Morning Star*, in Red Square

Russian icon of the Mother of God. Millennium of the Russian Orthodox Church, 1988

Star City, Moscow, June 1988. Group standing on steps of Mir space station includes Valentina Tereshkova, A. Lothian and Elizabeth Zolina

A. Lothian and Valentina Tereshkova with the space capsule, Vostok 6, Star City, on June 16th 1988 to celebrate the 25th anniversary of her spaceflight

Star City, June 1990. Left to right: Peter Lothian, A. Lothian, Dr Alyona Tereshkova and cosmonaut Alexei Leonov, Hero of the Soviet Union, the first man to walk in space

Floella Benjamin with dancers in national costume in the House of Friendship, Moscow, June 1990

Sir Fitzroy Maclean at the Eternal Flame on the Tomb of the Unknown Soldier, Moscow, June 1990

At the confererral of the honorary doctorate of Edinburgh University. The principal of Edinburgh University, Sir David Smith, centre, with honorary graduates, November 1990. Left to right: Neal Ascherson, William Brown, Valentina Tereshkova, Professor Heikki Raisanen *Courtesy of the Scotsman*

Valentina Tereshkova is welcomed to Abbotsford, the home of Sir Walter Scott, by his descendants Dame Jean and Mrs Patricia Maxwell-Scott, November 1990

The Space museum at Nikulskoye, near Yarolsavl. A replica of the house where Valentina was born

Valentina with her mother

Spacesuits worn by Soviet cosmonauts during the 1960s

Rocket launch from Baikonur cosmodrome during the 1960s *Courtesy of Novosti Press*

Vostok capsule of the 1960s, charred by re-entry *Courtesy of Novosti Press*

Part II: Conversations with a Cosmonaut

between pages 248 and 249

Early years, training and flight

Valentina's father, Vladimir Tereshkov

Valentina with her mother in Yaroslavl, summer 1963

Valentina's mother, Elena Tereshkova

Valentina's grandparents' house in Maslennikovo, near Yaroslavl

Class group, Yaroslavl 1950. Valentina third row, third from right

Airclub near Yaroslavl, August 1959. Valentina before her 22nd parachute jump

Valentina in the uniform of junior lieutenant, her first military rank, 1962

The four women trainee cosmonauts, 1962. Left to right: Tatyana Kuznetsova, Irina Solovyova, Valentina and Valentina Ponomaryova

Valentina with Yuri Gagarin, the first man in space, in 1962

Valentina undergoes a medical test during the training programme, 1962

Yuri Gagarin with Sergei Korolev, the Chief Designer

'Cosmic food' in the training capsule, 1963

Valentina at the Space Training Centre, 1962

The morning of the 16th June 1963. Valentina is helped into her spacesuit by specialists

Baikonur cosmodrome, Kazakhstan. Final farewell before Valentina enters Vostok 6

19th June 1963, just after landing in the Altai region. Valentina waits for the rescue plane

20th June 1963, after the space flight Valentina leaves for medical tests in Kuibishev

22nd June 1963, Moscow. Valentina with Nikita Khrushchev and Valery Bikovsky, pilot of Vostok 5, on the podium of the Mausoleum, Red Square

Valentina attends the World Congress of Women in the Kremlin, Moscow, June 1963. Nina Khrushchev far right

between pages 258 and 259

Meeting the World

Civic reception in Yaroslavl, 1963. 'A sea of flowers'. Valentina's mother sits on her right

Home to the Volga, 1963

Valentina with the president of the National Academy of Sciences, Mstislav Keldish, watched by Valery Bikovsky, Yuri Gagarin and other cosmonauts, 1963

Valentina with Yuri Gagarin in New York, 1963

Valentina with Fidel Castro and Wilma Espin, Havana, 1963

Valentina with Che Guevara, 1963

Valentina with the Indian Prime Minister, Jawaharial Nehru and his daughter, Indira Gandhi, 1963

Yugoslavia, 1973. Valentina with President Tito

Moscow, 1973. Valentina with Bussi de Allende, wife of the President of Chile

Star City, 1975. Valentina with Soviet pilots including Ivan Kodzhedub, three times Hero of the Soviet Union

New York, June 1982. At the United Nations headquarters with the Secretary-General, Perez de Cuellar

Star City, 1985. Valentina with the Indian Prime Minister, Indira Gandhi and her son Rajiv Gandhi

Washington, 1987. Valentina with the American astronaut Mary Cleave Courtesy of Marty Lamar

Valentina with the American congressman Jesse Jackson, 1988

Valentina with the American astronaut, Congressman John Glenn, 1989

Valentina attends the Congress of Peoples' Deputies, in the Kremlin, Moscow with fellow deputy, Metropolitan Pitirim, 1989

Baikonur cosmodrome, April 1991. Valentina with the French cosmonaut Patrick Baudry on the 30th anniversary of Yuri Gagarin's space flight

between pages 278 and 279

Valentina with friends

Valentina with the sculptor Grigory Postnikov preparing her statue for the Avenue of Heroes, Moscow 1963

Kirghizia, 1979. Valentina riding an Akhaltekhin horse

Valentina with a two-day-old pony watched by Yuri Gagarin's daughters, Lena and Galya, 1979

Addis Ababa, 1981. Valentina with the Ethiopian painter, Efevork

Moscow, 1986. Valentina with Samantha Smith, the young American girl who wrote to the Kremlin and was invited to Moscow. She died in a plane crash one year later

Valentina with the Russian actor, Alexei Batalov

Valentina with her pug Peppi, 1981

Valentina and her daughter, Dr Alyona Tereshkova, with a model of the space capsule Vostok 6, Moscow, 1991 Courtesy of The Sunday Times

La Scala, Milan, 1992. Valentina with Luciano Pavarotti

between pages 316 and 317

Valentina at work

Valentina delivers a speech at the United Nations conference on Disarmament, 1982

Valentina attends the United Nations conference for the UN Decade for Women, Nairobi, 1985

Valentina reports on the Halley's Comet project and the Soviet space programme, Leningrad, 1986

Tbilisi, 1988. Valentina addresses the Soviet–American conference

Moscow, January 1990. Valentina opens the Helsinki Commission conference on 'The Human Dimension of the European Process and the Role of the Public'

Valentina at the United Nations speaking on the new international order, 1991

Berlin, 1991. The Association of Space Explorers at the 7th Planetary Congress. Valentina front row, fifth from right *Courtesy of A.S.G.*

Berlin, 1991. The Space Explorers Congress. Valentina discusses the Mars programme *Courtesy of A.S.E.*

GRATEFUL ACKNOWLEDGEMENT IS DUE TO VALENTINA TERESHKOVA FOR PERMISSION TO USE PHOTOGRAPHS FROM HER PERSONAL ARCHIVES

Valentina Tereshkova

Valentina Tereshkova was born in 1937 in Maslennikovo, near Yaroslavl on the river Volga. Her father was killed in 1940 during the Soviet-Finnish War, leaving her mother to bring up three children, Ludmila, Valentina and Vladimir. In 1945 the family moved from the countryside to the city of Yaroslavl where Valentina went to school.

She left school at 16 and worked first at a tyre factory and then at a textile factory, 'Red Perekop'. During these years Valentina attended evening classes to obtain a diploma from the Textile Technical Institute. In 1958 she joined a local airclub and achieved 163 parachute jumps. After Yuri Gagarin's successful flight in space in 1961 she applied to join the Soviet space programme and was chosen as one of the first group of women to be trained as cosmonauts.

On 16th June 1963 a powerful rocket boosted the capsule Vostok 6 into space and Valentina piloted its 48 orbits around the Earth. She landed safely on June 19th, the first and only woman ever to accomplish a solo flight in space. This achievement earned her the title of Pilot-Astronaut of the USSR and Hero of the Soviet Union. She then travelled extensively at the invitation of world leaders visiting numerous countries including India, Cuba, Italy, America, Yugoslavia, Chile and Sweden. In 1969 after an academic course at the Zhukovsky Air Force Engineering Academy she graduated with a degree in technical sciences. After post graduate work there Valentina received a doctorate in engineering.

From 1968 to 1987 she worked as Chairman of the Soviet Women's Committee and was a member of the Central Committee of the Communist Party. In 1987 she was appointed Chairman of the Union of Soviet Friendship Societies, an organisation which promoted international cultural understanding. She attended meetings at the United Nations. Valentina continues to work for cosmonautics in Star City, the Cosmonaut Training Centre near Moscow.

Valentina is presently the Vice-Chairman of the Russian Agency for International Co-operation and Development.

She has one daughter, Dr. Alyona Tereshkova, an orthopaedic surgeon.

'Mankind will not remain tied to the Earth forever'

Konstantin Tsiolkovsky

PART I

Journey with a Cosmonaut

Introduction

On June 16th 1963, for the first time ever, a woman sang in space. The singer was Valentina Tereshkova, a twenty-six-year-old Soviet cosmonaut and former textile worker, and the song was about her homeland, Mother Russia. Valentina had left the planet human beings inhabit, with all its divisive frontiers, to become the first woman and fifth cosmonaut after Yuri Gagarin to pioneer a new order of living in the unexplored dimensions of the universe. For three days she orbited the Earth in a small, cramped capsule in conditions of extreme unpredictability, discomfort and danger, and then returned through the intense heat of re-entry to a hero's welcome from the whole world. She remains to this day the only woman to accomplish a solo flight in space for three days, a pioneer achievement which transformed her into an immortal who had earned everlasting fame.

The purpose of this commemorative chronicle is to celebrate with Valentina Tereshkova the thirtieth anniversary of her flight as she describes it and also to tell her life story for the first time.

But to understand why I was chosen to be the author, I must ask the reader to come with me on a journey which tells another story, about the force of friendship and how it can dispel harmful ignorance. It is the story of how two women met, one from the East, one from the West, and how both, being fearful that the antagonism between seemingly irreconcilable superpowers might lead to atomic war, tried together to build a bridge of genuine personal understanding and so prove that dangerous international ignorance and prejudice could be overcome. It is the story of how, during ten dramatic years for world survival, Valentina as a scientist and cosmonaut from Moscow, and myself as a journalist and wife of a government minister from London, came to trust each other and so work together for peace.

Friends who knew us both called ours a 'destined friendship' because it mirrored not only how, both from East and West, humanity travelled from the danger and darkness of the cold war to new 'rebuilding' hopes of perestroika and peace, but also how trust between individuals can break the international barriers which cause war. The people of the world hoped for this, and the hope was confirmed when, with the end of the cold war, America and Russia became allies within the United Nations.

For me, telling the story of a shared journey during this historic time as I saw it from the West has been both exciting and exacting.

Because of Valentina I was able to visit Russia, with the opportunity to record historic events first hand as I pursued my objective, which was to find out whether atomic war was inevitable. I saw important facts concerning the transition from war to peace which might otherwise have remained undisclosed. Then later, when Valentina broke the silence she had maintained since her flight by asking me to become her biographer, this gave me the opportunity to make known the experiences and views not only of a space pioneer but also of a remarkable thinker. It has been a challenge to try and describe an unprecedented decade in human history as I experienced it, and also to tell the story of an unprecedented human achiever as I heard her speak.

If readers are to share in this journey from the beginning, it seems necessary to remember world events in the years before 1984, when Valentina and I met for the first time. What had been the history of the second half of the twentieth century, now drawing near to its end?

The world Valentina returned to from space in 1963 was confused by conflicting developments. De Gaulle opposed the UK's entry into the Common Market. The Profumo affair shocked Britain and Kim Philby defected to the Soviet Union. Pope John XXIII died. President Kennedy supported Western Germany, declaring: '*Ich bin ein Berliner.*' The Sino-Soviet split became known. The nuclear test ban treaty was signed in the Kremlin. Martin Luther King's 'I have a dream' crusade swept the USA. A direct communication line was set up between Moscow and Washington to prevent another near-disaster like the Cuban missile crisis of 1962. Alec Douglas-Home became Britain's new Prime Minister, replacing Harold Macmillan. Beatlemania gripped world youth and Valentina's contemporary Rudolf Nureyev mesmerised ballet lovers in London. In November, President Kennedy was assassinated in Dallas.

The news of Valentina's flight was different. It inspired human unity. A woman had pointed upwards to show humankind an exciting new dimension to live in. From space she had seen the Earth as small, fragile, in danger of destruction; and had returned determined to do all in her power not only to encourage space research but also to work for global awareness of an endangered planet. She was the right person to attempt both objectives. In a world separated by divisions, looking up into the sky all human beings had felt suddenly united by one woman's achievement. That is why world leaders competed to meet Valentina.

But superpower rivalry continued, and developed into consistent hostility. The vision of a woman in space faded and the people of the West sank back into knowing nothing and believing nothing good about the Soviet Union, described to them as an evil empire from which they were separated by an Iron Curtain. The citizens of the Soviet East, told that the West was a cauldron of capitalist corruption, returned to feeling minimally secure within an empire which still retained much of the central control established by Stalin.

Stalin had been the hero of the free world. His wartime leadership had inspired the Russian people's heroic resistance to Hitler, a struggle which left twenty million Russians dead and twenty-five million homeless. The Nazis reached the gates of Moscow but were then driven back. The Battle of Stalingrad in January 1943, when nearly 100,000 German soldiers surrendered, was the turning point for the Western Allies' victory. But the alliance did not long outlast the war. In a renewed climate of suspicion, by 1949 fear of Stalin's expansionist ambitions led the Allies to contemplate the invasion of Russia. This did not happen, but the possibility increased Russia's long-held conviction that she was surrounded by aggressive enemies. The cold war had begun.

In 1956, Khrushchev, who had succeeded Stalin after his death, exposed Stalin's holocausts at the twentieth Congress of the Communist Party. Revision of Stalinist policies began, and his body was removed from its place beside Lenin in the Red Square Mausoleum. It looked as if, for the USSR, there was the prospect of a more prosperous and peaceful era.

However East-West relations remained strained and the arms race intensified. It had begun in 1945 when the USA exploded the first atomic bomb, followed by Russia's rival bomb in 1949. In the fifties both sides stockpiled atomic bombs and ballistic missiles capable of killing 900 million human beings. The international confrontation had extended to the Far East, where the United Nations supported South Korea in its conflict with China.

Then there was a respite. Eisenhower and Khrushchev agreed to aim for peaceful coexistence, and Russia ended its occupation of Austria. However, in 1956 the uprising in Hungary which the USSR suppressed and Britain's occupation of

Egypt to guard the Suez Canal swung the world back again towards war. The East Germans built the Berlin Wall, a symbol of the seemingly-permanent division between East and West. The world poets of the sixties, folk singers such as Baez and Dylan, seemed to be the only articulate mourners for environmental doom.

The cold war continued and US determination to drive Communism from Cuba led to the 1962 missile crisis. Matters came to a head with Soviet arms aid for Castro, and American reaction to Castro's Russian missile bases brought the world to within minutes of nuclear war. It is now known that, had Kennedy not responded positively to Khrushchev's last-minute appeal, a missile rocket would have been launched on the United States from Russia itself only an hour later. The crisis shocked both sides. Kennedy reminded the world that 'we all inhabit one small planet', and in 1963 the USSR and the Western Allies signed the Test Ban Treaty.

The development of rocket power had been central to the crisis. For the first half of the century, advances in this field had alternated between offering positive prospects for peace and horrendous possibilities for war. The first liquid propelling machines were developed by a nineteenth-century Russian teacher, Konstantin Tsiolkovsky, working in a small laboratory near his school in Kaluga. He dreamt of providing humanity with a vast new ocean of space in which to create environmental harmony and from which man could obtain all that was lacking on Earth. He was the father of rocket power, and his dreams were finally fulfilled many years after his death when in 1957 *Sputnik 1*, the first artificial satellite, was launched into space. Before that, however, his ideas had been adapted for the Nazis by Wernher von Braun and used to bomb London in World War II.

After the war, Tsiolkovsky's vision was taken up by Sergei Korolev, the Russian space expert and Chief Designer of the Soviet space programme whose triumph of *Sputnik* in orbit was followed by the first ever manned space flight by Yuri Gagarin in April 1961. The American reaction was panic – for the first time since Pearl Harbour the USA was vulnerable to direct attack, this time from space. A space race for military objectives ensued and seemed unstoppable until Neil Armstrong's moonwalk in 1969 proved that the Americans had established parity. Valentina's space flight happened in a year when cautious progress for peace was developing and Khrushchev's leadership was bringing many advances in Russia, notably in the consumer and housing industries as well as in the prestigious space programme. But then Khrushchev's other policies failed and he resigned in 1964, dying in a modest Moscow flat in 1971. The more conservative and less unpredictable Brezhnev succeeded him as the new Soviet leader.

Under the new regime, East-West misunderstanding closed in again. In 1973 the Arab-Israeli war led President Nixon to put US forces on full nuclear alert. A period of *détente*, which had begun in the late 1960s with Brandt's '*Ostpolitik*' and which had spread to the United States, followed. In 1972 Nixon travelled to Moscow to sign the SALT I agreement. But the arms race continued as a balance of terror with both sides amassing sufficient force of arms to assure them of instant victory before being wiped out by an equally devastating force. The likely victims of this interplay of hostility were hardly aware of the dangers. Average men and women in both East and West knew little of each other or of the actions of their leaders, who were convinced that the possibility of mutual destruction was justified if it protected the systems they served.

All this time, where was Valentina Tereshkova? What had become of her vision of humanity acting together to defend a vulnerable planet? She had remained convinced that space exploration must serve peace, not war, and that it could bring unprecedented benefits for humanity. But world leaders were needed who could persuade governments to promote peace in space. There was no sign of this in the eighties, while military scientists devised increasingly lethal weapons.

In 1963 Valentina had been a symbol of human unity and achievement. In the years that followed, however, she became

8

a legend hidden in silence. She worked on in the Soviet Centre
for Cosmonautics in Star City, she spoke for women's rights as
a member of the Central Committee of the Communist Party,
she visited countries throughout the world to promote inter-
cultural understanding as Chairman of the Soviet Friendship
Societies and she spoke on disarmament at the United Nations.
She also shared in the gradual movement of the Soviet people
towards social and spiritual freedom. But she refused to speak
about herself or her personal experiences. She saw herself as a
scientist, serving the Soviet Air Force so as to advance space
research. She loved her homeland, her family and her friends.
Self-promotion was totally alien to her character. Nevertheless,
she did not forget the planet which, from space, she had seen as
so urgently in need of protection and she continued to work
with cosmonauts and astronauts of all nations to establish ecological safeguards.

Then in 1987 there was a new Russian revolution. The
resolve of the Soviet people to find freedom found a spokesman
when Mikhail Gorbachev lit up the entire world with the
Russian vision of glasnost, a new openness to end dangerous
international and internal ignorance. This was followed by
perestroika, the 'rebuilding' to reform the Soviet Communist
system. These revolutionary aims were combined with proposals for definite disarmament. By the time of the Gulf War of
1991, the US and USSR were allies within the United Nations,
opposing Saddam Hussein's annexation of Kuwait. The last
decade of the century seemed to offer humanity the opportunity to unite and overcome increasing ecological dangers.

It was at this time, approaching the thirtieth anniversary of her
flight, that Valentina Tereshkova decided to break her silence by
telling the story of her life, speaking to me as an author she
knew and trusted. I felt very privileged. In the new century
ahead, if the planet were to be saved humanity must answer the
question: 'Peace – or perish?' Valentina was ready to contribute
her exceptional experience, and to suggest solutions. But why
did she choose to speak to me, a woman from the West?

To answer this, I have to introduce myself. Fifteen years older than Valentina, I had been one of the many who looked up at the sky in 1963 and felt proud that a woman was flying solo in space. I too then lived through the years of superpower hostility, fearing a final atomic conflict whilst knowing next to nothing about the other side of the Iron Curtain. During the Second World War I had worked as a nursing auxiliary. As the war ended I married, aged twenty. We had six children. My husband Peter, a member of the House of Lords, was appointed to various posts and served as a delegate to the UN, the Disarmament Conference, the European Parliament and as Under-Secretary at the Foreign Office.

After the war I began my career as a journalist. From 1960 to 1970 I worked as a current affairs correspondent for the *Scottish Daily Express*, and also as a freelance presenter and deviser for television and radio. In 1955 I founded the Women of the Year Lunches, to enable professional women from the widest possible cross-section to meet annually in London.

My involvement in public service included work for the Royal College of Nursing, the Royal College of Gynaecologists, and as patron of the UK National Council of Women. In 1989 I was elected a Fellow of the Chartered Institute of Journalists.

As a journalist I had met and interviewed many women of exceptional endurance, among them Coretta King, Mother Teresa, Indira Gandhi, Jehan Sadat, Odette Hallowes, Mary Barnes, author of *Journey into Madness*, an account of mental breakdown, and Sheila Scott, the first person ever to fly solo over the North Pole in a light aircraft.

My experiences with Sheila served as a useful preparation for interviewing Valentina, since the co-operation of both pioneers was difficult to capture. In the seventies I had devised a television series called *The Champions* and Sheila had agreed to be the first person interviewed for it; an important interview for me since it might persuade a television company to run the series. But travelling with me in a train to Manchester she was overcome by panic and announced that she was about to pull the emergency cord, stop the train and return to London.

I begged her to stay. 'If the series succeeds it will be a great break for us.' Sheila replied, 'If you think you can interview champions without finding them difficult, you will have to think again.'

However, having agreed to stay with me, on television she was cool, professional and inspiring. It was the same with Valentina. Her way of avoiding publicity was usually to say that she was somewhere else: 'going to China' or 'flying to Helsinki', when in fact she was safe in Star City, outside Moscow, protected from unwelcome intrusion. But when on duty she was always brilliant. Among the champions I had met she seemed to be the greatest, perhaps also because she turned my prejudices upside down.

During nearly all my life I had accepted the Western assumption that the USSR was intent on world domination and that this must be prevented because Communism would destroy freedom. Like so many others in the West I did not even believe in the existence of peace-seeking people in Russia, but in 1984 my ignorance was challenged when I met Valentina Tereshkova. From our first meeting mutual trust developed, despite the fact that we lived at the centre of two opposing power bases. During the subsequent years which turned the tide from the possibility of war to peace, she and I remained in regular contact and we were together at the time of many dramatic political developments.

I have called my account of our shared experiences *Journey with a Cosmonaut*. It is the chronicle of a meeting between East and West and how misunderstanding was transformed into understanding during ten years which changed the world.

But for me a major obstacle to telling the truth about our experiences was that, even after perestroika, there was still intense suspicion of Soviet motives in the West, and those reporting favourably on conditions in Russia were routinely told that they had been taken in by Communist propaganda. Obviously there was a need for caution on both sides, and facts had to be proved by pedantic provision of evidence. This is hardly the best recipe for a readable story, but I hope readers will understand that I have done my poor best.

When in 1991 Valentina asked me to be her biographer we discussed the possibilities and agreed that we could begin with interviews which divided her life into twelve important stages. This would provide a preliminary introduction to Valentina's life to mark the thirtieth anniversary of her space flight. A more comprehensive biography could follow later. We would call the interviews *Conversations*.

The interviews took place in the Friendship House dacha, outside Moscow, seven years after our first meeting. This was like reaching the end of a long walk through a vast building where we had met in action-filled rooms, and finally finding a small quiet refuge where Valentina and I could at last talk openly and at length about her life and her hopes and fears for the future.

In the *Conversations* Valentina describes her pioneer flight for the first time, and she speaks frankly about herself. She gives her views from the East and describes the post-Stalin Soviet Union which few in the West knew about, including the facts behind the Soviet space triumphs and the first involvement of women in the space programme. She also discusses the factors which led the Soviet people to perestroika. She describes the major events of her life. She identifies problems for the future, including the possibility of planetary catastrophe. She outlines her vision to use science well and the plans for landing on Mars in which she is currently involved. She speaks both from her experience as an international leader and from her super-terrestrial point of view. She explains how what she saw from space continues to inspire her to work with others to protect the planet and she sets out a plan for peace which could establish ecological harmony and make armed hostility obsolete. The *Conversations* are not only a first account of her life by Valentina, they are also a mirror for the hopes and anxieties of humanity confronting the challenges of the new century, when human survival will depend on world co-operation, particularly between East and West.

Understandably, until she spoke in this way, our previous exchanges had been mainly one-sided. When I spoke from the West I was independent and free of official constraints, although married to a British government minister. My impressions had been seen from a personal point of view and I recorded these for Valentina to consider so that she could either agree or disagree with my conclusions.

It was different for Valentina speaking from the East. Her situation was parallel, say, to that of Neil Armstrong, the first man on the moon, when he was serving as a member of his nation's space service and was unable to give political opinions without official permission. It was therefore a major breakthrough when Valentina, the pioneer Soviet woman cosmonaut, did speak when she felt it was right to do so.

For all these reasons I hope that my record of the events we were involved in during the ten years now described as having changed the world, will provide a piece of history which might otherwise not have been included in the jigsaw puzzle of developments at the end of the twentieth century which postponed planetary disaster.

But how did it all begin and then what happened?

The First Milestone

Meeting Valentina Tereshkova

Valentina and I met in 1984 in London because she had agreed to be the International Guest of Honour at a charity function, the Women of the Year Lunch, attended by leading professional women in aid of the Greater London Fund for the Blind.

With the George Cross war heroine Odette Hallowes and a distinguished magazine editor, Georgina Coleridge, I had founded this event for British women in 1955. The main aim was to highlight the value of women's work, at a time when equal opportunities for equal skills seemed far from being attainable. Women meeting in this way would bring together all categories of national influence with no barriers of colour or political creed. Five hundred guests attend each year under the banner: 'Every invitation a merit award' and guest speakers are chosen because of an outstanding achievement. Each year an International Guest of Honour, a woman of acknowledged world merit, is invited; for example Sally Mugabe, Petra Kelly, Jehan Sadat, and Coretta King.

In 1983, to prepare for the following year, the organizing committee nominated Valentina Tereshkova. The obvious reason for this choice was that she had been the first woman to fly in space. Two other reasons were less obvious. One was that some of us were worried by the continuing rift in the world of sport after British athletes were asked to boycott the 1980 Moscow Olympic Games following the Russian invasion of Afghanistan. At a time when world leaders were telling us that the only way to safeguard global peace was to threaten global war, we hoped that the presence of a leading Soviet woman supporting an occasion on behalf of Britain's disabled would prove that there could be friendship across frontiers.

Secondly, those of us who had been present would never forget the speeches made by two eminent women experts in science and ecology at the Women of the Year Lunch in 1980. It had been a quarter-century celebration with the theme: 'Twenty-five years back – twenty-five years on.' Margaret Gowing, Professor of the History of Science at Oxford University, spoke of a future in which a possible atomic holocaust would leave planet Earth desolate. She blamed the 'terrifying' arms race which increased the 'inventive fever' of scientists and resulted in a lethal build-up of atomic missiles and chemical and biological weapons. She quoted Churchill's verdict that 'survival has become the twin brother of annihilation.' Barbara Ward – Baroness Jackson – President of the Institute of the Environment and known throughout the world as a leading economist and environmentalist, also spoke. She ended her appeal for humanity to unite and save 'Spaceship Earth' with the words: 'We either love or die.'

I knew something of the background to these fears. In the early seventies, when my husband was UK Under-Secretary for Disarmament, I had sat with our student daughter in the conference hall in Geneva, and I remembered how helpless and fearful our reaction had been to the long official reports on how the superpowers were amassing atomic bombs, it seemed to us, like golf balls. The Big Bang could happen and indeed it was difficult to see how it could be prevented.

Thus, in 1984 the first woman in space was not only an outstanding choice because she was one of the most remarkable women in the world, but also her views would be particularly interesting to those who were anxious about planetary survival. As seen from the West, two of the most respected scientific and environmental experts had estimated that the end of the planet could be imminent. Would Valentina's view from space confirm this? Was the East equally apprehensive?

We waited for her reply to our invitation. We did not know if she would attend a charity occasion. But two people were working on our behalf: the first, Diana Makgill, Vice-Chairman of the Women of the Year and Chief of Ceremonial at the Foreign Office; the second, Yuri Mazur, Cultural Attaché at the Soviet Embassy, who had told us that Valentina was coming to London to address the Royal Aeronautical Society at about the same time. Together they used their powers of persuasion on the Soviet Ambassador in London, Mr Popov. When I met him five years later in Moscow he still remembered how they had encouraged him to advise Valentina to accept.

Some of us have short memories and may want to recall what else was happening in 1984.

It was a year of crisis for relations between Russia and the West. Soviet athletes boycotted the Los Angeles Olympics in retaliation for the US boycott of the Moscow games four years earlier. It was the year Orwell had predicted would see world domination by an extreme form of Communism. In the USSR Yuri Andropov died, and after the elderly Chernenko's brief interregnum, Mikhail Gorbachev became General Secretary of the Soviet Communist Party. In Britain miners were on strike in protest against pit closures. An IRA bomb blasted the Grand Hotel in Brighton during the Conservative Party Conference and Margaret Thatcher narrowly missed being killed. Gorbachev and his wife Raisa visited Britain on a fact-finding tour. Richard Burton died. Bob Geldof launched BAND AID so that rock and pop musicians could raise money for famine relief in Ethiopia, and this inspired worldwide action and

17

co-operation. In the USSR the Russian physicist and Nobel prizewinner Andrei Sakharov went on hunger strike to demand reform, and Stalin's daughter Svetlana returned to Moscow from America. In India, government troops stormed the Sikh Golden Temple, and three months later Indira Gandhi was assassinated by her Sikh bodyguard. She was succeeded as Prime Minister by her son Rajiv. At Bhopal, a chemical leak due to industrial negligence killed two thousand and blinded many thousands more. In the USA, Geraldine Ferraro became the first woman to be chosen as a Vice-Presidential candidate, and Ronald Reagan was re-elected President. The US space shuttle *Discovery* was launched successfully. Bishop Desmond Tutu was awarded the Nobel Peace Prize. In China, free enterprise policies became part of economic reform. Also in 1984, the chairman of the Lunch Committee, Ann Dickinson, was advised by the Russian Embassy in London that Valentina Tereshkova had accepted the invitation to attend the Women of the Year Lunch.

As I was President for the occasion, the next step was for me to call on Yuri Mazur and make the necessary arrangements. The organizer of the event, Joanna Forrester, drove me in her car. I rang the bell of the front door where, having joined a protest rally in 1980, I had held up a sandwich board calling for Sakharov's release.

We noted that, unlike the US Embassy, there were no gun-on-hip guards, just a television camera above the door. The gate opened when we leant on it and we walked in up the steps of a dull-looking brick residence in the private road in Kensington, known as Millionaires' Row. There was a small lawn and a few bushes for a front garden. Inside the entrance hall a lugubrious attendant, who in subsequent calls grew ever more gloomy, not unlike a music hall comedian, took our names and notified Mr Mazur.

In the car Joanna Forrester and I had discussed how to combine persuasion and caution. We both felt apprehensive and in fear of the prevalent reputation of the KGB. It was reassuring when Yuri Mazur helpfully came out to welcome us.

He took us past a large portrait of Lenin to talk in the official sitting room, furnished like a Victorian hotel. I glanced up, I hoped with diplomatic restraint, at the small television camera overhead. Coffee and biscuits were brought in. It felt like a long way from KGB dragons – more like the Mayor's parlour in a Midland town. I had to keep remembering the reports on dissidents in psychiatric hospitals and the war in Afghanistan, although I had reminded Joanna that the latter should be seen in proportion to similar land grabs in South America, Lebanon and Cambodia, which the West condoned.

The meeting was formal. We discussed timetables and the press conference, and we left a letter for Valentina Tereshkova explaining that our chosen theme for the speakers was 'How to be first'. As international guest of honour she would be speaking with the first woman Lord Mayor of London, Dame Mary Donaldson; Brenda Dean, first woman General Secretary of the trade union SOGAT; and Antonia Fraser, the historian who had charted the course of many women 'firsts' including that of Mary the first Queen of Scotland, who had her head cut off. The Duchess of Kent was to attend as Royal guest of honour. We hoped Valentina would describe what it had been like to be first in space. We emphasized that because the occasion was for charity there must be no reference to politics or to religion.

Our proposals were accepted with courtesy. Our next meeting was to be in three months' time at a press conference at the Savoy, and Yuri asked us to attend a reception for Valentina at the USSR Embassy the same evening. The fund-raising function would be held on the following day.

Joanna and I were silent driving home. Leaving the Embassy I had picked up a copy of *Soviet Weekly*. In it I read a speech by Gorbachev calling for improved family standards. Half to be funny I said, 'It could be a speech from the Mothers' Union.'

Joanna did not comment, but we both now suspected that there was a lot of prejudice on both sides to be overcome. Since Hitler's time there had been only one major enemy to be opposed, and it had never occurred to me that there was any other option. If the Free World was to survive, Russia must be defeated, because otherwise Communism would obliterate freedom. To change this conviction was like changing character. To trust the Russians seemed to be out of the question; some Christians even believed that Khrushchev could be the Antichrist.

Now unexpectedly I felt that such prejudices needed a jolt. If individuals could contribute anything towards avoiding atomic war, East and West both needed to arrive at understanding based on accurate information and not on ignorance. I felt very ignorant. Puzzled, I was now seeking the truth on uncharted seas. My only reassurance was my journalist's training that facts can be established by observation. I must wait to see what Valentina was like.

This was my outlook before the first meeting with Valentina, at the press conference which was to publicize the Lunch at the Savoy. There had been so much interest in Valentina's speech that it had been decided, provided she agreed, to arrange for media representatives to meet her the day before. I was in the chair and there was a large attendance of journalists, including an American woman reporter I knew well. Valentina sat on my right. She looked like the pictures I had seen of her: she was dignified, self contained, and wearing a blue and white check suit. She said afterwards, 'made in Moscow – very well made isn't it?' My American friend led with the first question, an aggressive criticism of the Russian invasion of Afghanistan. This was translated to Valentina by her interpreter, Elizabeth Zolina, with an astonishing command of English.

Valentina's reaction was not unexpected; she obviously resented divisive politics being brought into her support for a British charity. But others took up the question of Afghanistan. With Elizabeth translating I stood up to intervene. I reminded my press colleagues that if they continued to ask political questions about Afghanistan, I, as Chairman, would have to give Madame Tereshkova an opportunity to counter these with questions on US actions in Vietnam, and that this would destroy the purpose of her attendance as a guest of honour in aid of our charity, which was grateful to her for proving that one of Russia's greatest women wanted to help the disabled British blind.

To my relief, the threat of discussing Vietnam silenced the American contingent. But after the conference my American friend said: 'I never knew you were so pro-Russian.'

Was I? I had thought I was on the side of justice. Valentina, who had seemed distant, even suspicious, at first meeting me had given me a long look from the platform. As we went outside for photographs she took my arm. Sisterhood among women had not happened with my American friend, but it had happened between Valentina, Elizabeth and me.

The same evening I went to the reception for Valentina at the Soviet Embassy. I felt nervous, as I was on my own and the only faces I knew by sight were famous politicians. By a side wall I saw a table where Russian women who were obviously Embassy wives were sitting. With experience of many similar diplomatic gatherings it was not difficult for me to recognize the Embassy wives: kind, patient faces and not involved in active diplomacy, which they left to their husbands. To their dismay, the strange apparition with the black eye patch sat down beside them. I asked if they were from the Embassy. Yes. I said I had six children, did they have families? That made genuine contact, and I was told about family worries like measles in Moscow and grandmothers who had telephoned: 'It is either me or Alexis, he is too difficult to live with. I am too old. Take him away.' Then one of the wives asked me if I had heard Ronald Reagan say on television that Russia must be bombed back into the Stone Age. I said I had, and that it was meant as a joke. My questioner did not believe this excuse; she had become white with anxiety.

Valentina was at the other end of the room surrounded by VIPs. To my surprise she saw me in the corner and came over with Elizabeth to sit beside me. The Embassy wives vanished like morning mist. Valentina said: 'You were very fair this morning. I was grateful to you.' I replied that if anyone was grateful it must be me, on behalf of the charity. She seemed to want to talk and we did, with Elizabeth translating at surprising speed.

I told Valentina that the theme for speakers was 'How to be first'. I asked her about what she would like to say as I had been told that Soviet speeches nearly always included political propaganda. Valentina said she might refer to Soviet difficulties in promoting peace because of American policies. Feeling I had little to lose I said that this was too political and that I hoped she would speak on what being 'first' had meant to her when she had seen the Earth from space. She described how beautiful the planet had looked, how fragile, how easily it might be destroyed by atomic flames. I begged her to convey this vision in her speech.

To the surprise of the other guests at the reception, Valentina continued to talk to me on a wide range of subjects. I said I believed in God and that perhaps His protection would save the planet. She answered that she was not a believer, but she hoped I was right. Elizabeth asked me if I had met Mrs Thatcher, whom Valentina and she greatly admired. I said, 'Do you know anything about Florence Nightingale?' Elizabeth said she did, and I said I thought that the two women with their genius for administration were very similar and that I made the comparison because I had tried to write a life of Florence Nightingale. I told Valentina about my family and she told me about her daughter Alyona, who was training to be an orthopaedic surgeon. Then she left, to address the Royal Aeronautical Society.

It had been alchemy. Perhaps it was due to my defence at the press conference, but I felt we both trusted each other completely. Certainly we were able to talk easily, as though we had known each other for a long time.

The next day the Women of the Year Lunch was everything I had hoped for and looking back I realize how both East and West met with a warmth of mutual understanding neither side had anticipated.

The Top Table guests of honour included the singer Joan Armatrading; government minister Lynda Chalker; Professor

Margaret Gowing, a previous speaker in 1980; nutritionist Prue Leith; Labour MP Oonagh McDonald; *Vogue* magazine editor Beatrix Miller; Joan Ruddock, the campaigner for nuclear disarmament; Olympic javelin champion Tessa Sanderson; dress designer Caroline Charles; actress Julie Walters, and throughout the room five hundred women mirrored the same unique cross-section of influence and interests.

Knowing that at the lunch I was to introduce Valentina, I had tried to find out beforehand facts which could be helpful to both East and West. To counter the humiliation of the Moscow Olympic Games in 1980, the Soviet sports organisations had held their own games in 1984 in Eastern Europe. So I rang the Women's Editor of the *Morning Star*, Mikki Doyle, whom I knew well. I asked her for a list of the Eastern gold medallists. At the lunch I named each one, saying that sportswomen from the West saluted their sisters from the East. Tessa Sanderson joined in the applause and she leant across the Duchess of Kent to say to Valentina, 'Ask me again to your Games. I won't refuse.'

The Duchess of Kent spoke to Valentina about her flight and ended by saying, 'Yours is a large country, mine is smaller, but some day I hope I can show you Yorkshire.'

When Valentina spoke she appealed for protection for planet Earth, saying, 'Unless it is prevented, the merciless fire of nuclear war will not spare a single nation or a single continent. Our planet is big enough for us to live in peace on it, but it is far too small to be exposed to nuclear menace.' At first hesitantly, the women in the room stood to applaud her. Valentina's speech had increased East-West understanding, not least on the dangers threatening the globe. Then it was over. A large black car drove Valentina away. I did not think that I would ever see her, or Elizabeth, again.

During the days after Valentina's departure I became hopeful that there might be work for peace which we could undertake together. Events had confirmed that humanity and its planetary home would be obliterated unless the superpower enmity which was building up to nuclear war could be overcome. Misunderstanding must somehow become understanding. This would only happen if bridges were established to enable opposing sides genuinely to exchange experiences and points of view and then, possibly, to prove that there was no need for war. The West must travel to the East and the East to the West to see facts and come to know people and situations at first hand.

Politicians were failing to achieve unprejudiced dialogue. Could individuals succeed where politicians failed? Perhaps if Valentina and I could meet again we could work out how much separated us and compare it with how much we could share, and learn how people in the West and East could replace enmity caused by ignorance through finding out more about each other. I had become very conscious of my own ignorance about the USSR.

However a member of the Embassy staff had not been optimistic when I told her I hoped to see Valentina again. 'She is a very private person. She can be contacted at work but otherwise she usually keeps herself to herself. She is well known for her dislike of personal publicity, and because she never gives interviews to journalists some have called her the Greta Garbo of space.' This did not encourage my hope that through meeting Valentina again I could somehow contribute to building a bridge of East-West understanding. In any case how could I know whether she would wish for it?

At the time I could only imagine what Valentina's impressions of our first meeting might be. This is what she wrote later:

My first feeling, after receiving your invitation to come to the Women of the Year Lunch, was one of surprise. For my official work I received many invitations for conferences, symposiums, seminars, meetings of organizations and lectures in universities and in academic, scientific and technological societies, but never to speak at a social occasion. Why would I be speaking to an important audience at a lunch and not a seminar? Why not a lecture? For Soviets, meeting for a meal was something which was formal and according to protocol. It did not seem serious or appropriate to share one's experience with the public at large without a proper structure. I then asked myself whether Soviets had their own concept of public life which was quite different from that of the West.

I was preparing a lecture on the Soviet space programme for the Royal Aeronautical Society in London where I would be describing high technology, new materials, sophisticated space devices and apparatus. I would be speaking to my fellow professionals and sharing with them my assessment of the present situation in aeronautics and the future for humanity. But I had also come to believe that technology by itself does not guarantee a better world, and that humanity needs a moral compass to guide technology. So my second feeling was that I should strive to understand the purpose and the people involved in an occasion which was unusual for Soviets.

I was given a brief on the occasion, and on you, by our Embassy in London. I was impressed by your activities for women and for the handicapped. Yours was a different way of helping humanity from the one familiar to me, but I decided that to follow my vision of the moral compass needed to guide humanity for a better future, my understanding of your meeting was part of that moral compass. So I accepted your invitation to speak to Britain's professional women and by so doing help the handicapped in Britain.

It has always been a strong impression for me that in every country there are people who want to build bridges of understanding with other nations, while others want to destroy them and tear them down. Meeting you and your friends in London in 1984 made me sure that builders of good bridges were numerous in the West, and that tolerance, travel, thought and time were what was required to unite West and East. Then when you and I met we built a personal bridge of love and friendship.

My only unfavourable impression was of Western mass media. After the press conference in London, British journalists wrote trivial things about me. One even said, inaccurately, that I was too afraid of heights to fly into space again. To my mind, decency and ethical behaviour should be compatible with freedom of expression. It seemed ironic that, while the media in my country were not telling the truth because they were not free, Western media were doing the same because they were free to say what they wanted to, even if it was not true. But my overall impression was good. When I read the guest list I saw how many different professions and ethnic groups were represented and that what you had said was true – it was 'A wide cross-section of working women from Capitalist to Communist.'

Added to this there was my first impression of you. My expectation had been that you would be typical of the wives of government ministers I had met in the West, but remembering the lunch I can say that the greatest impression left with me was of your personality. From our first meeting I had a spontaneous wish to speak to you and to share my vision of the world with you. That is why, even in our first conversation at the Soviet Embassy, we so easily exchanged our thoughts about my experience in space, about religion, about women's activities and the need to help the disabled. We immediately understood each other. You say you have learnt about Russia through me. In the same way my relationship with you deepened my impression of Britain. Human contacts are more important than sightseeing, they are like a fire which brings warmth and light into relationships which otherwise would be cold. I have often said since, 'My friendship with Tony, an outstanding, talented and discerning woman, helped me to know the Western way of life better. It encouraged me in my wish to be unbiased and tolerant.' I can tell you sincerely that since our first meeting, our understanding, which has become even deeper, means a great deal to me.

Valentina's impressions of our first meeting confirmed that the alchemy between us had started with mutual trust at a time when it was in short supply within the fortresses of East and West. Perhaps this was the beginning of an equal exchange of unprejudiced information.

Meanwhile, I could only hope that waving goodbye after the Women of the Year Lunch would not be my last opportunity to exchange trust with Valentina. But how?

After the lunch there were numerous letters from those who had heard Valentina speak and who wanted not only to thank her, but also somehow to build further on the new British-Soviet connection. So I wrote to Yuri Mazur to ask if he could tell her about the enthusiastic response. He said that if there were any photographs I could leave them at the Soviet Embassy and he would send them on.

This led me to another unexpected discovery: that making contact with a national leader in the USSR was sometimes easier than a similar assignment in Britain. Three days before Christmas, I found myself with an unusual undertaking. Before leaving London for Scotland and family festivities I needed to deliver gifts to two very disparate international leaders – the Archbishop of Canterbury, Robert Runcie; and the Chair of the Soviet Women's Committee, Valentina Tereshkova. I set forth in dark, deep rain by taxi.

The Archbishop had supported *Christ's Words*, a Bible publication I was involved with. To thank him I had found an exceptionally fine transcript of the Creed made by the nuns of Stanbrook Abbey, where contemplatives live by a timetable which combines prayer with calligraphy, usually the illumination of manuscripts. For Valentina, I had collected photographs of the Women of the Year Lunch in a small album bound in red leather. I put both gifts in carrier bags.

Contact with Lambeth Palace took a long time. I rang the bell and imagined I could hear old Father Thames rolling along. It was dusk and a dim light threw shadows on the gates. No one answered the bell. I felt guilty about disturbing a doorkeeper the week before Christmas but I rang again. I was pleased to have a fine present to give the Archbishop and I had described it in a covering letter. I hoped to leave it personally because it was too large in its oak frame to post.

After about ten minutes I felt that there was no future in personal delivery – I must think of some other way. But a voice broke the silence on the intercom. I explained who I was and what I hoped for. Neither the voice nor I found my explanation convincing, until I added that I was cold. This resulted in a kind elderly man in a dark suit opening the gates and taking the carrier bag. I never heard again about my wet presentation.

It was much easier to get into the Soviet Embassy. I rang the bell of the outside gates and saw a face at the curtains. I spoke into the intercom: 'Lady Lothian with a gift for Madame Tereshkova.' If a camera was monitoring my weird appearance under the umbrella, in a black leather jacket and wearing a black eye patch, it must have looked surprising. After a few minutes a sleepy doorman, still hurriedly buttoning up his striped coat, came out to unlock the gates. Perhaps he did not want to get wet, since I was not asked to provide identification. He took the bag, thanked me, and disappeared. The gates closed behind him. The rain continued to pour down and I returned home.

A month later Yuri Mazur sent on a letter from Valentina, who had been delighted to receive the photographs and hoped we would meet again. Once more the assumption that there could be no communication with the Soviet Union had proved too pessimistic. For me it had been easier than trying to contact a prelate in the UK.

Meanwhile there seemed to be no other reason why I would see Valentina again. In the early eighties tourist groups were visiting Russia under surveillance, but it was unusual and suspect for individual Russians to come to London or for a UK citizen to visit friends in Moscow.

A shared human anxiety led to our next meeting. In 1985 my son-in-law, young, active, a fine footballer, found he had become ill with multiple sclerosis. It seemed impossible to accept this blow, but as he is particularly brave and unselfish he inspired all his family somehow to rise to his example of courage. Then a friend told me that the *Financial Times* had published a report on how Soviet scientists were hoping to find a cure for MS. My son-in-law asked, 'Do you know anyone in Russia who could tell you more?' I immediately thought of Valentina. As Chairman of the Soviet Women's Committee she had great influence, but it also meant she was very busy and difficult to get hold of. Would she even remember me if I sent her the *Financial Times* press cutting, told her of our family anxiety and asked her if she could provide Soviet medical information?

Once again I found myself at the gates of the Russian Embassy, having asked Yuri Mazur to see me and perhaps send a letter to Valentina. His response proved that compassion does have no frontiers. I hardly knew Yuri then, but his concern could have been that of a brother. He would send my letter immediately. One of his cousins had MS. He hoped the Russians were on the way to a cure, but he was not entirely convinced.

The reply from Valentina came within a week. She warned that a cure had not been found, but she offered my son-in-law a bed in the Moscow hospital where the research was being done, and if it was not possible for him to travel to Moscow she would arrange for the Soviet Ministry of Health to send the precise prescriptions for the vitamins and drugs being used to a relevant doctor in Britain. If necessary they would be sent in kind. Valentina no longer felt remote. She was a friend in need.

Within the month the medical documents were received by the doctor in London, who confirmed Valentina's caution about not yet finding a cure, but said that the vitamin treatment seemed hopeful. We were all very grateful to Valentina and to thank her I wrote the first of what was to become a series of letters in which I tried to describe my life in Britain and so extend the sincere conversation we had had at the Embassy reception. It was becoming increasingly obvious to me that East and West knew dangerously little about each other.

Two years later, in 1987, as President of the Women of the Year Association I was notified from Moscow that the Soviet Women's Committee would be inviting a representative from our organization to attend the World Congress of Women. I was pleased when Yuri Mazur then rang me to ask if I could recommend more British women's organizations and I asked him when the delegates would need to travel. 'Next month.' I replied that this was ridiculous, a large and important organization needs at least six months' notice to arrange for delegates to be appointed and travel. He said that some organizations needed less time, and named them. The majority mentioned were unrepresentative of the British mainstream, and biased on the side of Communism. A press colleague recently returned from Russia warned me: 'They are all there for the beer. They love VIP treatment. Mainly they come from minorities and pressure groups. Leading Socialists shun them.'

I was learning again about the mechanics of misinformation which deepened the division between East and West. The Soviet side did not seem to know how Britain's great democratic institutions operated. Similarly, on our side, when I suggested that Russian delegates should be invited to women's conferences in Britain this was criticized as being too innovative. Some of the organizations with which I worked were left of centre, but they had no intention of supporting Soviet Communism.

On behalf of the Soviet Women's Committee Yuri arranged for an invitation to be sent to the Women of the Year Association. The joint chairpersons were Dr Erna Low, travel and leisure expert, and Pat Gregory, the first woman manager of a football team, and they agreed to my going as the representative provided I would not charge any costs to the Association. Later Yuri sent me a one-way ticket from Valentina.

I felt no hesitation in accepting, except that I was worried about not speaking Russian and not knowing any of the other delegates. As usual when looking for reliable advice I rang my friend Mikki Doyle, Women's Editor of the *Morning Star*. We had met working for Women in Media, a radical group of feminist reformers. We all called each other Sister, but it really became true of Mikki and me. She and her husband Charlie, and Peter and I, genuinely loved each other, so much so that when asked who he would want to be with on a desert island, Peter replied without hesitation, 'Mikki and Charlie Doyle.' The outside world saw our polarised philosophies, Christian and Communist, as not to be reconciled, but in actuality Mikki and I sometimes feel like one person and we even look and dress alike. Certainly we both worry about the deprived and believe that we cannot stand on the sidelines unmoved and inactive.

Mikki had been asked to attend the World Congress but had refused. She was in Prague working for Radio Czechoslovakia. I was almost on my knees to her to change her mind. I begged: 'I won't know anyone. I can't speak Russian.' She gave in and said she would join me as soon as she could leave Prague.

Now the decision had been taken. I would be flying out on Aeroflot, into the unknown arena of women's Communist activities world-wide. It would also be my first experience of Moscow, or, for that matter, of the USSR. 'You must tell the Foreign Office and the British Embassy that you are going,' I was advised repeatedly. But that seemed to me to be a breach of trust with Valentina. 'You will be all right,' Yuri had said cheerfully. He also reported that Valentina had been appointed head of the Union of Soviet Friendship Societies, an organization similar to the British Council – she was no longer chair of the Soviet Women's Committee. A journalist with knowledge of Russia told me that some of the men in power would like their wives to be in Valentina's place. But the informant had added that Russians were very suspicious of 'wives'. Valentina's unique status was that her preferment had been earned by a genderless achievement.

By this time it was well into May. I was to be in Moscow from June 23rd to the 30th and I myself had said that one month was too short to prepare in. The days flew by for me, trying to find out about visas and Russian money. Yuri was unfailingly helpful, even writing out a message in Russian to say that, if I was lost, whoever picked me up must tell Valentina. But he was certain that my fears about getting lost were groundless.

Although I looked forward to going to Russia for the first time I found little encouragement. My optimism was not shared by the harbingers of gloom in Britain. I told one cab driver I would soon be in Moscow and he was full of foreboding: 'You may never get back.' My husband's attitude was neutral. He has a peaceful outlook on all that happens: 'I don't think it can be as difficult as people say; after all, tourists come and go from Russia.' Our large family seemed too preoccupied with their own problems to worry about my journey into the unknown but the grandchildren said it was 'brilliant' and 'cool'. The only friend who was enthusiastically in favour was Elizabeth McLeish, the administrator of my husband's office in Scotland. With typical Scottish lack of fuss she had recently travelled to the Far East with her husband by car and caravan.

I put my trust in Valentina but a vision of myself half-blind, arriving alone in Moscow, not knowing where to go and unable to speak Russian, remained alarming.

In the weeks before leaving for Moscow, to counter possible criticism when I brought back my report, and knowing that I would be accused of being taken in by Soviet propaganda, I tried to assess the international political landscape in the context of West-East hostility. When Valentina Tereshkova and I met again what would there be to unite us while the barons of power on both sides – the autocrats in the USSR and the money men in the USA – seemed impervious to alteration, like granite?

I knew that she represented the best result of Soviet formation: solid patriotism, a high level of education and training, awareness of global needs, knowledge of classical art and literature and unparalleled courage. Her epic pioneer and scientific achievement also meant that she had met many world leaders and as Chairman of the Soviet Women's Committee she had firsthand knowledge of women's problems. For twenty-five years she had been a leading Soviet woman on her own merit and she was still a serving Soviet cosmonaut.

I could claim familiarity with all that was best in the West: individual freedom, fraternalism, pride in democratic processes, and willingness to accept social reforms which increased greater equality for gender, race and creed. As a journalist and the wife of a government minister I had observed high-level action, and sometimes actively participated. I too had met influential world figures. I too had been involved in supporting women's interests.

There could be much in common to build on together but a century of genuine even if ill-informed patriotism separated us – fundamentally. We were both open to an honest exchange of different points of view but East-West fundamentalism continued to block individual communication on both sides of the divide. Our separate worlds had not yet been turned upside down.

Throughout this time of preparation before leaving for Moscow an indelible impression from my childhood kept recurring. On summer seaside holidays the highlight had always been to visit funfairs. There was only one terror: the ghost train on Brighton Pier. The high point of panic came when, in the darkness, the train hit a seemingly indestructible black wall, but just before disaster, the wall opened and the train travelled safely into the light on the other side. I took trouble to find out how it happened. The wall was an illusion: two separate panels opened on impact and afterwards came together again. For me, ever since childhood the straightforward explanation became an enduring reminder of the light on the other side of darkness after fear had been shown to be unnecessary.

Preparing to visit Russia I remembered the Black Wall. It encouraged me not to accept barriers as insurmountable.

Certainly a main barrier between West and East was demolished for me on a historic day when I found myself in Moscow with three thousand woman delegates, mainly Communist, from all over the world, hearing Gorbachev explain his ideals for glasnost from the Kremlin platform. Later that summer, taking time off by the Black Sea, he was to write his 'explode an epoch' appeal for perestroika which unexpectedly made the leader of the Soviet Union the twentieth-century prophet for peace. After that the world would never be the same again, as the hands and hearts of human beings who longed for peace were held out in response: from East and West from Germany to China; to South Africa and, indeed, from all the continents of the globe. Human hands tore down stones as with the demolition of the Berlin Wall, and human bodies confronted armoured cars as did the martyrs of Tianenmen Square. The defiance of dictatorship spread to Poland, Czechoslovakia and Hungary. But what had happened quietly – almost unnoticed – in Austria and Spain, the orderly transition from autocracy to democracy, then exploded through violent disruptions in the Eastern bloc of European nations, and not, as Gorbachev had hoped, through orderly reform.

But before I heard Gorbachev describe and explain the resolve of the Soviet people to achieve increased freedom, while I was still in London, preparing for a first experience of the Soviet system, I had to ask myself about the extent of the crimes of Soviet Communism, which the West insisted were monstrous. During previous decades I had been deeply disturbed by news about the suppression of religion, including the Baptists seeking to provide Bibles who were sent to psychiatric asylums, and Soviet dissidents, like the physicist Sakharov, accusing Stalinist policies of suppressing and brutalising the human spirit. In Moscow would I find disturbing evidence of affronts to human rights?

In the West I had stood up to be counted against instances of man's inhumanity to man, past and present, such as the holocaust of soldiers' lives to win the First World War, German

34

genocide of the Jews and the British war-time policy to destroy civilian targets, with forty-three thousand dead in one Hamburg night, and the culminating horror of Hiroshima. I had also opposed imperial arrogance when controlling colonies: the pigment prison of apartheid, the plunder of global ecology by rich consumers and too little redress for other betrayals of human justice, such as the denial of equal opportunities to women.

Obviously I would welcome an opportunity to stand up and be counted against cruel crimes in the East. But as cruelty was worldwide, and not confined to one country, I believed that all crimes against human rights, no matter where they happened, should be condemned as equally evil. The problem was that while in the West I could show repugnance which was based on available evidence, as far as the USSR was concerned, my only opportunity to protest against cruelty for which I had evidence had been the 'Free Sakharov' rally outside the Soviet Embassy in 1980. During the week in Moscow I would attempt to become better informed.

An effective civil servant had once advised me: 'Before you take on an investigation, grind out the grammar beforehand,' and it seemed sound advice. So the night before leaving London, not least because I was representing the Women of the Year Association, I tried to tidy my thoughts by writing out my objectives. First why I was going, secondly what I hoped to find out, thirdly how could I present objective impressions obtained during the conference to those who were certain that I would return deceived by Soviet propaganda?

In my early training as a journalist I had been taught: 'Action stations means no time to think – quick reactions – quick impressions as accurate as possible – just tell it how it is.' To identify the most important issues to be investigated on arrival I needed to sort out beforehand the questions I would try to answer in Moscow.

This is what I wrote down:

How can I separate true from false information? I am going to Moscow as a delegate representing professional women in the

UK, but also grateful to be the guest of Valentina Tereshkova, Chairman of the Union of Soviet Friendship Societies which aims to promote peace by cultural exchanges. My exchange of experiences with Valentina aims to bring knowledge into the ignorance of East and West about each other, which is intensifying the cold war. Will I be told the facts or convenient half-truths?

In Britain I am constantly being warned not to be taken in by deceptive Soviet peace propaganda ultimately designed to win wars. If my final report is to seem credible I will need to discipline my impressions through a dependable two-point focus throughout my stay.

On the one hand I must guard against being prejudiced against Communism, as this would prevent me from seeing clearly. I must set what the West says about life in Russia against what I actually find for myself. Staying in Moscow I will be experiencing in a privileged way the results of an amazing seventy-year social, economic and political experiment to transform and govern an area the size of almost a quarter of the world. The USSR covers a vast area with fifteen far-flung Republics, a semi-European continent which before Communism had been undeniably underdeveloped and despotically ruled. Will I be able to learn in a short stay, surrounded by Communists from all over the world, what really has changed for better or worse since the Tsar's rule? Is administration in the Soviet Union still only possible through a severe system of central control?

Until I establish facts to answer these questions I must not be hypocritical if I find faults in contemporary Soviet control. I must remember that throughout this century Britain has had to exercise repressive measures in its colonial administration, and now in Ulster, to impose order. Obviously Russia's totalitarianism has been cruel and inhuman. But does this mean that it can never change or indeed that no progress has been achieved? Has the best of what Lenin planned for been obtained? Was Stalin's time the lost time? Also – in seventy years what would the Tsar's regime have done? The only enviable comparison which must haunt the Soviets is the USA, but it has taken three hundred years and a civil war for North America to achieve its current prosperity and even recently the Southern States had to be forced to grant democratic rights to their black citizens. In Europe it took centuries for the EEC to transcend national enmities. I must recognize and record facts which I find to be progressive in the Soviet system.

On the other hand, the second requirement for my two-point focus must be not to be deceived. It obviously suits a strong armed superpower which desperately needs money to spend on social improvements, to try to persuade possible rivals, and even possible victims, to give up expensive deterrent weapons. Hitler went on arming while the rest of Europe dreamt of disarmament. When he exploded into aggression to extend his empire, a partially-armed world was nearly conquered. Will I hear truth or lies on disarmament? Will I be listening to a replay of the temptations to appeasement at Munich during the thirties, or will I be watching the beginning of a genuine breakthrough into a millennium without nuclear war? Is a new-type Communism emerging in Russia? Japan's prosperity is based on the productivity which does not 'waste money' on armaments. Why do Russia and America still want to be military superpowers?

Looking back, this pedantic appraisal of the propaganda implications appears almost ridiculous. But in 1987, as an independent observer without official support, my precautions to avoid being deceived by Communist propaganda were in fact seen as not radical enough. That I would become an instrument of sinister Soviet intentions was not just thought of as a possibility, it was assumed as a certainty. If I was to report the truth about any favourable experiences in the Soviet Union facts had to be capable of withstanding the closest scrutiny. And there were so many questions – I could only begin to look for a few answers in one week. Nevertheless, sorting out questions beforehand had helped me.

Also there was, for me, another question I was anxious to ask and answer in Moscow: the international challenge as to the best way to help the Third World. In Moscow I would be meeting and hearing the views of three thousand women delegates representing 150 nations, not only from the First and Second but also from the Third World. This chance to meet the Third World in Moscow was the experience I most anxiously anticipated.

It was common knowledge that, while the West's food mountains had never been so high, never had so many people gone hungry and that although the Green Revolution can feed the victims of famine, they are too poor to buy food. I found it deeply dispiriting to know that those who have will not give their surplus away to those who have not, and also that, because the South needs to repay huge debts to the North, this means that when the North provides financial assistance this is far less than the repayments required in return.

Certainly for me this was the most important question on which I hoped to find an answer at the World Congress of Women. The Third World is neglected and it is too poor – too hungry – too destitute – too ignorant – to save itself. How can it travel from its present poverty to some form of adequacy? In Moscow I would be asking: should the Third World copy capitalist policies – or Communist policies – or is there another alternative? Is there a compromise to be found between the Christian dream of one world family with one father God – or the dreams of capitalist materialism – or the Communist dreams of a state-controlled productivity and distribution?

At a London conference on the Third World a Brazilian delegate had told me, pointing towards the black delegates: 'They are sitting on fortunes underground. So are we, but who will help us to dig out minerals as the Arabs have done? We must make money for ourselves – and not for our exploiters from abroad.'

In his book *Small is Beautiful*, Fritz Schumacher had taught that by intermediate technology the poor could achieve their own sufficiency and survival. But would there ever be proper assistance to do so? Must the major part of the world die in dereliction while the minor part is committing suicide from self-indulgence?

With all these thoughts in my mind I did not sleep well. Packing suitable clothes was also a worry. The timetable indicated evening receptions as well as long workshop hours. I felt thankful that I always wore my own kind of uniform, usually black and white, and this would make it easier if there was no time to change. There was another problem. In 1970 I had lost my right eye because of cancer, and I had found confidence and comfort by wearing a black velvet eye patch. In a crowd or amongst strangers it brought sympathy and not annoyance if I ran into them, or stumbled, or directed water or food in the wrong direction. Would it look like wanting to attract attention if I wore the black patch in Moscow? I decided that attention, no matter how embarrassing, was less alarming than annoyance. I would wear the patch. How could I keep my hair tidy? I put in an alarm clock to wake up an hour early so as to set my hair. I also packed a small electric kettle to make tea – would the plug fit? For added comfort I put in a hot water bottle. Thus protected, I regained confidence, and even before leaving London I started to describe my crossing of the Iron Curtain and possibly the most interesting week of my life. I wrote my impressions as a day by day diary of the journey I had begun to meet the Soviet system in Moscow for the first time, and also to try and find Valentina Tereshkova again.

The Second Milestone

The World Congress of Women, Moscow 1987

THE FIRST DAY

I leave home at what feels like dawn. An Aeroflot official meets me inside the Heathrow Terminal in the room for the Moscow flight. The usual lost American tourists are looking for their cheerleader. A very roomy aeroplane. On the aeroplane, jolly Neapolitan music: 'Torna a Sorrento'. One of the most comfortable flights I have known, and not too long at 3½ hours. Delicious rice and chicken, linen cloth and napkin, orange juice, no alcohol on offer but a variety of soft drinks including the inevitable Coca-Cola.

Having been apprehensive on leaving London with only a one-way complimentary ticket from the Soviet Women's Committee and entirely on 'Tereshkova trust', it is extraordinary that I feel no anxiety on landing, just like getting to Edinburgh. I wonder who will meet me: if there is no one there I will not know where to go.

Arrival

At the end of the passage two women are waiting, and introduce themselves as my interpreters, Natasha Kritchiguina and
Albina Bogomolova. In their fifties, they look and talk like
dons' wives at Oxford. Natasha, thin, well dressed and self-
possessed, is an economist studying the development of
capitalism and is a senior researcher at the Institute of World
Economy. Albina is a language teacher at the USSR Academy
of Sciences; she is tall, fair and an extrovert. She says Albina is a
Polish name but that she is very Russian. She is holding a
bunch of daisies and bluebells: 'nice and natural, a bit dead but
we will get them to life again in the hotel.'

They find my suitcase, and we drive away in a big black car.
'You are one of the honoured guests,' Natasha says.

We pass a monument of wooden crosses – plain and rugged –
where the Nazis were turned back from reaching Moscow. All
along the road there are high-rise flats and they seem very
proud of them. 'That is the institute which trains astronauts,'
points out Albina as we pass blocks of Victorian-type buildings.

I say how much I would value a chance to get to Mass if
possible in the morning, and hesitantly explain that anything
helpful which happens in my life usually follows prayer. 'The
monastery is a museum,' Natasha says, 'but there are services in
other churches.'

She does not seem critical or surprised. I gather they trust me
because Valentina trusts me – they seem in awe of her, but at
the same time proud of her. I sense Natasha has higher status
than Albina. She is trying to think of a church she can take me
to in the morning. She says a very good choir sings in one near
her home and she will ring up the priest about the services. She
says she knows nothing about religion – only economics. When
I ask, 'Can I go to Communion?' there is a blank reaction, but
combined with an obvious desire to assist if possible.

The hotel

It is very modern, like any large European hotel. Albina says it
was built by an American firm and it is called the International.

Later I am told that the cost of building it was covered by Armand Hammer, the American philanthropist trusted by Lenin but who made money when he supported Lenin. There is a suite for me: two bathrooms and a sitting room, and, to Albina's excitement, some red roses. 'That must be Valentina.'

They have both been to London, Paris, Rome, New York. Natasha is a health enthusiast and believes diet can cure cancer. We try to see if Mikki is on the delegates list. Apparently not. But as they had expected a friend to come with me, there are two beds and two television sets in my rooms.

The three of us have dinner in a dark dining room. We have a corner table for six. Later I find most of the other tables are for the Hospitality Committee; in charge is a serious young man who is important in the young Communist movement, the Komsomol. Good plain food: clear soup, fried fish, trifle. In the restaurant all the Russians noticeably drinking orangeade. Apparently this is Gorbachev's newest change – to educate a generation which is not poisoned by drugs.

'He is very pure,' Albina says. 'He wants sober Russians.'

She is so proud of all that we see: for example, a cock that crows each hour in the hall of the hotel. When the floor manager of my floor gets my window open she says, 'Russian women – real champions!', again flying the flag for Russia from the heart. She is very pretty, wearing an up-market dress, as from a London City store. I am told later that the team which looks after guests has to be well-dressed and it is one of the rewards.

In the streets it had been reassuring to notice similarities with the West, for example the unifying effect of wearing denim, the clothes Esperanto which signals the fraternity of those who want to feel comfortable.

There are no signs of any other delegates but Albina is not worried. 'Only honoured guests are in this hotel.'

I suddenly realise I am a sort of 'combination' delegate: on the one hand a delegate like the other 3000 (with a standard official label round my neck saying 'Antonella Lothian – England'); on the other hand, as Natasha tells me seriously: 'You are also Valentina Tereshkova's personal guest and she wants you to be looked after.' This worries me, I feel so old and tired and uninspiring. Will I let Valentina's trust down?

Mikki has not yet arrived. Her visa has been held up in Prague. Natasha says she is surprised the Women's Editor of the *Morning Star* is my friend. 'You must be a very kind family – your husband and your eldest son are both with Mrs Thatcher.'

I call her and Albina 'my two professors'. Natasha is amused. She and her husband have a house in the country as well as in Moscow, and she loves gardening there. Perhaps I could post her a book on English gardens? She shows me a picture of her beautiful daughter who is a physicist, her son-in-law: 'I love him more than her, I think'; and her fair-haired grandson of five with big blue eyes like her own. 'In the country he gets into bed with me in the morning and I read him fairy stories.'

Albina is always laughing. She is thrilled to have got us tickets for a special concert. No other honoured guests are going or, indeed, have had the offer made to them. That will be on Thursday.

I look out of the window last thing. Raining – the river is glistening – the lights soft. Surprisingly I feel at home. Albina has arranged her wild flowers in a wild way in a jam pot. They have come to life and look 'natural', unlike the luxury hotel. I suppose that if the Communist experiment is ever going to replace capitalism it will only be done by winning hearts and minds. I remember the advice on caution but it seems ungrateful to be on my guard, I feel sure with no good reason. Bed is very welcome. I set the alarm to give me time to set my hair in the morning.

THE SECOND DAY

I meet Albina at 9.30 after making tea with my electric kettle. Natasha is envious of the kettle. Together we visit an exhibition of Russian paintings – 'Women's Portraits from Private Collections', starting with some wonderful icons. Albina has brought her student daughter Elena. The big black car is at our disposal, with Sasha, a helpful young driver. Albina says she knows I like 'church' so we then go to the Church of the Holy Trinity, where two candles are lit by Albina with me and she buys me a little canvas triptych from the church warden, who has one in his wallet. Then Albina's daughter shows us the University, where she has just taken her mathematics degree.

I ask, 'Why so many famous men on pillars but no women?' She smiles, and agrees that there must be more women. Science is like a new religion and Elena, who has just sat her mathematics exams, loves art. She is very, very tired after her exams; thin, kind and floppy – Albina's pride and joy. She asks me in very slow English if I agree with her teachers that if you have no 'talent' for art you should not waste time on it, but concentrate on mathematics instead. I had not thought about it before but said some parents in the West were very ambitious that their children should pass exams. Albina says that in Moscow most families have only one child. I remember the loneliness of being an only child. What will a generation of 'only one' children be like?

Back at the hotel we meet Natasha for lunch. Then we go to the Pushkin exhibition. Natasha praises the Decembrists: 'the only Revolutionaries who never had anything to gain – in fact everything to lose; and wives followed husbands to Siberia.' We look at a memorable picture of Pushkin, small and defiant, with his wife. Natasha says, 'She was a great success with the Tsar, while Pushkin felt a misfit. He started by being too romantic – admiring Byron – but he became more mature.' She quotes his poems and there are tears in her eyes. She says I must visit Leningrad.

Outside we find boys kicking the smart car with our driver in it, as often happens in London. Natasha stops at a bakery to buy me some buns for tea, also sugar cubes and a carton of milk. Albina seems to earn a much lower salary. They only met each other for the first time yesterday. I can't make out what their role in the Reception Committee is, but Albina says she offered to do it because she 'would meet interesting people.' I feel inadequate again.

At lunch Natasha comments on Gorbachev's crackdown on alcohol and says that alcohol poisoning is a major health hazard in the USSR. Now no officials drink, men or women, only the visitors can buy alcohol in bars. 'Children who don't drink now will never miss it,' she says, but her husband doesn't like the long vodka queues in the shops. I say I think the Indian and Asian delegates may be relieved to find so much orangeade.

Natasha asks me if I am missing my husband, whom she calls 'Sir Peter'. I try to ring Peter in London and Mikki in Prague – two hours' delay for both calls.

I am down punctually for dinner at 7.30 to find Elizabeth – Valentina's London interpreter – in the hall, with Valentina's daughter Alyona, who is on her way to collect her doctor's diploma. Alyona is tiny and reminds me of a young actress, dressed in a white shirt with a red bow tie, a white coat and a black slit skirt. 'My mother loves you,' she says simply.

Elizabeth seems just the same as when we first met and really pleased to see me – then she takes Alyona off to her great occasion. Tomorrow she will be Dr Tereshkova – a trained orthopaedic surgeon. She is 23. She says her mother wants her to look after me and be with me 'every day'. Natasha points out later that this is very kind of Valentina. She has not met Alyona before and is keen to talk to her. In a way I feel I should be protecting Alyona, so trusting, innocent and anxious to protect me.

THE THIRD DAY

Woke at six. Couldn't believe I was in Moscow and would soon be sitting on stage in the Praesidium just behind Gorbachev and Raisa and Valentina, with 3,000 women in the hall in front of me. It is a bit like Woody Allen – can it be me? I try to remind myself of all the organizations I have worked for, all doing particularly important work, and that I must not feel too inferior. Natasha and Albina arrive punctually at 8.30. We drive off in the car and on arrival at the Kremlin Palace they stay by me, saying they have never had to look after anyone as anxious as me.

45

The Honoured Guests go in by the side door. Fortunately in the reception room Sally Mugabe and Terry Marsland recognize me and give me a genuine welcome. The other delegates are a bit puzzled by the black patch. I wear a white shirt, black tie, black pleated skirt. Natasha says, 'That is really smart,' and points out that the Russian deputy organiser wears exactly the same outfit, but no black patch.

While we wait to go into the Palace of Congresses the widow of the Liberator of Angola tells me she had a tummy pain all night. The wife of the President of Afghanistan is rather stern and large. All the women round me are very capable administrative people. We are called out on a list of names to which is added each honoured guest's particular achievement. 'Lady Lothian' has none. Sally Mugabe gives me a solitary round of applause. I still feel inferior. I am No. 40 on the platform towards the end of the row behind Gorbachev, with Madame Couturier, heroine of the French Resistance, on one side and a young Philippine delegate in charge of the United Nations department dealing with apartheid on the other. In the interval she tells me that strong sanctions could solve apartheid quickly. At the end of my row there is the Italian delegate, lame with a stick, a tough-looking lawyer. Behind me sit rows of women far more important than me. In front of me in the rows of faces I see Alyona sitting with the Soviet officials. She waves and blows kisses. To my amazement Gounod's 'Ave Maria' is played as background music, and then an emotional American cheerleader dressed in white robes calls on us all to 'Save children from war.' At this point a happy army of children marches on – just like ones in Glasgow or Birmingham – and gives the platform party a lovely bunch of red roses each.

The chairwoman, Freda Brown from Australia, makes a moving speech, including among the world's future dangers that of genetic engineering. Gorbachev and Raisa arrive. There is a wild welcome.

When Gorbachev spoke he delivered a series of ideological shocks – like electric signals – in the large, listening hall. He was describing the new Soviet vision of reformed Communism, and his speech repeatedly referred to morals. It was too surprising for anyone to really take in that he was also describing a new Communist revolution.

Thinking back, I know now that I was there when Gorbachev first proclaimed not only glasnost, but also explained his ideal of international rebuilding through perestroika. I do not think any of us present realised that this was the curtain going up on events of immense magnitude and that the world would never be the same again. The speech was Gorbachev's proclamation of a new revolution for Communism wanted by the Soviet people. It was a call for self-discipline, family life, help for mothers and wives, eternal values, equality for men and women, the protection of children. For the last ten minutes he spoke on disarmament, saying that it was disappointing that Russia's disarmament offers were rejected by the West. Natasha told me afterwards he was being brave with his own generals, who wanted to keep parity with the USA.

I remembered I must ask myself, 'Is this propaganda?', but I felt certain that it was better to believe and be disappointed than be cynical and miss exceptional opportunities. If Russia is opening the door, can we slam it shut? The Russians I have met seem to be easily hurt by any form of criticism – even of the erratic hot water in the hotel. To criticize or question Soviet sincerity could be deeply dangerous. The overall reaction from the audience is delirious. Everybody kisses everyone, particularly Freda Brown. The Congress has certainly been given a fantastic send-off.

I go back to the hotel for lunch with Alyona and Natasha and Albina. Alyona is very pleased with her degree, and also that I know the Hippocratic Oath which she heard read out at the academic ceremony.

Then a shadow falls. Valentina rings and says her mother has had a heart attack and Alyona must go to be with her. I hope she can come back. She was going to stay the whole week with us and we were going to see Valentina together. Poor Valentina – Alyona tells me that she loves her mother above all else and she is shattered by the news.

Meanwhile the saga of Mikki being prevented from travelling goes on. The Women's Committee is keeping a room for her. She rings from Prague to say that she has her visa but now she cannot get a seat on the aeroplane. I do wish she was here.

It is teatime, and while I am preparing to go to the anti-apartheid seminar after dinner, Natasha brings me news of another shock. She has arranged for me to be received by the Metropolitan of Minsk – His Eminence Bishop Filaret – tomorrow morning. I had only asked to go to church, but that has inspired this added religious honour. What can I talk to him about, and why should he see me? Will this 'experience of a lifetime' turn out to be my death from worry?

Before dinner Natasha and I drive to Red Square, where we walk and sit in the hot summer sunshine. I tell her of my anxiety about Third World dereliction. She says she studies contrasting economies and visits experts all over the world, including distinguished professors in Oxford, London and Edinburgh. She asks me if I support privatization. I say I see it as one of the most effective 'Thatcherisms'.

Red Square gives me a feeling of Rome. I don't really like the Cathedral of St Basil – in fact I only half like Red Square, possibly because it was counterproductive to be told at home that it is one of the wonders of the world. What I love in Moscow are the bridges and the buildings and the old churches. Often a bit like Rome again.

After dinner Albina goes home and Natasha and I go to the anti-apartheid meeting. This is very African, and packed with delegates. It starts with a strong speech by Sally Mugabe and a rather too long and angry speech by Oliver Tambo's wife. This does not impress some young German nuclear disarmers, who prefer peace to violence. There is singing, dancing, rage, revolution. I am glad I am there. A deep division is evident between developed and underdeveloped nations, exemplified by the delegates. I like the black ones best – responsive and calling for real priorities.

Natasha is silent and thoughtful. I suspect she does not know many Africans, and that she is not overworried about injustice to the Third World: she prefers investigations into capitalist and even Chinese economic systems.

She says she does not mind being late: she goes home by underground. The car is only for me. Alyona drives herself.

THE FOURTH DAY

Get up at 7 a.m. to be ready for church. Natasha has found a daily service in the church 'The Joy of all the Afflicted'. She says it is well known for its choir and that it is small and near her home. It is really lovely – icons, candles, incense, the chant of the liturgy. I feel a grip of the heart seeing the sincerity of the elderly poor, unlike St Francis betrayed by the rich Basilica of Assisi. Old and young are crossing themselves, standing, bowing and kissing the wooden floor. The seemingly endless chant of the liturgy. The thin candles. The icons – particularly of Longinus, the centurion saint who witnessed: 'Surely this is the Son of God', a saint whom I had never found anywhere else. The young priest looks a bit like Lenin. At one stage he reads from the Bible then the Sacrament is brought out to worship. Is that the Consecration? There is a feeling of Absolute Presence.

Natasha asks an old lady if I can go to Communion. She gives a firm answer, 'For Communion you must have been to confession first. The priest will give you both sacraments but you must wait till the service is over.' We can't wait, as the service takes four hours every morning and Communion comes at the end. As we leave, the babushkas are making a ritual round of the icons, kissing them and crossing themselves. I feel certain that if the Mother of God spoke to them from an icon they would not be surprised.

Back in the hotel we find Albina, Elena and Alyona. Her grandmother is in hospital and still very ill. As a group we drive to a meeting with His Eminence Metropolitan Filaret, to be welcomed by his assistant, a sort of Russian Terry Waite, and Nina Bobrovna, the totally dedicated administrator, burning with belief in the spirituality of the Russian Orthodox Church.

I am told to ask Nina questions. I ask about endurance for a four-hour liturgy: is standing an ordeal for so many old people? Nina says it is the glory of the Russian Orthodox Church that spiritual worship matters most. We are taken to see a beautifully restored church near the Metropolitan's house.

Then we arrive for tea with the Metropolitan, big, kind and welcoming. Everything I say to him is carefully listened to by my four young Soviet companions. Nina acts as interpreter and says the Metropolitan wishes to be asked questions. I ask if he has met Professor Torrance, former Moderator of the Church of Scotland and leading Biblical scholar, and if he knows about his writings on the Creed. He says he does not, but tells me of the coming Millennium – the Jubilee Celebrations in 1988 of the 'Baptism of Rus', marking the official beginning of the Russian Orthodox Church.

I say I wish we could go back to early Christianity when the Christians shared all they had. We discuss whether or not there is a need for 'liberation theology'. Then I say that it is wonderful to see how much Russians love and respect the Mother of God. This he takes for granted, as do the young Soviets.

Metropolitan Filaret then says he often visits the Archbishop of Canterbury. He is taken aback that Alyona is Valentina's daughter. Alyona listens with great sincerity and simplicity. Albina's daughter Elena asks the Metropolitan why God gives artistic talent to some and not others; she is really unhappy that she has to follow scientific studies when she prefers art, because the State needs scientists. We are told that at the celebrations next year the most famous Russian painter of icons, Rublev, will be made a saint. I say I love the ideals of St Francis of Assisi because he uncompromisingly followed the poverty of Christ. Metropolitan Filaret says that St Seraphim was like St Francis in his love of poverty. I remember that Tolstoy railed against 'the diamond-encrusted church'. My four companions listen to it all. I desperately suggest they might ask the Metropolitan questions, but they reply, 'We like listening.'

The Metropolitan seems a bit puzzled by our group and gives us each a book by himself called *Choose Life* and a record of

Russian church music. Unexpectedly, the choir in the record is of the church Natasha and I were in earlier. Valentina is being kept waiting, but Alyona keeps ringing her to say where we are. I tell the Metropolitan that I am president of the Order of Christian Unity where Christians from all denominations study the teaching of Christ and then together try to uphold His Commandments. It sounds as genuine as I know it to be and convincing for us all. My memory of the Metropolitan is of a conventional Orthodox priest, a good choice to keep Church and State on the best possible terms. But I don't know what the terms are.

We then drive on for our meeting with Valentina. I had last seen her in London but we had been in contact through Embassy messages and by letter. We met again now in the big office from which she runs the Union of Soviet Friendship Societies. Seeing her again is a reminder that she is not only one of the bravest women in the world but also that she holds in her heart and mind the values that the world needs. In the room where she works, Valentina shows me a model of the space vehicle she travelled in and a photograph of planet Earth given to her by the American astronauts' corps with a dedication of admiration, calling the picture 'The Blue Planet'. Valentina asks me about my son-in-law Donald's illness and what more she can do to help. I believe that is why I am her guest here now: she was pleased that I trusted her to help Donald even though she was so busy and so important. Her reaction to calls for help is not only to give but to give even more.

Afterwards, having left her, I felt I had not made the most of our meeting. If only I had followed Donald's reasonable advice: 'Don't talk — listen.' There was so much I wanted to tell her, and tried to; particularly about the need to make Russia better known in Britain to a wider cross-section of people. She agreed. I also said that the world is waiting for a lead on transnational challenges — plagues like Aids; pollution; chemical poisoning; atomic annihilation — all transcending frontiers.

Valentina listened. As always she was calm, sympathetic and self-controlled. It was like talking to a wise physician. There was not time for me to hear enough of her views, but she did tell me of her plans for a Russian Exhibition in Birmingham the following year, and that she would try to find out more about MS. She said she was working for more exchange of medical knowledge with an increase in scientists travelling between the two countries. I suggest artists, sports people and philosophers as well.

I try to say that what she has arranged for me during this week is my ideal of hospitality, and, if I dare to believe Alyona, also love. I tell her that I wish I could arrange for her and Coretta King to appeal for peace together; one from Russia, one from America. Valentina says she has tried to meet Coretta but she has never been able to accept an invitation to visit Moscow. We briefly discuss the other subjects mentioned in my letters.

Then she presents me with a beautiful porcelain samovar. I give her a small Crown Derby dolphin for her bathroom. I tell her how sad I am about her mother, and that I will pray. With so many onlookers it is hard to be as genuine as I want to be. Valentina says, 'We will see each other again – we will not say goodbye.' Obviously she is heartbroken about her mother being so ill.

I leave feeling really sad. I owe her so much trust and kindness, not least for obtaining the Soviet treatment to help Donald. As in London I feel I have known her all my life. Alyona says she has given her mother daily details of what we were doing together. She assures me that I am not a new foreign friend, much more like a close relative she sees in Moscow every day. She has been talking to her grandmother about how genuinely we all trust each other, and hopes she may be well enough to meet me next time.

Back at the hotel, Elizabeth Smith, from the Scottish GB-USSR Association and wife of the Labour Party politician John Smith, comes to say Mikki has arrived and has been taken to

Elizabeth's hotel. Alyona and I go together to the first work-shop, where Terry Marsland, a trade union leader I know in London, is the chairperson. It is on 'Women and Work'. Terry refers to the audience as 'Comrades'. I suggest 'Sisters' would fit in better, as there are non-Communists present. Terry laughs, as I mean her to, but later calls us 'Sisters'.

From the statements made and simultaneously interpreted, the unbridgeable divide is evident again. The gap between Third, Second and First Worlds shows in each speech. 'Developed' world statements saying, 'We are destroyed by consumer goods' contrast with the Third World saying, 'We suffer without any'. Certainly in this vast assembly a regional landscape emerges, with the Capitalist World apparently polarised from the Derelict World. Possibly the USSR, the vast continent which has experienced seventy years of violent change, could be the Middle World – a bridge between the other two? I ask myself again, if I was living in the Third World, and encased in the cement of hopeless poverty, would I seek relief in Communism or Christianity? Which system would move the log-jam of misery? A young African asks me in English why the Scandinavians complain about pollution from refrigerators when in her country there is no water to refrigerate.

After the meeting I am driven, again in a Friendship Society Zil, to the British Embassy. In last-minute recognition that many delegates come from Britain, the ambassador has asked some of us for a drink. It is a pleasant evening and the Embassy garden is well kept and attractively English. Enoch Powell is one of the guests. He is surrounded by ready listeners. He seems to respond to Soviet goodwill and to understand current Soviet problems better than most British politicians. I meet members of the press corps, who seem either arrogant or condescending in their attitude to the Congress. They are sceptical about Jon Snow's reports from Russia and say he has been 'taken in'. They appear to suspect that as a friend of Valentina's I must be a fellow-traveller. How can I persuade anyone that all I want is to find out how nuclear war can be avoided and also what will help the Third World?

On my return to the hotel I find Alyona waiting. She stays till dinner and then goes to her grandmother who is a little better. She says that with so much happening, 'It is like a dream.' I feel the same.

After coffee in the bar of the hotel, we try to find family gifts in the hotel shop where a group of Italian tourists can't make up their minds. Then I have a really long talk with Natasha. Mikki tells me that she is a Party member, whereas Albina is not and so does not have the same ideological responsibilities. Natasha says she knew Donald Maclean and helped him write a book and that he was sad and lonely when he died. She really liked him. I say that he should not have betrayed his country. She agrees but insists that he was an idealist. She is deeply interested in Thatcher economics, which are her speciality, and says privatization interests her most and that the Chinese are trying some sort of labour shares with profits. I don't understand.

THE FIFTH DAY

We go first to the hotel that Mikki has been taken to. Mikki, already surrounded by old and new friends, is bold as usual in white jacket and trousers. We move her to our hotel, where she has a room to herself instead of sharing one. Alyona is with us again, but Elena has been dropped. Albina says there was criticism of too many 'hangers-on'; she loves her Elena, so she is crestfallen.

Today we start with a visit to Lenin's tomb in the Mausoleum. There is a long queue way down the road to Red Square. Natasha gets the car parked in a VIP enclosure and says we can slip into the queue near to the front. We talk to families up from the country – they are more forthcoming than the Moscow citizens.

Mikki says Lenin's body is a feat of science it is so well preserved. When we reach the room it reminds me of a saint's tomb in Italy. Lenin lies there – small, dapper, white and stiff, like a wax model. I remember reading about his dream of a 'workers' state to function as a producers' democracy', and that his grandfather was a surgeon and his father a Civil counsellor – both bourgeois intelligentsia. He wanted the workers to oppose capitalism as the bourgeoisie had opposed feudalism: 'The overthrow of the bourgeoisie can be achieved only by the proletariat becoming the ruling class.' When he was dying he hoped for a successor other than Stalin: 'Someone more patient, more loyal, more polite, more attentive to comrades, less capricious.' He liked Bukharin.

Just before Lenin died in 1924 he was trying to adjust extreme measures and rectify mistakes. 'One can only be as radical as reality.' His last hope was a Cultural Revolution, making the people so enlightened that they understood the advantages of everyone participating in the collectives. He was trying to overcome the division between the urban commodity producers and the more independent agrarian workers. At the same time he remained a ruthless revolutionary, resolved to remove opposition by brutal means if necessary. These had been surpassed by Stalin's terrors.

I had talked about it to Natasha in the garden outside the church, when it was already official that Gorbachev was seeking new economic reforms. She was pleased I knew something of Lenin and Marx. I reminded her that Lenin had warned that the Russian bureaucrat is 'a rascal and a tyrant, with whom workers will drown like flies in milk.' Is Gorbachev the type of leader he was looking for? Natasha says that Andropov was wise and that he and Gromyko supported Gorbachev becoming Party General Secretary.

Out in the sunshine again having left the Mausoleum, I wonder where Father Georgy Gapon is buried but do not dare ask. He organised a workers' appeal to the Tsar for reforms in living and working conditions, and in St Petersburg on Bloody Sunday, January 9th 1905, troops were ordered to fire on the petitioners. A thousand were killed and injured with blood on the snow. 'There is no God any more, there is no Tsar!' Father Gapon had shouted. Did the insulated Tsar hear him?

We walk past the Heroes of the Revolution: carved heads on their plinths, one by one along the Kremlin Wall. Khrushchev is missing. I still respect him more than any other Soviet leader so far. Mikki said she will always have 'a soft spot for Uncle Joe'. Natasha looks disapproving. While Albina maintains unfailing cheerfulness, Alyona and I feel tired. But we go on together to the meeting of the Commission on Women and the Environment. Mikki heads back to the hotel to rest.

The Commission on Women and the Environment is chaired by an intense Finnish doctor with a blackboard and diagrams. Alyona listens to the simultaneous interpretation in Russian; mine is in English. It is a relief to get back for lunch.

In the afternoon we go back to the Trade Union Hall to listen to the Commission on Women and Technology. It is a most interesting workshop with statements from delegates on control of computers as compared to control by computers. There is a succession of different attitudes from all over the world, the aim of the Congress.

This evening the Belgian delegation is showing a film on genetic engineering, *Tomorrow's Children*. 'You will not want to eat after it,' the delegate sitting beside me says anxiously. She is worried about new possibilities for altering the human species. I am sorry to miss it, but Albina insists on the concert.

We go back to the hotel for dinner and then Alyona leaves to see her grandmother in hospital. She is weaker today and Alyona is very worried. Valentina is taken up with meetings at the Kremlin. I am told this is the week major reforms are being proposed by Gorbachev, who is bringing in new executive members to support him.

Albina's longed-for concert is all she hoped it would be. It is held in the Conservatoire Great Hall. The conductor is Gennady Rozhdestvensky and the soloist Natalya Goosman, to whom the famous composer, Schnittke, has dedicated this first performance of his Concerto for cello. The programme starts with Haydn marvellously played, then run-of-the-mill music, then Schnittke's cello piece. It is brilliant, full of changes from crashing, break-one's-heart-movements to lovely melodies, with an ending which I can only call miraculous, Goosman leaving the last note hanging in the air long after she stops playing.

There is great applause. The audience looks like any similar musical audience but possibly more restrained. Schnittke comes on to the stage: sad, clever, thin and young. Apparently he has a brain tumour. He is the idol of young Russian musicians. It was such a perfect evening, we feel particularly united in our appreciation of the music. Natasha says, 'Schnittke makes you think and suffer as well as listen.'

THE SIXTH DAY

This is 'Moscow Day' on the Congress programme. We set off to tour the city with the group Mikki calls the 'big shots'. Mikki behaves like the biggest shot and is kissed by the mayor of the New Town – an arm-twisting handsome man reminiscent of big business in Glasgow. Mrs Kaunda and the other VIPs all have sore feet and sit whenever there is a chance – like me. We visit the Co-op shop. It is very unconvincing: few shoppers, even fewer goods for sale. I ask why. The reply is that it is not shopping hours. I remember Mikki's colleague, the London Communist journalist, warning us, 'Don't let them give you bullshit on everything being ideal.' This store is like an empty stage set, but with delicious brown bread for sale, perhaps to impress the big shots.

People in the New Town look comfortably dressed, with sensible shoes and healthy faces. They live in egg-box high-rise flats. I particularly like two councillors, like similar councillors in the UK – a man and woman, proud of their New Town. It is beautifully planned: swimming pools, children's playgrounds, green belts.

We also visit a well-equipped sixth-form school where a really genuine anti-war elderly headmaster begs me to find generals and admirals in Britain and appeal to them to end war. There are peace slogans everywhere. The peace campaign must be dripping into the children's minds psychologically: it is almost obsessive. Is the Soviet Union taking a gamble on peace? It hardly seems a gamble, because these children will never want to go to war. It is not like Hitler's hypocrisy about peace: once again I decide to trust the Soviet Union.

We next visit the infant school with its waving and singing children. It is an ideally planned school, down to the 'rest beds' with yellow covers for children who have a sleep in the afternoon. Every classroom has a nurse's room as a clinic. In the swimming pool, small heads with green bathing caps bob up and down.

The children are very like children in Britain – mostly fair hair and blue eyes. They dance and sing the quack-quack song and look reproachfully at me because I don't know it. Mikki does. One little boy asks his teacher to dance. The other children disapprove.

Then our small group breaks away from the main party to visit a flat in the high-rise building and have tea with the young woman who sold bread in the Co-op. It is holiday time, so her son is at a seaside resort. She has a steel samovar and provides teacakes; she cries when she shows a photograph of her mother, who died last year. Otherwise she is very dignified and passionately proud of the New Town. She would like my grandsons to come and stay: she is sure they would enjoy a trip round Moscow by bus.

'Most Moscow people have only one child,' the woman councillor says, 'and it throws out calculations when couples are so happy in the New Town they have up to four, and then they have to have two flats!' There are not many old people in sight in the New Town.

We drive on to see a sports complex with a modern bicycle stadium, 'where many records have been established.'

Alyona is really enjoying it all and she repeats that it is 'like a dream.' It seems as new to her as it does to me, but then in London I stay in my own corner and do not see what visitors see.

In the car I ask Mikki how the UK delegation has been organised. She says the 'mastermind' is a UK woman Communist who usually asks her own collaborators only.

Back at the hotel, I am told that the vice-chairman of the Novosti Press Agency will see me in half an hour in his office. Alyona and Natasha will come too. I feel very uncertain again. What am I supposed to achieve? Natasha does not know.

On arrival, received in his study, I decide to tell him that in the UK we need to hear less about disarmament and more about what the Russians have achieved in medicine, art, conservation, sport. Also more about Russia from historians like Dmitri Likhachev, who Natasha says is a great thinker. The vice-chairman says that in America, documentaries on Russia are increasingly popular on TV, but that in the UK there is less interest. Having worked for television, I question whether that is not simply a failure in communication. All is said through an interpreter. The large formal office reminds me of the BBC. A young second-in-command, Pyotr Sylantev, gives me his card and says to get hold of him about TV documentaries. I suggest the icon-painting saint next year. The Vice-Chairman seems surprised when I introduce Alyona; he says that Valentina is one of the greatest Russians. Alyona tells me afterwards she would have preferred to remain anonymous – just a young Russian surgeon, as she is. The Vice-Chairman does not like me saying that propaganda is counter-productive. He makes a long statement about the presentation of facts being wrongly described as propaganda. But all official conversation seems to return to one theme – nuclear disarmament; and that the West opposes it.

Driving back in the car I ask Natasha, 'Why did I work so hard for the USSR?' Surprisingly she unbends and replies, 'You genuinely believe in justice.'

At the hotel Mikki has arranged for me to be interviewed by Kate Clark of the *Morning Star* and also by the *Trade Union International Journal*'s reporter, Mikki's friend from Prague. I make notes beforehand of the highlights for me, such as my appreciating the chance to meet world women; my support for the priorities Gorbachev had picked out in his speech for the future of human security; and also my own belief that, as some of the best ideals in Communism and Christianity are so similar, in the next century they might combine. At both interviews I am asked what I think are the major dangers for the next century and I identify atomic annihilation, nuclear tests, pollution, chemical poisoning, genetic engineering and dereliction in the Third World. Afterwards Mikki says, 'You did well.' I had done my best.

Back in my bedroom, Natasha interrupts contemplation by coming to tell me that the Novosti press agency has asked me to write a message for *Pionerskaya Pravda*, the newspaper read by all Soviet schoolchildren aged 10-15 years. Would I give my impressions of the Congress and my hopes for peace? Another difficult task, but I really want to speak to Soviet schoolchildren and this is an astounding opportunity. I was worried to find the right words.

I postponed writing but before leaving Moscow I wrote:

Dear Pioneers!
This is a letter from a grandmother in England.

I write this to you having been in Moscow for the great meeting of women from all over the world which happened between June 23rd and 27th 1987.

I am so grateful that I have this chance to tell you – the young people of the USSR – some memories which will stay in my heart and mind forever.

For example – the opening occasion in the Kremlin Palace of Congresses when you welcomed nearly three thousand delegates – and also the memory of the closing concert when from fifteen Republics you sang and danced not only with the Bolshoi but also almost as brilliantly as the Bolshoi. You certainly inspired your world-wide audience to return to their homes and work for peace.

As I write this I have in front of me the picture of the monument to Yuri Gagarin and I see in him a picture of you all – the champions of the world's future without war.

I am the grandmother of many grandchildren your age and during my stay in Moscow I feel I found them again when I met Soviet young people. I had left students in England who were tired after exams and looking forward to holidays in the mountains and at the sea. I met them again in Moscow. I had left young people in England enjoying sport and television, singing and dancing and happy with their families. I met them again with you.

I work as a journalist and for television and the World Congress of Women has enabled me to bring back to England from the great and generous motherland of Russia the certainty that we can be Citizens of One World as well as loving our own motherlands. I think the Congress proved that the world can be one family. I feel your leader, Mikhail Gorbachev, spoke for me as my leader when he told the world's women that humanity has not yet realized how much it has in common, including the challenge to help the hundreds of millions of people all over the world who never have enough to eat, cannot read or write, and have no roof over their heads – as well as the urgent necessity to overcome dangerous environmental poisoning and disease.

From what I see in England, I know that wanting to help and to share happiness and love is an ideal which burns strongly in the hearts of all young people, and since I have been in Russia I feel even more sure that the young people of the world who enter a new century will unite as brothers and sisters to make our planet a better, safer place to live in.

When your Hero of the Soviet Union Valentina Tereshkova visited London in 1984 she told Britain's women: 'Unless it is prevented, the merciless fire of nuclear war will not spare a single nation or a single continent. Our planet is big enough for us to live in peace on it, but it is far too small to be exposed to nuclear menace.'

I agree.

Please allow this grandmother to hug you – hold your hands – and say these words with you to make a future safe for your own grandchildren.

ANTONELLA LOTHIAN

Lady Lothian, Journalist and Broadcaster.

When I wrote this I wondered whether suspicion of propaganda works both ways. Would adults in Russia and the children themselves believe that I wanted to tell the truth? The letter was published in July, and Yuri Mazur rang me up in London from the Soviet Embassy to say his son had seen it. Yuri had not known about it. His son had approved.

After a demanding week I now feel tired. I plan to watch Moscow television in the living room, but Natasha arrives bringing 'Active Against Alcohol' posters and badges. Kate Clark has asked Mikki to dinner and rings to say she can't buy wine so Mikki buys some in the hotel hard currency shop. Natasha says there is a big chance for sales of alternatives to alcohol but Albina has a glass of vodka with Mikki in the bar – poured from a secretive china jug. I am given a really good ginger-and-fruit cocktail – one of the many new Russian alcohol-free favourites. On my way to my bedroom a young Russian stops me by the lift and says he saw me on the television which covers the Congress and recognises the black patch.

It is late, and I need to sort out papers and myself. Albina has ordered supper in my bedroom – roast chicken and rice. Sitting on the balcony looking over Moscow's river is rather like being on Chelsea Embankment, except that there are fewer cars and therefore cleaner air. The sky is blue and it could be London: opposite is a Victorian brown-and-white building with a red slate roof; skyscrapers beyond but solid buildings as well and on either side of the hotel two ornate buildings bigger than a Victorian castle, built in the same style. Mikki says one is the gasworks. She has gone out and taken Albina with her. Wherever she goes people laugh, and usually like each other.

A sightseers' boat is going down the river. It could be the Thames. It most certainly is Europe. Everyone from drivers to housekeepers is kind, even if some pedestrians look a bit glum, but so do they in any UK city.

Natasha says that, geographically, Russia is Europe and that Russians feel increasingly European, and before leaving me she shows me the USSR on the world map, pointing out that one republic is the same size as India, and there are fifteen. It is obviously a huge undertaking to impose control on such a vast area, and if Soviet rule ends what would Western democracy replace it with? I return to my anxieties about the Third World where the only question must be which form of administration increases or decreases misery. Third World delegates can see for themselves that in Russia misery is not increasing. In comparison to famine I wonder how much they mind about losing intellectual or religious freedom. If only democratic ideals did live up to what they preach, the rich North would save the poor South.

THE DAY OF THE GRAND FINALE

The Congress ends today. There is a very full timetable. Natasha collects me at 8.30 to go to the Praesidium for the final session. Raisa Gorbachev will be there and Robert Mugabe from Zimbabwe will be speaking. The honoured guests have now become more familiar to me by sight but not yet their names and countries. They are often introduced as 'The widow of the Liberator of . . .' and I can't hear where. Many of them have given me cards and are expecting me to visit them. Carmen Pereira of Guinea-Bissau hopes I will stay with her. I wonder if it is a long way to go.

Our big black car arrives to meet us – Mikki says we have the largest and most important car. Alyona comes with us. She says her grandmother is worse. She looks even smaller and more fragile. At the reception I talk to an honoured guest from Ethiopia: young, smart and intelligent. She says European civilisation disorientated Africa. She only has one child and misses the original matriarchal African society. She is very modern, and not impressed when the widow of the Liberator of Angola says she has six children and that a united family is essential. On the platform I am in the front row again. I feel a bit faint but luckily I have an old bottle of smelling-salts in my bag. The French lady welcomes me grimly, the UN Philippine delegate gives me a warm welcome and the President of Women Lawyers in Italy is pleased to see me. Someone asks if I am in the House of Lords. I say it is my husband and I feel worried again. Will they wonder why I am sitting where I am?

63

In the huge assembly in front of me I can't see Mikki, Alyona or my 'two professors' but I can now recognise other members of the Reception Committee in the officials' row. They have all held, or are holding, important official posts and most of them now know me and smile – perhaps Mikki and I, 'Mutt and Jeff' as she describes us, are a bit out of the ordinary, the Christian and the Communist. Mikki has been telling everyone, 'If we can get along, anyone can.' The reaction has been happy and sympathetic, even from strangers, and most of all from black strangers who give us a hug.

Waiting for the speakers to arrive, it is inspiring seeing women of every colour and in every national dress. Apparently a group of Greenham Common feminists present objected to male speakers, even Gorbachev – what will they say of Mugabe? He makes a sincere speech on behalf of the non-aligned nations and speaks about men needing women, and gratitude for nine months in his mother's womb. The black delegates approve of this human fact but many white faces look disapproving and the Greenham women walk out after a noticeable demonstration. Where were they for their first nine months?

There is a good summing up by a West German and an inspiring final speech by a young USA delegate. Then Madame Pukhova brings the 1987 World Women's Congress to an end. We all hold hands and sing 'We Shall Overcome'. I find myself believing in what I am singing, that peace will be possible and that pressure from women has a major part to play.

We leave the Praesidium and all delegates assemble for a buffet lunch. The African delegates give me cards and ask, 'Address please?' The delegate from Zimbabwe is delighted I liked Mugabe's speech – she is very proud of him. She gives me a pottery bird carefully wrapped and says she will ring me in London. It is amazing to see so many nationalities really behaving like one family. The only criticism I hear is when a Third World delegate points to a group of prosperous-looking sisters and whispers, 'Fat cats'.

In the early afternoon we return to the Palace of Congresses to attend a spectacular concert as the grand finale. The Moscow

Philharmonic plays Tchaikovsky and the Bolshoi Ballet dances. Then from every Soviet Republic literally hundreds of 'small Bolshois' aged from four upwards fill the huge stage in national costumes, dancing their regional dances – bursting with self-confidence and wholeheartedly sharing in all the family feeling that has developed. Natasha whispers, 'We must give children what they hope for but I wonder how we can.' It is her first admission of anxiety, but she is not alone. In the Third World there are millions of disappointed children, and even in the First World children without a secure family life are seriously deprived. Alyona says she wishes Valentina could have been with us. I agree. I owe this important week to Valentina.

I ask Alyona to tell her that I am learning about Russia. I then have to say goodbye to Alyona who has to return to her grandmother's bedside. After four days with her constant support I will feel lonely without her. She is so unspoilt and genuine. Will I ever see her or Valentina again?

Before I go to sleep I think of the concert and above all of Soviet children. The Bolshoi danced like gods, but the children, even small ones of four, danced like the Bolshoi – all in the traditional costumes of their own Republic. Can anyone deny that all the shining confident faces singing about peace must be good for the future? Is Leninism justified by the education that all the children in all the Republics have received?

Perhaps unreasonably, I am overcome by anger at the complacency of Christians. All this week solutions have been put forward with no reference to religion. If, in a moment of holy madness, I could have cried out to the vast crowd in the Kremlin chamber – so many of them post-Christian – what could I have said about Jesus Christ's solutions for life that would sound convincing? That He had been crucified on two wooden boards covered with horse-flies because He loves us all so much that in this way He conquered death and by rising from the dead enabled us all to do the same with Him? Would that promise be welcome because no other question on the mystery of death provides so much hope when it is answered? Could I also have said that Jesus said it was easier for camels to

65

get through needles than for the rich to reach Heaven, and that to neglect the least was to neglect God? If I had appealed, "This is Christian truth, compared to ideologies," would it have sounded as true as I believed it to be?

I had come from the free world which proclaimed the right to religious worship as sacrosanct. I was now in a totalitarian state which repressed religion, but how much depth had spirituality in the West gained from freedom?

This is my diary on the last day before I return to London. Natasha collects me at 9.30, and first we struggle over Mikki's visa back to Prague. There is no way of getting in again from Russia unless the Czechs let her. It certainly is not all one Union to the bureaucrats. Then, with Natasha, I drive back to the small church with the icon of St Longinus and the beautiful singing, for the Sunday service. I remember what the Metropolitan said: 'In our Church even old people stand for three hours.' I manage one hour, then go and sit in the garden outside with Natasha, who has been standing as long as I have, deep in thought and discreet in a corner. It is strange – I feel she serves the Communist Party as I try to remember the teaching of Jesus, both committed to an ideal which we believe is worth living for.

The congregation in the church of 'The Joy of All the Afflicted' seems to me like an island of intense testimony, standing, and presumably suffering from sore and swollen feet like me, for such long hours to worship God and to love the Mother of God and God's friends the saints. The babushkas kiss the icons and cross themselves. Here in this church the temporal and the eternal are united. Time somehow is not relevant. In a way the faithful are like trees, steadfast towards the sunshine of sacramental adherence and belief. Absolute faith in the presence of God. 'If you find ten just men will you spare us?' Abraham had asked God. It is true in many of the world's communities. There are always the few who serve with silent sacrifice – their mission one of prayer and faith, like contemplative monks and nuns worldwide. I read somewhere that

Gorbachev's mother worships regularly in her own church. In Moscow the faithful kissed the wooden floor. I did too. It seemed the least I could do. Natasha thinks it is not hygienic.

After the service the car leaves us at the Underground. It is much more like a palace than the Rome Metro, but all around us the faces remind me of Rome, with mothers telling their children not to point at my black patch. Everyone looks ordinary, but comfortable. I feel a sameness, but a comforting sort of sameness, like feeling less guilty on a fibre diet because it is nearer to Third World food than rich Western food. If I was really sincere I would begin by drastically lowering my own expectation of luxury. Why does the West insist that luxury is progressive? Perhaps, if the USSR can now save money on nuclear armaments, in the future Soviet children will get more of the material advantages they so obviously and enthusiastically expect. For the time being there are only a few basics available.

Albina comes to meet us for lunch at the hotel. Mikki has had a long lie-in. At lunch she tells us how she became a member of the Communist Party, having started life as a Jewish tailor's daughter in New York. Aged seventeen she married an Englishman and they had two children. When he left her she became involved in her father's socialist causes, and joined the Communists working for the blacks. Then she married Charlie Doyle – her great love – the Communist trade union leader from Glasgow.

Now most of the Honoured Guests have left and the members of the Reception Committee are conferring, but they all come over to listen to Mikki and to say goodbye to us. Elena arrives to give me her favourite record by Schnittke. I feel sad to leave her and Albina. I have learnt about Russian youth from Elena. She is tolerant, romantic, studious and very dependent on her parents. She is puzzled when I say that the titles used by noble families are an illusion. For her, a 'Marchesa' is an artistic symbol. In poetry, literature and ballet she wants classical figures to wear titles just as they wear beautiful clothes. She says there is nothing to resent or ridicule. For me this is a novel point of view and I put it down to Elena's intense involvement with all things artistic. But I do remind her that, not least in theatre, a beautiful actor is needed to make the most of beautiful clothes. Her mother laughs and says, 'I don't think Tony is interested in fashion.'

Mikki goes to the hotel shop. I return to my room to pack my suitcase and again to sit for ten minutes by the window over the river. It gives me time to ask myself what I have found to respect or criticize this week in Moscow, when so much has been offered to me and for the first time I have come into personal contact with the other side of the Iron Curtain. That was my main objective: to find out whether East-West prejudice and hostility were justified or whether they were unfounded. Now that I have met the East, how do I reply?

Obviously it has not been long enough to find out details about living situations, but how often do I do that in the UK? I can only record fragmented impressions. On the debit side, I have found it sad to see young people channelled into the skills most needed by the State, even if these are not their natural talents. I have heard the complaint of a musician pressurised into becoming a mathematician. But isn't that the same in the rest of Europe, where parents expect children to excel even if it sometimes causes breakdowns? Admittedly totalitarian bureaucracy has suppressed free expression in the USSR to a deep degree, but not in children. Children in Russia seem to be really loved, most families having one and that one is often spoilt. People tell me as a joke that Georgia is the republic most like Italy and that I would be happy there. Georgians have four children. Also, when Natasha says Russia is 'European' does that mean she hopes that Communist-type rule could be a contribution by the Soviets to the European collective? Can she not see that this would diminish hard-won European freedom unless Communism changed? But perhaps Soviet Communism is changing.

In Moscow, unlike the cheerful children most adults seem to keep a low profile, almost as if to say, 'If you don't give trouble you won't get into trouble.' In fact Moscow feels rather like a particularly strict school with recreation available but exams at the end of the road. Does this prove that the capitalist world enjoys much more freedom? Obviously freedom of choice, if you have the money. It cheers me up to think that in Britain we have achieved something very close to equality as well as freedom. Natasha wants to know more about the British: they are a puzzling people, she says; Marx and Lenin thought so too. She agrees that British democracy has been rooted in religion – as with the Quaker 'Levellers' and Methodist chapels. I energetically conclude that Britain is best after all.

To try and sum up my impressions of the other side of the Iron Curtain in these seven Soviet days, my main feeling is that I have witnessed a movement here in Moscow which genuinely rejects war. When she spoke at the 1984 Women of the Year Lunch, Valentina Tereshkova warned against nuclear destruction and called for international progress towards peace. In the London audience there were many who called that propaganda, and all this week in Russia I have been depressed to remember the West's suspicion of the Soviet wish for peace. Atomic deterrents have arguably contributed to parity and to forty years without war because the use of these weapons could annihilate the globe, but humanity still stands at the edge of the nuclear precipice. If the USSR is now making a positive move, for whatever reasons, to reduce the risk of annihilation, it must be dangerous negligence for those in authority to discourage it.

Added to this, positive actions seem to be proving that Soviet statements on reform are genuine because so many rigid Communist ideologies are being removed. Many Russians fear this may be opening a Pandora's box by diminishing central control over a vast continent, but the Soviet government remains on the side of the new revolution. So why is the West waiting before giving the Soviet people the support they need to implement democratic reforms? On this last day in Moscow, it seems to me that in the interest of world peace the new Soviet aims for disarmament must be encouraged. The West is too often hypocritical. For example, it justifiably criticizes denial of human rights because of the way the USSR deals with what it calls 'anti-Soviet propaganda' by putting dissidents in prison. But I remember how commercial interests in the neutral nation of Switzerland opposed Stanley Adams for disclosing that a multinational chemical company was under suspicion. This threatened the State's financial security which depended on industrial contributions. In the USSR the security measures taken to protect State interests are certainly fiercer than in Switzerland but is not the motive to safeguard basic assets similar?

Certainly this gathering in Moscow of 3,000 world women has been run with faultless efficiency, admirably matching the highest standards in the West for accommodation, food, transport, rallies and workshops. On behalf of women the Congress has raised awareness so that, working, meeting and thinking together for a week, decisions look likely to follow discussions and then action can follow decisions. Returning to many diverse areas of the world, the participants have been strengthened in their belief that women can obtain positive improvements in living standards by means of a day-to-day struggle against forms of injustice. Also, I have found some reassurance for my despair at the Northern surfeit of riches compared to dereliction in the South, seeing both North and South trying to understand each other in Moscow. To sum up: women from all over the world have cared about human needs together.

Heading for home, I am finishing my Moscow Diary in a BA aeroplane bound for London. The week has been a minute-by-minute challenge. It seems strange that this should have come my way in late middle age when I am feeling tired, blind and rather ill. But I did try to keep my wits about me, my brain as clear as possible, and my heart open. So often in my life I have struggled to defend what I have seen as a true situation and others have been certain that they knew better and that I was a fool to believe too easily. Am I really going to start all over again about Russia, trying to say why I respect many aspects of the Communist experiment even if I would like to live and die for Christian solutions? Here in Moscow I suspect that I have seen the beginning of the end for an epoch as revolutionary for humanity as Chinese, Egyptian, and Roman domination. I believe that I am observing what may be the last gasp of a gigantic empire which attempted to establish a new form of collective civilization. If so, I respect many of its final admirable achievements.

Valentina has sent her former secretary to drive down to the airport with me – a wonderful old lady whose father was illiterate. The last sight of Mikki was her waving from the sixth floor. At the lift door, the leader of the Young Communists was waiting to bring me five carnations. I asked him to come and see us in London.

In the car, Valentina's friend tells me that Valentina's mother is dying; Valentina is very sad but sends her love. She asks me what I thought of the Congress. I say it did not have enough non-Communists to be fully representative. She answers, 'Would they come if we asked them? When I was in London someone said the Russians had dropped the bomb on Hiroshima – that was five years ago and the English seem to have forgotten that we were allies in the War.' Her wound had not healed. I suggest, 'Ask the Women's Institute and the Girl Guides next time.' I said it seriously and she considered it seriously. Could I give Valentina the names of more women's organizations in Britain?

She and Natasha and Albina had stood at the door to the aeroplane waving – the stern old Communist, the jolly obedient Russian teacher who is not a Party member, and the committed Communist economist Natasha: academic, clever, controlled – but underneath it with the emotion which 'suffered' at the concert and quoted Pushkin's poem for his Nanny because it was so sad and so beautiful.

Waiting to take off, I recalled how Alyona had said soon after we first met, 'My mother really loves you, she is so happy you have come; but my grandmother is very ill and we are so worried.' This was the first time I had heard about the most essential person in Valentina's life – her mother. It had been a tragic time for Valentina and my being in Moscow when she was sad about her mother's illness contributed another element to our friendship. On the first day of the Congress as she sat in a place of honour on the platform in the huge hall of the Kremlin, I had known why Valentina looked so distant from worldly acclaim. The human being she relied on most was slipping away.

That was also the day Gorbachev had opened the Congress with the speech announcing his hopes for perestroika and peace. The people of the Soviet Union had found expression through him. I was there when the century changed.

When we next met in London I asked Valentina what she had thought of the Congress. As usual she was direct; her main memory was of her mother's illness and the anxiety and grief it had brought her, but the success of the Congress had meant a great deal to her. She described her memories and I wrote these down.

> I was proud to see the hall of the Kremlin full of women from all over the world. My dream had become true. Just after my space flight I attended the 1963 World Congress of Women, and for the first time I met women from all over the world. Some of the participants in 1987 still remembered my appearance as a young and enthusiastic cosmonaut on the stage of the same hall. This time it was sad for me that because my mother was ill she was not able to attend the Congress, as she had done in 1963, but I will always remember the genuine warmth and fraternalism of this 1987 Congress.

My own most vivid memory was of the welcome she had herself evoked. The delegates loved and admired her. A colleague of Valentina's on the Women's Committee told me the

World Congress of Women had been a special project for Valentina. She had been working out the event since 1985 and it had been on her personal initiative that the Congress was called in Moscow. She had worked on the agenda and on the list of participants and she was finishing the preparatory work for the Congress when she was appointed to another post, to direct the Friendship Societies.

I hoped I could bring a true picture of an outstanding occasion back to the West with me. I knew that the black wall of prejudice still stood strong. I was reassured that, after the Congress, world opinion confirmed that the dramatic week for women had also been a dramatic week for the world and that from then on Gorbachev had proclaimed more revolutionary proposals for the reform of Soviet Communism.

On my return to London I wrote a short, formal report for the Women of the Year Association. It was published in the Association newsletter, and I was pleased that it was well received. I wanted my impressions to give first-hand information on the positive aspects of Communism in Russia. I had tried to tell the truth. But how many readers would dismiss my analysis as 'taken in by propaganda', and how could I prove otherwise? Unlike the government-approved UK delegates I did not have an official brief. I had to find out for myself and make up my own mind and what I had found was very different from the picture of Soviet Russia being given in Britain. It seemed indubitable to me that the World Congress of Women had exemplified the best of what had been achieved by Soviet Communism up to perestroika – the opportunity for women representatives from different areas of the world to meet; the ever-present peace campaign; the order and system with which 3,000 women and their workshops were superbly catered for and planned; and the Soviet delegates' fraternal feeling within the Soviet system including many different republics and ethnic traditions; the excellent education of children and students; and most of all the undeniably determined movement surfacing from within the Soviet Union itself to reform corruption and find a new road to freedom. I had seen much in Soviet Communism which seemed very good indeed.

As I was boarding the BA aeroplane in Moscow I had asked the rather formidable stewardess, 'Is this Aeroflot?' She answered, 'If you can't see the difference it is time I resigned.' All round me people were expressing relief at the sight of alcohol again. 'Have the Russians got an alcohol problem?' the stewardess asked me. She had no apparent notion of our own. In fact the travellers' talk was mostly about Gorbachev's determination to make alcohol as difficult to obtain as any other drug. The three Russians whom I had left at the air terminal were anxious in case this made Gorbachev unpopular – not least because it shut out Russia's income from vodka. I told them many of us in the West were anxious because alcohol is made to seem essential for well-being by the manufacturers who make billions out of sales. But no use telling the BA tourists, now knocking back gin and whisky, that advertising in the West is a form of brainwashing so as to make money. Once again the Iron Curtain between West and East of 'My philosophy is best' had descended. Western tourists wanted to believe that brainwashing only happened in Russia.

In London I found myself frustrated by the complications of communicating with Valentina which meant waiting to hear from an Embassy official with a message from her. As the weeks went by I became increasingly anxious because of my lack of news about her mother. How could I find out, as she had never given me a private telephone number? If we could not communicate how could I sustain our balanced exchange of experiences and of trust between West and East which, while I was in Moscow, had been heightened daily for me? When Valentina and I first met there had been a deep and dangerous division between our nations, but that had been changing fast since 1986, the year of the Reykjavik Summit, and the beginning of the end of the cold war. It was also the year of the

Chernobyl atomic disaster and a fund to help the victims had been established in London and had been well supported. What new moves to build further international understanding would Valentina propose now? I wanted to write to her but I was not sure how.

Then to my relief Yuri Mazur rang me. He said he hoped to deliver a present from Valentina, a small cup and a wooden spoon. He also told me that he had been recalled to Moscow to be replaced by Gennadi Fedosov. He had no news of Valentina's mother, but he could take back a letter from me. This was the pattern of Russian exchanges: letters by hand, usually person-to-person; presents; followed by plans for meetings, all hopeful and haphazard communications until one arrived in Moscow, to find everything perfectly arranged. But I had no immediate reason to travel to Moscow; my only consolation was that now I had a reason to write to Valentina.

Our next meeting happened a year later, when, at a week's notice, Gennadi Fedosov rang me to say that Valentina was coming to London as a member of the Soviet official delegation, led by Gorbachev. She hoped we could have supper together. Gennadi also gave me the news that Valentina's mother had died.

We had a home-cooked meal in a friend's flat – just Valentina, Elizabeth and me. She had spoken on British television and had been to Oxford to attend a seminar, where she had met Mrs Thatcher and Mother Teresa who surprised her by speaking on the 'tragedy' of abortion, which Valentina did not think fitted the occasion.

After supper we looked out over the roofline of London to Big Ben. Valentina liked the Post Office Tower. She hardly ate at all. She was devastated by the death of her mother, who had asked her to read a poem by Pushkin as she was dying. A Patriarch in the Orthodox Church had promised prayers for her mother's soul and said she was eternally alive. This was of great comfort to Valentina. She was thoughtful, and did not appear to see clearly what benefits perestroika could immediately bring to the USSR, which urgently needed improved food supplies and more consumer goods.

She supported the Soviet disarmament proposals and reminded me that, as a strong proponent of the peaceful exploration of space, she had spoken about the dangers of Star Wars for every nation. In 1986 she had lectured at a conference organised by a friend of hers, Lydia Schmidt, chair of the Union of Women of Luxembourg and former deputy chair of the Socialist International, and had warned against Star Wars.

After dinner, she asked me if there was anything that might lead me to make another visit to Russia. I answered from the heart: 'The Millennium of the Russian Orthodox Church. To be there, for the liturgy, the music, the ceremonies of the Church celerating its hope for freedom as well as its ancient glory, would be like a miracle for me.'

'I don't have strong ties with the Church,' Valentina answered, 'but I know the Patriarch and I will ask him.' She added, 'This year is also the twenty-fifth anniversary of my flight.'

This made Elizabeth say, 'And no one will hear about it, because you will never co-operate with journalists.' Valentina smiled, unmoved. Her rejection of personal publicity was too well known for her to deny it.

Once again we had met as members of the same family, and our hope to prove that a strong bridge of personal understanding could be built between West and East had been confirmed as possible. Now another historic milestone on my road to learn more about Russia seemed to be ahead of me if Valentina could find a way for me to attend the Millennium.

After Valentina's return to Moscow I wrote two letters on some of the subjects we had talked about, and sent them to her through the new Embassy counsellor Gennadi Fedosov, who dealt with Friendship Societies' affairs. I tried to convey the impressions made on a Western woman like myself watching the succession of conflicts which were bringing bloodshed all over the world. I had been with Valentina during the cold war when it had been a revelation to me to find so much to admire in the changing Communist system. But did East and West now see more or less disorder and difficulty resulting from the new collaboration which had replaced superpower confrontation? Would both sides continue to uphold the ideal that democracy was worth any price it might require?

In my view the explosions of nationalism seemed to shout for individual freedom, demanding that separate national identities should not be obliterated by central control. This could be justifiable. On the other hand, the violence against any form of restriction, even necessary discipline, was worrying, particularly among young people. It was happening in Russia, Africa, Europe, Asia and in America. There had been a similar ignition in 1968 when French students had revolted, taking de Gaulle by surprise and stunning their own countrymen who did not know that they were inspired by the nihilistic writings of Herbert Marcuse advocating anarchy as the only way to replace defunct structures of power.

Certainly anarchy was one way to pull down the mighty from their thrones, but the girl from Nazareth, in her revolutionary song known throughout Christendom as the 'Magnificat', had found another alternative – the way of spiritual freedom. I wondered if a return to genuine 'love of your neighbour' religion could provide the unifying factor most likely to satisfy those who, in the countries which had revolted against Communist or right-wing domination, now showed young faces holding lighted candles or singing hymns. To me this suggested that spiritual need should not be underestimated. I suggested to Valentina that a Russian Orthodox Church reformed and renewed might unite many people, not least because it had traditionally upheld the virtue of asceticism.

I accepted that mine continued to be a one-sided correspondence. In contrast to her openness when we met personally, Valentina's only letters to me were typed, formal official acknowledgements with her signature in precise, elegant, scientific handwriting. I reminded myself that if, as a Russian, I had tried to contact a high-ranking military officer in the West,

I would have found myself barred by restrictions, no matter how reliable I could prove myself to be. I was treated with unfailing trust by Valentina, who was similarly officially constrained. I realized that this was a privilege and I was satisfied by her assurance that some day soon she would 'tell me the truth' about her life and outlook.

Now that international events were further evolving to transform East-West relations, the rules for communication were also changing between the Communist and democratic systems. There was a far wider exchange of information. Even so, until Valentina could give me her views on the matters I was writing about, I had no way of knowing if she was in agreement with me. I was writing in the dark and for the time being I knew that I could not and must not ask for more than she could correctly concede.

When I tried to telephone Elizabeth in Moscow I sometimes succeeded, but usually the lines were engaged and when we did speak her advice was nearly always to wait for Valentina's spokesman at the London Embassy to tell me how and when Valentina had arranged our next meeting. This could be when she was in the West for conferences, so that if she was travelling through London I could meet her and Elizabeth Zolina at their hotel. I assumed that this repetitive pattern of protocol was required by Soviet regulations, although as with all things Russian, there were surprising exceptions. It was like the front door at the Embassy, which was either locked and barred or flew open at the slightest pressure.

The fact that Valentina and I trusted each other, and that we were in regular contact, increasingly mystified those who had come to know of it. My media colleagues thought it would make a good story and wanted to publicize it. Others hoped to use the contact for their own Soviet projects. The West was waking up to many unexpected and interesting aspects of the USSR which had previously been blocked out. Women's publications wanted me to bring back an exclusive interview with Raisa. My response was that for me to press for any of these requests would diminish my special relationship with Valentina. This was thought to be out of proportion. 'What is it you are trying to defend? What sort of relationship is it?'

It was a question which I had not yet answered for myself. Why were we such firm friends? 'You are not unalike in character: both independent and strong minded,' someone who knew us both well told me. I thought about it. There was a sameness in our reactions to people and events; we were both intelligent but not intelligentsia, in the sense that we were not attracted by the closed circle of so-called intellectuals who exclude those who do not think on the same lines as themselves. I had told Valentina how Lord Attlee once said to me: 'The intelligentsia hate the British public but not half as much as the British public hate the intelligentsia.' She understood.

We both believed in responding to the challenge of basic human choices on right and wrong. Valentina often spoke about morals. On a television panel, Malcolm Muggeridge had once introduced me as a moralist. It had made me indignant until he told me that Thomas Aquinas had defined morals as 'the right use of reason'. This was certainly true of Valentina, who was always concerned about moral choices, but required choice to be founded on balanced and careful reasoning. We both also believed in the interconnection of responsibility between human beings and she was always anxious for children to be trained to think about the results of right and wrong behaviour towards both their neighbours and the environment.

Another resemblance was that we valued merit earned by personal effort. Valentina had never felt part of an establishment elite, or known childhood within the Soviet *nomenklatura* as described by Sakharov's widow, Elena Bonner, in her book *Mothers and Daughters*, where she tells of growing up in the thirties under Communism with servants, plentiful food and comfortable housing. In comparison, Valentina had served her country as a military technician.

My father's family had been Yorkshire doctors, soldiers, lawyers: all professionals, and I worked as a professional journalist.

79

Valentina and I both knew that for efficient administration there was no choice but to deal with the next detail. We both enjoyed working and recognised this in each other.

But did such shared beliefs, including our fear of nuclear war, explain why we found it so easy to understand each other? Was it because we were also similar in outlook in that we both valued family ties, children, and country life as opposed to city life, although our work was city-orientated? I tried to identify other similarities but failed, not least on the level of courage, where there could obviously be no comparison.

There were dissimilarities. I had always felt a loner, an outsider, resenting any attempt to categorize me, because above all I wanted to be free to belong to any community which would accept me. Valentina was the opposite. She never seemed to doubt that, no matter how genuinely she appreciated other nations and cultures, she remained a four-square Russian from the Yaroslavl region which, when she described it, sounded like the northern Italy of Luciano Pavarotti to which she felt deeply drawn. In fact it struck me that if she had not been Russian she could have been Piedmontese. Perhaps the Italian factor was another link between us. As Vittorio Zucconi, a leading Italian journalist, had written: 'Italy and Russia are very similar. The Russian organization is like the Italian Post Office but with atomic power.'

Because Valentina was interested to know more about my upbringing and because, as she often said, we had been educated in different 'cultures', I told her my life story.

My early childhood had been spent in Egypt, where my father was a British medical administrator. My mother was Italian, the daughter of a soldier who eventually became Governor of the then Eritrea. She was small and brave, and was still sailing the oceans at the age of seventy in a boat without an engine.

My mother and father had separated when I was eight years old, and I had suffered the sundering experiences common to all children of divorce. After this I stayed regularly with my grandmother in Rome and with our family housekeeper in her smallholding in the Tuscan hills. It was here that I first experienced life in a dictatorship. The thirties in Italy were ruled by Mussolini. But Italian-style Fascism often meant disregarding all regulations, so for me dictatorship meant only that, provided no one asked disturbing questions, those who wished to live in peace could do so. I remember that one of my two uncles, an uncompromising soldier, was never promoted because he opposed Fascist corruption in the armed services, but the only time I can remember being frightened by Fascism was when Mussolini, copying Hitler, issued decrees which discriminated against the Jews. I had never distinguished between Jews and Italians before then, and was shattered when a young friend who wanted to train as a scientist told me that her family must emigrate to Argentina to escape persecution. Sadly, when I met her sister after the war she told me that my friend had been killed in a car accident. She had kept a diary, found only after her death, and on one page she had written: 'Poor Tony, always wanting to know why. What will happen to her?'

After my mother remarried I had lived mainly in England with her and my stepfather, another British soldier. This gave me happy, conventional country-based security, educated at home or in Army schools. During the holidays I either travelled with my half-sister back to Norfolk, my stepfather's home, or I joined my father in a rented villa in the health resort of San Remo, where he had been obliged to retire because of chronic asthma. It was a comfortable British lifestyle, remote from the challenge of social injustice in the wider world with its strikes and unemployment which always worried me.

This security had been shattered when I was sent to school in Germany just before the war. The persecution of the Jews was relentless and to witness how they were categorized as sub-human by the description 'Semite' and denied dignity as individuals transformed my thinking. I had become a very uncomfortable member of the school, particularly when I followed up carefully concealed rumours of atrocities against the Jews told to me by a house cleaner. I challenged the upright

Christian citizens who befriended me to share my repulsion but they did not want to know. What they did know, and I was finding out, was that in a dictatorship, repulsion and security cannot be combined. I had seen it in Egypt, Italy and Germany: to live in peace it was necessary to stay in step with people in power and with their bureaucracy. This made me increasingly indignant with those who built barriers around themselves to avoid seeing the cruelty suffered by outsiders.

At this time, with the prospect of war, I had also felt I must find an answer to spiritual as well as social challenges. Many of my friends, hardly twenty years old, faced the likelihood of death, not in the acceptable rhythm of old age but at life's beginning. I asked myself – would their short existences end like snuffed-out candles? It cost agonies of uncertainty before I took the simple decision to be certain of eternal life, as promised by Jesus Christ. This continues to be my deep faith in the context of St Paul's challenge that faith is the substance of what we hope for and evidence for what we cannot prove.

In the war years I had worked as a nursing auxiliary and lived through the death of friends who had not wanted to go to war. We often shared the same sadness that the First World War poems of Wilfred Owen and Siegfried Sassoon had spoken for, and many of us remembered the heartbreaking evidence of human unity when, on Christmas Eve, soldiers on opposing sides in the mud and blood of the trenches had sung 'Silent Night' together. But patriotism had become realism in the Second World War. It was the only alternative to evil conquering the world.

After the war there had been marriage, six children and involvement in national and international affairs both as a journalist who supported Socialist reforms, and as the wife of a Conservative government minister. But peace had not brought social justice, and through my mind in these years ran the now-familiar thread of anxiety watching human progress being obstructed by unnecessary barriers. The same question persisted: why build barriers? Why did the people I liked and met in many varied situations actually enjoy living exclusively within their own tribe? The tribes inevitably conflicted. I could not see how the security afforded by being fenced in made conflicts worthwhile.

Seeing the Jews suffering in Nazi Germany had sown in me a seed of motivation to try and protect the helpless. I believed wholeheartedly in the ideal of reverence for life taught by Albert Schweitzer. I came to feel this particularly about black friends, as my work enabled me to meet many from the Caribbean. The history of the black people haunted me – removed in thousands from their own continent, culture and traditions, carted like cattle across oceans, dumped in cotton and sugar plantations to be exploited by God-fearing tyrants, yet still singing their incomparable spiritual songs. I often asked myself, why did so few white people afford them proper respect? My memories of Germany continued to hurt a corner of my conscience, and after the war I had constantly found other forms of oppression and discrimination. It seemed to me that, having defeated the Nazis, the democracies of the rich North now adopted similar master-race attitudes in their dealing with the poor South. There were too few positive educational or financial measures to help the new second-class citizens of the Third World whose resources had been sequestrated. If my ideal was to be on the side of human unity and reverence for life, what was I doing which contributed to justice?

My response was usually inadequate. The only solution I could think of was that barriers must be broken, and that people must meet even if this caused disturbance. The definition of discrimination is 'to distinguish unfavourably'. To remain undisturbed, it was essential not to see and not to speak. But the antidote to unfair distinctions was the exposure of facts, and I hoped that I could discover and present facts which led to human unity.

I had been fortunate in that, during the fifties and sixties, the circumstances of my life enabled me to meet an exceptionally wide cross-section of people. As well as my press contacts I also met medical workers through my work for the Royal Colleges of Gynaecologists and of Nursing. Then my husband's political duties took him as a delegate to the UN in New York, the

Disarmament Conference in Geneva and the European Parliament in Strasbourg, and travelling for the Foreign Office in Africa, so with him I met top-level politicians from all nations. When I became actively involved in the campaign for equal opportunities I also met many influential women leaders. These varied contacts proved to me that when disparate people know more about each other they become tolerant in practice, even if they do not agree in principle. There were opportunities for me to bring disparate groups together and I was encouraged when I was told, 'You create a friendly talking atmosphere.' The ideal of human unity was a slow road to travel on but as time went on I had found more fellow-travellers, and also now in the Soviet Union.

Valentina had been interested to hear this past history and to know more about me. She was right. Our cultural circumstances, superficially, had not been similar, but if we understood each other's different upbringing, dissimilarities in education and background could be proved not to separate those who share the same ideals.

On reflection I decided that the major unifying characteristic which lifted Valentina and me above conventional time-serving was that we both genuinely wanted to know the truth. I believed that telling Valentina the truth as I saw it from the West was the most important contribution I could make to our friendship, and she spoke the truth to me.

But an unsolved mystery remained. In Russia it was given the same description again and again: *Destiny*. Why had we met? Was there some work we were meant to achieve together, or was it just a happy coincidence that our lives had been uplifted by an unexpected encounter? To Russians it seemed natural to describe ours as a 'destined friendship'. But what did destiny mean? What did it expect of us? Where would it lead to?

I looked up 'destiny' in the dictionary; the definition was: 'Fate considered as a power.' Some sort of power did seem to have helped to develop our friendship. But why? I found my usual refuge in setting out and trying to answer two questions on paper.

For a start: if an explicable meeting between two people leads to an inexplicable unfolding of extraordinary results, before it can be said that there was intervention from a source of power, two elements need to be confirmed. The first is that the destined friends have to be in an appropriate place at an appropriate time so that the unexpected meeting can happen. Secondly, the chemistry between the destined friends needs to include a catalyst which facilitates necessary results in exceptional circumstances. Our relationship did seem to fulfil these two requirements. Was ours a destined friendship?

When I eventually read this analysis to Valentina, she smiled. She reminded me of the Jewish friend who had written: 'Poor Tony, always wanting to know why.'

But then a photograph of Valentina taken with her mother proved that there was a catalyst which united us. My childhood had been centred for a time in living with an Italian foster-mother: our Tuscan family housekeeper, Selide. She was both ordinary and extraordinary. There are many others like her, the dedicated family women of the world, who in every nation hold communities together. This does not exclude the essential place of unselfish men, the father figures which are exemplified perhaps most positively by the patriarchs of Israel who also hold families together. But the unselfish family mothers seem to be even more important because not only can every colour, race and creed provide its own examples, but a common factor unifies them all; with their patient work they are clever enough, and strong enough, to hold communities together.

The one I knew best – Selide – was poor, proud, talented; at ease with the highest and critically observant of the weaknesses of both high and low. She was queen of her own kingdom, a smallholding in the hills, as her mother had been before her. She understood everything, knew everything and could govern everything; from putting into place the smallest pieces in her own life's jigsaw puzzle to finding a solution for global problems. She did not need to study philosophy because by instinct she set principles in their right perspective. She was self-sacrificing to a heroic degree for her family and friends and an obsessive love for children was the only passion which lost proportion. She was familiar with classical music, literature, works of art. It was innate in her to comprehend levels of sophistication which a school or university might never impart. I have found these strong family women in the same mould, all over the world. They are at their most typical as grandmothers whose family years have been spent fighting an unrelenting incoming tide. Unquestioning, they have not only undertaken the treadmill of family work: mending, washing, cooking, carrying, but they have also served the ugly sides of the human condition, the convulsions of birth and death, and the demands of dealing with disease. With wrinkled faces, capable worn hands and bright, discerning eyes, they are hardly ever taken in, except as willing victims of their grandchildren. They represent humanity at its finest and furthest from triviality, counterfeit and indifference to neighbours' needs.

That is why, for me, the photograph of Valentina's mother explained that there was a catalyst for our similar outlook on life. We both recognised in her a hero of humanity – one of the family women whose hands I had wanted to kiss in Portugal, in Canada, in Italian churches, in an Arab crowd in Jerusalem, among West Indians, waiting for relatives at the Cyprus airport, in the Glasgow tenements and on island crofts everywhere. Sometimes I found one among the rich who practised self-denial; and these were 'as different from their peers as a diamond amongst pebbles, the common hallmark usually being not to have the unfair advantage of easy beauty but to share a nobility of features carved by endurance. Black clothes and headscarves, the first that come to hand, make the thin and the stout look the same: functional. This could also be true of a film star, nurse, doctor or scientist who is a loving family woman; but usually the common denominator for these heroes of humanity is adversity and poverty.

When I saw the photograph I realised why Valentina was convinced that her mother possessed infinitely greater intelligence than, and was innately superior to, those whom the world presented as superior. Valentina relied on her mother's power. It was power I had so often sensed as spiritual, no matter whether the spirit within was Buddhist, Islamic, Hindu, Jewish, Christian or Communist. Seeing the photograph of Valentina with her mother I knew why she was not only lovable but also invincible. The small thin woman in a black dress and working shoes, her grey hair tied back to a neat head in a bun, is looking at Valentina in her hour of global fame as she must have looked at her when she came back from the factory: with understanding, no trace of awe – just a close relationship, and the assurance of never-failing support. I saw all this in the photograph, and Valentina knew I knew. The two of us knew the same truth – without words.

At our sustained meetings, whether in Russia or Britain, Valentina and I did exchange words, speaking through Elizabeth Zolina as interpreter. Our trialogue had a rhythm of its own: the question, then the translation, and then the answer. The interpreter is, in a way, taken advantage of by both sides, but with Elizabeth alchemy happened again and our trialogues were usually surprisingly thoughtful, constructive and real. Alyona had also become an interpreter, her sweet intelligent face strained with the will to convey true meaning.

Strangely, illogically, however, there was often no need for words. I was not able to speak Valentina's language but it was as if Valentina and I were meeting on some kind of sound wave, like the pictures on television which do not always need translated captions to make the meaning comprehensible. We seemed to exchange thoughts in a strange dimension of perception and Elizabeth was often surprised that I was regularly ahead of her translation. It was the same with Valentina: although she does understand English because she has learnt it for scientific research, our exchange of similar ideals did not always need language to make it understandable. That is why our shared intuition of what her mother represented had provided a crucial key.

For me it also explained the extent of Valentina's contact with reality. It had worried me to find how many Russians in the professions, the ones I was meeting, seemed to be cut off from the humble, anxious-looking elderly women I had seen in the churches. Later this was confirmed when I saw Soviet officials taken aback and even terrified by the fierce determination to reach the Communion rails of old women in headscarves, who were there in huge crowds at the Millennium services. Obviously it is the same all over the world. The privileged are usually sealed off from the poor, particularly by city living, and I remembered how in Nazi Germany and Fascist Italy this separation had become sinister and punitive because of the suppression of free speech.

I was free to speak and free to question, and so I could tell Valentina the truth as I identified it from the West. The world of Soviet cosmonautics was a limited scientific community, and the welcome she received as a celebrity was sometimes artificial. Like all people in power she was not always told the truth by those who worked for her, who, in any case, feared her as an acute observer of all they were doing. I could only hope my honest accounts helped her.

But Valentina did not need to hear the truth from me as much as she needed to hear it from her mother. While her love remained centred on her mother she remained in contact with women of the same calibre, who in their millions, without living at the centre of official power, possessed true power; and, with ground-level information through the network of their families, represented reality.

It was a great relief to me to find that Valentina and I shared this illumination. It brought me back to the definition of destiny. We had met and our understanding and respect for each other had developed in an extraordinary way. We had proved the two individuals who trusted each other, one from the East and one from the West, could break apparently unbreakable barriers. I now believed that it was reasonable to have faith in the fact that we were destined, together, to provide a voice for the voiceless women of the world who wanted peace and dreaded war.

The Third Milestone

Millennium of the Russian Orthodox Church

In 1988 I was once again on my way to Moscow by Aeroflot and again I owed it to Valentina. She had arranged for me to receive a formal invitation from the Metropolitan responsible for the international delegates to the Orthodox Millennium. He welcomed me as the President of the inter-demoninational UK Order of Christian Unity.

It became typical of all subsequent happenings in a spiritually dramatic week, that I arrived at the reception centre in Moscow at the same time as the Archbishop of Canterbury, Billy Graham, Archbishop Tutu, Dr Busack and four Vatican cardinals, and that I received the same hospitality. Certainly attending the Millennium celebrations was one of the most moving experiences of my life and it seemed like a miracle that the events I participated in were happening within an atheist autocracy.

Valentina had arranged that throughout the week Natalya Semenikhina, the daughter of the Soviet General Batov who had been made a Knight of the British Empire in the war against Hitler, would look after me. Valentina was always worried that I was partially blind. A black Zil car was at my disposal for special transport, but not surprisingly this caused suspicion. Waiting for the hotel lift I heard three Italian priests who were with the Vatican delegation say: '*Attenzione – e certo una collaboratrice.*' My British image had masked the possibility of my understanding Italian. I kept quiet. It was now becoming second nature to me in my friendship with Valentina to have to hold onto the integrity of my own intentions, while I was increasingly suspect on all sides. The Archbishop of Canterbury, charismatic with courtesy and much respected by all present, had greeted me with surprise: 'What are you doing here?' My ally throughout was the Very Rev Dr Duncan Shaw, former Moderator of the Church of Scotland, a distinguished theologian, extremely well informed on international Christian activities and particularly Orthodox Christianity in the East. He knew all the leaders of the Christian battalions and I was thankful that he and I were together most of the time. I was not particularly inspired by the professional Christian administrators from the West.

My participation had begun with a telex in May from Metropolitan Filaret of Minsk. It read:

> Dear Sister in the Lord cordially inviting you to attend celebrations dedicated to the millennium of the baptism of Russia to be held by the Russian Orthodox Church from June 4 to 6 1988 kindly inform the invitation accepted and cable birthdate and passport number for entry visa arrangements we shall meet your stay expenses in our country our address 113191 Moscow Danilovsky Val 22 respectfully Metropolitan Filaret of Minsk and Byelorussia Chairman Department for External Church Relations Moscow Patriarchate May 12 1988

Metropolitan Filaret was the bishop I had met when I was attending the World Congress of Women. Then he had given

90

me his book *Choose Life* which had widened my slim knowledge of Russian Orthodoxy and how it began in 988 when Grand Prince Vladimir, 'Equal to the Apostles', investigated Islam, Judaism and Christianity, three religions based on one Holy Book, to find one to unite his people. The Greeks in Constantinople, 'who worshipped God in such splendour and beauty that their God seemed to dwell among men' were preferred, and today prayer and patriotism continue to remain the hallmark of the Church in Holy Russia despite a century of suppression by tsars and commissars.

For the Millennium the four hundred international guests of honour were in Russia seeking inspiration as well as information. I recognised many famous faces, but more important was the guests' international influence. Nearly all represented thousands of fellow faithful, and the ones I spoke to from Japan, India, North Vietnam, Samoa and Kentucky reacted fraternally to an Apostolic Church which bridges East and West through a disciplined form of Christian worship within sacramental structures. There was also the opportunity to compare Russian spiritual-secular problems with similar problems as dealt with in democracies where secular laws prevail. This encouraged an exercise in honesty, including the reminder that it did not suit Christians from situations of material surfeit to criticise lack of luxury in Russia.

The ten-day timetable was taxing but each occasion was food for the soul. On the first day there was the Church Assembly in Zagorsk outside Moscow with Orthodox delegates from East and West and speeches of praise simultaneously translated; bells ringing, elders with strong faces listening, and multi-coloured clerical gear – white, blue, red and plum – covering the handsome young priests' carefully combed hair. The Russian Orthodox Church is strong in clergy: priests, deacons, monks and nuns, and seminarians. It is also strong in patriotism. The majority of saints were defenders of Mother Russia, and prayers for the fallen in Afghanistan reminded me of Imperial Britain and the hymn, 'I Vow to Thee My Country': 'The love that asks no questions.' The speakers and dioceses echoed Bible history; Antioch, Jerusalem, Alexandria, Cyprus and Armenia, but Athens and Constantinople were absent.

That same evening, never to be forgotten, there was the Festive Concert in the Bolshoi Theatre at the invitation of the Patriarch. Raisa Gorbachev sat in the front row. The Creed was sung first by a massed choir – all watched live on Soviet television, with the backcloth of Prince Vladimir like a triumphant Canute rising from the river. Next came religious music and songs of extraordinary power; Communist state choirs alternating with monks' choirs – an affirmation of secular and spiritual unity with Tchaikovsky's 1812 Overture transcending in an explosion of energy. This was no normal theatre performance. It was traumatic – a cry for a new century of belief by a whole people and now it could be heard by the whole world as well as throughout the Soviet Union.

When I next saw Valentina she told me she had been inspired by the concert and that it had confirmed for her that spirituality remained deep in Russia.

The evening following the concert, Duncan Shaw and I attended three local Moscow churches for the all-night vigil. The babushkas were there with their families, standing, bowing, crossing themselves, kissing the icons; the priests in their gold vestments, the incomparable singing, their majestic repetitive sacramental prayers in slow movements: the gifts of Russian Orthodoxy to the world.

The next morning, perhaps most moving of all, we shared in the open-air Mass at the newly-restored Danilovsky Monastery, 'For all the saints who shone on the land of Russia.' The weather was wet and windy but the crowd which packed the square was undeterred. We heard the great bell ringing, taken up by lesser bells, after all being silent for seventy years.

The aged Patriarch Pimen's voice dominated even the singing. Rows of priests distributed Communion to the crowd, which seemed to be a sea of headscarves, evidence that the babushkas were present with daughters, sons-in-law and grandchildren. With difficulty I reached the altar, hoping to receive

Communion, but obviously I did not look Russian and the priest asked me, 'Orthodox?' I said no, so he just blessed me. That seemed Orthodox. Round the altar, dignitaries with gold mitres and vestments were interspersed with the black and white of Evangelicals and Protestant bishops and cardinals in red. It was all broadcast throughout the Soviet Union. I asked a Russian friend if I was intruding on a Russian occasion. There was no reply.

In contrast, probably the most significant political act happened in the afternoon: the Prime Minister's reception at the Kremlin with a personal question-and-answer session. Patriarch Pimen was sitting beside Gromyko, who welcomed all the churches participating in the solemnities and said that, while the 1917 Revolution had been a great historic necessity which united a multi-national country, new thinking was now needed for the nuclear age. He did not dodge difficult questions, as on job preferment for Party members compared with believers. It seemed unprecedented that cardinals of the calibre of Willebrands and Casaroli could ask controversial questions in public of the Head of State of a superpower and receive constructive replies. Gromyko also gave an assurance that all religious restrictions would soon be lifted. It was difficult to take in fully the implications of this meeting which were in fact revolutionary for Soviet relations between Church and State.

To end the festivities we were given the choice of three pilgrimages – Kiev, Leningrad, or Vladimir and Suzdal. I chose Vladimir, a destination which became exceptionally interesting for me. It felt like leaving London for Bath and Glastonbury, and it was like a rural microcosm of the solemnities in Moscow. There was the same hospitality, even larger helpings of simple food, even more frequent bursts of choral singing, even more bearded impassive Orthodox prelates and friendly young priests, and also the same interminable international messages and the same four-hour-long services. Vladimir's art treasures are unrivalled and provide continuing religious education because there are icons everywhere, sometimes so close together that they look like patterned gold wallpaper.

At the first Mass held in Vladimir Cathedral the babushkas pressed forward in a benevolent but irrepressible tide. There were moments of panic when a dangerous crush seemed unavoidable. No question of ticket holders here.

For the church reception we were met by horn players in a beautifully simple monastery square with its whitewashed cathedral, star-encrusted onion domes and green fields. The church organizer in a flowery cotton dress might have been a member of the Townswomen's Guild. At the banquet held in the ancient kremlin with polished wooden tables and benches, a woman's choir in Tudor dress sang, the priests sang, the horn players sang, everyone sang. It ended at midnight. Mass was at 7 a.m. in the open air next morning, with swallows diving in the blue sky.

Now my participation in the Millennium celebrations was ending. In Vladimir-Suzdal our group included a cardinal, a bishop from North Vietnam, a Russian Baptist leader, a Lutheran professor, and a victim of Hiroshima, and we had found the Russian regional celebration more personal and merrier than in the capital. We parted with regret to make our way back to the controlled comfort of the Ukraina Hotel in Moscow.

Because Valentina expected us earlier, Natalya and I were driven back in an official Zil car while the other pilgrims travelled by special coach the next day. The Zil drivers seemed to be a race apart, accustomed to halving the time of long-distance journeys by using the fast lane which on all Soviet roads was reserved exclusively for official cars. This gave the drivers confidence, and the interpreters seemed to be in awe of them. But I always found them very friendly and they were amused when I appealed for help because I was a babushka. On our drive back from Vladimir to Moscow there was an unexpected confrontation. Natalya and I were tired and we fell asleep. The driver had been interested in the celebrations we had attended and he obviously wanted to hear more. Suddenly we were woken up by the car coming to a halt. 'No oil, no water,' the driver announced. Natalya became agitated. We were already late for the next appointment in Moscow. We sat in the car, presumably expecting to be rescued. Natalya argued with the driver but it had no effect. I tried a different approach. I asked her to describe the religious ceremonies in Vladimir to him while we were waiting. The driver said he had wanted to tell his mother. He started the car. There was oil and water after all. We drove on at high speed but no longer in silence or asleep.

Was there a constant and particularly inspiring thread running through the Millennium celebrations? For me it was the babushkas. Taking part in the Orthodox celebrations left me convinced that if faith and fidelity exemplify religion, no one in Russia had a greater right to enjoy and celebrate the Millennium. Aged between fifty and seventy, these grandmothers of all Russia are irreplaceable in each community. At home they cook, find food, nurse the sick, scold, advise and listen. In church they pray, move furniture, and attend the Sacraments. They also often contribute a third of their pensions to Church needs. For the Church this is formidable 'granny power'.

Gorbachev had written in his book on perestroika: 'Today our main job is to lift the individual, spiritually respecting his inner world and giving him moral strength.' I had become certain that Western Christianity would be guilty if it hurt this hope, and undoubtedly now that freedom for religion would benefit all Russians, a political leader with battalions of babushkas behind him could well become invincible. After seventy grey years for the babushkas there was now a promise of spring. A right reward for real religion.

Witnessing the revival of religion in Russia also reminded me of a still unsolved spiritual mystery. I had noted with deep, and, for some, possibly disproportionate interest, the message given in 1917 by the Mother of God to three Portuguese children minding sheep at Fatima. She told them that Russia would be converted, but only after it had spread errors throughout the world. The message to two young illiterate girls and one boy brought them only suffering, humiliation, and punishment from the secular authorities, but they would not betray their story. They maintained that the Mother of God called humanity to pray so as to prevent the terrifying consequences of world-wide wickedness, which she warned could culminate in global catastrophe. In the light of nuclear dangers this was not improbable in the future but had the first part of the message now been justified?

I already felt depressed thinking that on my return to the West I would find that people remained sceptical about Christianity not only being still alive in Russia but even able to lead the world in a religious revival, which I believed could be true. Throughout the Millennium I had heard the remark: 'I am not a believer but my grandmother had me baptised.' Returning from the service in Zagorsk Cathedral with Natalya, our driver, not the same one as before, asked if we could stop at his grandmother's dacha to give her the holy image he had been handed in the cathedral. We found the grandmother in her log house in the woods and at the door there was a candle burning in front of an icon of the Mother of God. I reverently kissed it and the grandmother hugged me warmly. 'You are both believers,' Natalya said. In fact we were two Communists, two Christians, for that moment, united as friends. It seemed to me that the Orthodox Church was probably the only unifying factor which could hold within its widespread network all ages and conditions including non-believers in the Soviet Union. I hoped that it could become a positive influence for global good.

After the Millennium, when I was back in Britain, in a letter to Valentina I suggested that many problems of injustice and misery might be solved by a worldwide attempt to practise true Christianity and that the Russian Church, purified of its former materialism, might inspire this. There are one hundred million Orthodox believers throughout the world, and there are seventy million in the USSR – more than there are Communist Party members.

I told Valentina that Gandhi had said: 'I love Jesus Christ but I do not love Christians because they are so unlike him.' If only there were enough Christians who were like Christ, this could bring about understanding not only with Islam and Judaism, faiths which share the same holy book, the Bible; but also with the Communist ideals so often close to Christ's teachings. I wondered if another religious benefit for humanity might be that because spirituality usually encourages a frugal way of living, this could provide an antidote for many of the perils which accompany materialistic excesses, such as pollution and other ecological hazards. It could save mankind from environmental disasters to follow modest expectations where so many Christian humanists, such as Mother Teresa, already lead the way.

I had no way of knowing what Valentina as a scientist thought of the questions I was asking her, but I knew how much she hoped for unity through the exchange of inter-ethnic cultures and that her main religious concern was how divisive the religious fundamentalists were proving themselves to be.

Throughout the Millennium, together with many others, I had been inspired by all that was best in what we saw as an Orthodox Church reformed by suffering. Discussing this with an Episcopal bishop from America he said he agreed but added: 'In the West will anyone believe us? They did not believe Billy Graham when he told them at home about the revival of religion in Russia.'

Then something totally unexpected happened. Another remarkable experience resulted from my being in Moscow for the Millennium. I found myself being asked to take a historic message to Margaret Thatcher.

Natalya said that, during the week, Valentina had been anxious that I should meet Metropolitan Juvenaly of Moscow who had been to school with her in Yaroslavl. At one of the evening church receptions Natalya persuaded him to receive Dr Duncan Shaw and myself privately the next afternoon.

It turned out to be not only an inspiring meeting but also one of historic consequence. To start with, in the Metropolitan we found a genuine pastoral priest, one of the most distinguished of the younger Orthodox theologians living in and looking after the famous Novodevichy Convent, and then at the subsequent interview he confirmed for us how, after seventy years of suppression and persecution, the Russian Orthodox Church was about to be set free. The convent is in a beautiful setting overlooking the Moscow river and it contains an unrivalled collection of church treasures all exceptionally well-conserved. I introduced Duncan Shaw as a former Moderator of the Church of Scotland and a distinguished Calvinist theologian. The Metropolitan said it was an honour to meet him and that he was happy to meet me. Over tea and cakes Duncan and I described the Gromyko seminar to him and how, in the presence of Patriarch Pimen, he had given an assurance of increasing religious freedom. I admitted that, as always, the Western delegates had wondered whether to believe it, because solidified prejudice left little room for the virtue of hope. Metropolitan Juvenaly replied that the truth was in fact very hopeful, and that during the same week Gorbachev had met the Orthodox bishops and he had told them that the Church could now practise religion without restrictions. We heard this news with awe.

Then, to my surprise the Metropolitan asked me to write down a message and take it to Mrs Thatcher. He remained unmoved by my protestations that I did not know her. 'Pray and try,' he said. His message was that he wanted her to know that the Russian Orthodox Church was now free because she had enabled America to look at Russia and Russia to look at America and this had made perestroika possible. I was also to take her a record of Russian church music and the seal of Saint Vladimir. Having left the Metropolitan, Duncan and I discussed his request and we agreed that as the message was so sincere and of such historical importance I had no choice but to take it to the Prime Minister.

One of my problems would be to explain my involvement to her, but I remembered the Metropolitan's advice to 'Pray and try' and when I returned from Moscow to London I wrote to Mrs Thatcher's secretary saying that Metropolitan Juvenaly, whom she had met on her visit to Russia a year previously, had asked me to bring her a personal message and gifts commemorating the Millennium. I described the gifts: a record of his cathedral choir, and the Millennium Seal, all in a plastic bag with St Vladimir printed on it. Would the police allow me to leave it at No. 10? I added that the message he had asked me to convey to her was of his gratitude for her personal initiatives to inspire a Soviet-American dialogue and consequently the 'miracle' of perestroika in Church-State relations.

I did not expect to see the Prime Minister face to face. However her secretary, Mrs Gaisman, replied to my letter and proposed a meeting: 'No. 10; Thursday July 7th; 6 p.m.'

It seemed to me that once again my 'rebuilding' perestroika journey was getting out of hand. I was not a Conservative. I consistently criticised the Thatcher cut-backs in the social services. I had never joined the prevalent chorus of admiration for the Prime Minister, but now I was to give her a message from Moscow which indicated that she had saved humanity from atomic war. I felt very sincere in doing so, but what would her reaction be?

As it happened, our meeting took place on the same day as the *Piper Alpha* oil rig disaster. I almost hoped the Prime Minister would cancel it, but Mrs Gaisman telephoned again to say would I go to the House of Commons instead.

Sitting in St Stephen's Hall waiting to be summoned I felt very unprepared. I remembered that the last time I had spoken to Margaret Thatcher was thirty years earlier to discuss her speech at the Women of the Year Lunch. The theme was 'If not you – who?' and she had chosen Anna, teacher of Victorian values to the King of Siam. Then she had been a conventional Conservative politician, not well-known and only recently appointed to the Board of Trade. Now she was one of the most famous women in the world – not least in Russia.

Outside Parliament the news headlines were about the death toll on the oil rig – inside, the customary complacency had been taken by surprise. There was an atmosphere of agitation.

The Prime Minister's Parliamentary Secretary came up and introduced himself. 'She has a lot of unexpected meetings today. I hope she can fit you in.'

Upstairs in a room overlooking the river, another Parliamentary Secretary was at a desk writing. He briefly said hello. While waiting, the Member of Parliament who had met me discussed perestroika with me. I suggested that there were historical turning points when youth will not be pushed further than a given point, as in the USA with Vietnam and in Europe when war between European nations every twenty years was suddenly unacceptable at grass-roots level, which made the EEC inevitable. As I had seen it, Russian youth had now reached a frontier of non-acceptance of war and austerity. He did not appear convinced.

Then the door opened from another room and Mrs Thatcher, hand outstretched, gave me a kind, unpretentious welcome. She looked red-eyed and tired but the sort of sympathetic listener one could talk to.

I read her the message from the Moscow Metropolitan. She listened carefully. I gave her the plastic bag and we took out the presents as if it was Christmas. I had to kneel on the floor to get the record out; she knelt to help me. She seemed genuinely interested in my impressions of Moscow on two very different occasions, the World Congress and the Church Millennium. She smiled when I told her that at the Congress the Communist delegates, having asked me what political party I belonged to, had been puzzled by my reply: 'Floating Voter', but when I had added, 'I have voted for Mrs Thatcher,' they all reacted with, 'She is a very clever woman.'

I also told the Prime Minister the story of my friendship with Valentina Tereshkova, how I had defended her at the press conference when American journalists had attacked her about Afghanistan and how later she had sent Soviet medical information to help our son-in-law. Mrs Thatcher said this showed trust in British medical implementation. She too had met Valentina, 'a very fine person,' and she knew about her space achievement. I told her that Valentina hoped that a candidate from Britain would train as a cosmonaut. The Prime Minister asked her parliamentary secretary to take account of this request.

Then I decided I had nothing to lose by stating what I believed to be true about Mrs Thatcher herself, which was that although in the future her current triumphs would probably be forgotten, our grandchildren would thankfully remember the part she had played in solving the crisis of misunderstanding between the USA and the USSR, which might have culminated in atomic war. She replied, 'Yes, but we must not let down our guard.' Then she said in parting, 'This has been an unhappy day for me because of the oil rig explosion, but the Metropolitan's message has made me happy.'

I cannot quote more of our conversation without her permission, but I remember the impression she gave me that, even with confidence in perestroika, she wanted the West to stay strong to defend itself. I replied that I had reminded my Russian friends that I did not want to live in a Europe used as a football by the USA and USSR, while both superpowers remained protected from ultimate destruction. Mrs Thatcher looked thoughtful. Throughout she had been sincere, humble and wise. I wished Valentina had been there too.

I left the Prime Minister's office hoping that history would remember Margaret Thatcher's outstanding contribution to peace, in that she had been sufficiently discerning to make up her own mind about the possibilities of perestroika. As the Metropolitan had said, she encouraged the Russians to meet the Americans and the Americans to meet the Russians and this had been the turning of the tide in East-West relations. But I wondered whether the politicians who surrounded the Prime Minister would ever believe any good news involving the Soviet Union.

After the World Congress of Women I had tried to give media colleagues my favourable impressions of the perestroika movement in Russia. A plate-glass barrier of suspicion had been the only response, with the accusation that I had been taken in by propaganda. Now a world statesman, Margaret Thatcher, had halted the headlong haste of too many political leaders to act on fear. Fear might have led to the annihilation of our fragile planet by atomic weapons used irresponsibly or even accidentally. One woman had altered the direction towards dialogue instead of destruction. It was an achievement of immense magnitude. Would it ever be fully recognized?

As our interview ended, the Prime Minister's office had become intense with decisions and discussion. I saw myself out alone, and met a cleaning lady in the lift. 'I really like the Prime Minister,' I said. She replied, 'Yes, so do I – but the men will see her out before long.' For me taking a historic message to Margaret Thatcher will remain one of the most unexpected happenings of my life.

All this took place following my return to London from Moscow. But to revert to what was happening to me in Moscow, when I reluctantly agreed to take a message to the British Prime Minister I told the Metropolitan that I did not see myself as a reliable carrier pigeon. This had caused a brief problem for Natalya who was interpreting. Were there no carrier pigeons in Russia? She solved it by describing me as a migratory bird. I seemed certainly destined to travel further afield, because the next milestone for me on my road to perestroika was a long way from spiritual revival. It was to see at first hand the achievements of Soviet space technology, and all in the same week as the Millennium celebrations.

A. Lothian, October 1984

Below: Valentina Tereshkova. Lecture at the Royal Aeronautical Society, London, October 1984

Above: Mikhail Gorbachev addresses the World Congress of Women in the Kremlin Palace of Congresses, Moscow, June 1987. A. Lothian third left, middle row

World Congress of Women, June 1987. A. Lothian and Mikki Doyle, Women's Editor of the *Morning Star*, in Red Square, Moscow

Russian icon of the Mother of God. Millennium of the Russian Orthodox Church, 1988

Star City, Moscow, June 1988. Group standing on steps of Mir space station includes
Valentina Tereshkova, A. Lothian and Elizabeth Zolina

A. Lothian and Valentina with the space capsule, Vostok 6, Star City on June 16th 1988 to
celebrate the 25th anniversary of her space flight

Right: Star City, June 1990. Left to right: Peter Lothian, A. Lothian, Dr Alyona Tereshkova and cosmonaut Alexei Leonov, Hero of the Soviet Union, the first man to walk in space

Left: Floella Benjamin with dancers in national costume, in the House of Friendship, Moscow, June 1990

Sir Fitzroy Maclean at the Eternal Flame on the Tomb of the Unknown Soldier, Moscow, June 1990

At the conferral of the honorary doctorate of Edinburgh University. The principal of Edinburgh University, Sir David Smith, centre, with honorary graduates, November 1990. Left to right: Neal Ascherson, William Brown, Valentina Tereshkova, Professor Heikki Raisanen

Valentina Tereshkova is welcomed to Abbotsford, the home of Sir Walter Scott, by his descendants Dame Jean and Mrs Patricia Maxwell-Scott, November 1990

The Space museum at Nikulskoye, near Yaroslavl. A replica of the house where Valentina was born

Valentina with her mother

Spacesuits worn by Soviet cosmonauts
during the 1960s

Rocket launch from Baikonur cosmodrome
during the 1960s

Vostok capsule of the 1960s, charred by re-entry

The Fourth Milestone

In Star City

I had not seen Valentina during the Millennium week and our reunion was for an occasion which made me particularly proud because we were celebrating the twenty-fifth anniversary of her flight. The venue was in the heartland of Soviet space research: Star City.

No one alive at the time could forget the panic in the West in 1957 when *Sputnik 1*, the first artificial satellite, was launched into space; not by the powerful US technicians, but by mainly unknown Soviet engineers. President Eisenhower was on holiday playing golf and when he heard he called it a 'silly ball game in space,' and Nikita Khrushchev is reported to have said: 'I never thought it would work.' Then America took in the implications and terror ensued.

Up to this time the USA had relied on its superior deterrent, the atom bomb, for protection against the long-range devastation possibilities which continued to govern the situation in Europe. Now America had become as vulnerable as Europe and Russia had achieved parity in its defence against the atom

103

bomb. This was due to a dedicated group of Soviet scientists working in Star City and led by their Chief Designer Sergei Korolev, whose brilliant teamwork achieved man's first positive step into space.

The realization that a satellite could carry an H-bomb and reach America gave immediate impetus to the American arms programme. It became imperative to launch an American manned missile into space which could rival the Russians. The determination to match rocket for rocket was punishingly costly for both superpowers until rivalry cooled at the time of the positive Soviet disarmament proposals. At the same time, the Soviet space advance had shown the West that technicians of exceptional capability were working in Russia on a most exciting opportunity for mankind. They were opening up an entirely new element in which to live – the vast ocean of space, in which the American astronauts were eventually to excel, reaching the Moon in 1969.

Valentina's service to the Soviet space programme had been in the post-Khrushchev era, as he resigned in 1964, shortly after her space flight. She worked on after the Test Ban Treaty, when the Soviet space pioneers no longer seemed to be a possible means whereby the USA could be destroyed. But Star City, the training centre near Moscow where Valentina still lived, remained the headquarters from which Americans had formerly believed that sinister threats were being planned against them. Now I was Valentina's guest in Star City in a new era of peace for the USSR and the USA, when superpower hostility had been replaced by mutual respect and co-operation so as to achieve further space advances together.

The Training Centre had housed those involved in the Soviet space programmes since the first twelve cosmonauts, including Yuri Gagarin, had arrived in March 1960 with technicians, instructors, aviation engineers, doctors and workers.

After their personal flights most cosmonauts, including Valentina, continue their daily work on space flight programmes and live in Star City with their families. I knew that

Valentina was happy to do so, in the countryside she delights in, with many friends as neighbours, and with her mother buried nearby. Cosmonauts use the Star City school for their children and there are shops for day-to-day purchases and a club which includes a museum of cosmonautics.

This was the venue for the twenty-fifth anniversary celebration of Valentina's flight, and it became one more milestone on our shared journey of friendship. If I had not had any knowledge of Russia before I met Valentina, I was certainly making up for it now. I had been part of the revival of religion in Russia; now I was in Russia's technological city of the future with my friend, one of its pioneers.

I had driven down with Natalya who had been my interpreter during the Millennium week. Elizabeth Zolina came with us. She was pleased about the reason for the celebration because she was very proud of Valentina after working for many years as her interpreter and assistant. But she was worried: in Moscow there had been calls for interviews and photographs and Valentina had disappeared.

Valentina gave me the usual affectionate welcome. She had stood bare-headed in the rain at the gates waiting to meet us. 'This is where cosmonauts live and prepare for space flights,' she explained. 'It is our family home.'

We passed green woods, driving up a long gravelled road. It was very like Scotland and Valentina proudly pointed out the finest trees. The vice-presidents of the Friendship Societies and the Chief of Protocol were waiting for us at the door of the building which contains the cosmonauts' flats. Valentina looked forward to a celebration with her friends.

I felt empty of energy, but trusted that I could cope with the contrast from the spiritual to the secular because in Russia I had already found so much spiritual in the secular. Elizabeth said, 'It is destiny that you are in Moscow for the Jubilee celebrations of Valentina's flight when Alyona is on duty in hospital and, for the first time, her mother is not with her.'

105

On her own in Star City, with her colleagues, I saw Valentina as a cosmonaut. She humbly showed us the model spacecraft which looks like a child's cardboard igloo with a window in it, surviving travel through intense heat and in which she had returned to earth, back to her beloved Mother Russia. This was the real Valentina, committed to cosmonautics.

The cosmonauts' flats are small and up several flights of stairs. A cleaning lady helps Valentina once a week and occasionally cooks unwillingly. Valentina asked her to sit with us for lunch but she did not want to, 'because I don't like one of the cosmonauts.' She is called Hope but she is not an optimistic character.

Everything in Valentina's flat is very simple. We wash, then go to the cosmonauts' training building. Valentina says, 'Very few visitors see what you will see.' I feel unreal again. A cosmonaut called Peter – his chest covered in medals – is on the doorstep to congratulate Valentina. We go to a huge room where cosmonauts are trained. The model spacecraft dominates the floor. It is in two parts with the second ship fitted on just as it is in space. Russian cosmonauts are in space at this moment: Peter says, 'We have just been talking to them. They have had a good sleep ready for descent tomorrow.' It is the longest stay in space so far.

I keep saying I would have been frightened but there is always the same answer: 'We don't think of fear, we only think of responsibility.' Valentina and other cosmonauts used these same words at different times.

The director of the space programme is in charge of safety in space but has never been in space himself. He also wants to congratulate Valentina and comes into the spacecraft to be photographed with us. For the men in space above us I feel relieved when he leaves us every ten minutes to check on developments. I have my Polaroid camera which intrigues the official photographer. I call it 'Charlie Chaplin', but everyone is impressed by the instant results. Valentina says Alyona was given one for her birthday.

Valentina is at home in Star City. Here, where life on a new world such as Mars is being planned, the atmosphere is surprisingly down-to-earth. Once again I admire her integrity. She cannot cope with pretension. She says the hardest thing for astronauts is the transition from being 'ordinary' professionals to being glorified by the world. There is special training for them to handle this with self-control.

I am given sample packets of the food cosmonauts eat during the flight in space – a tube of fish paste, 'very nice', and small packets of bread 'because all objects fly in the air with weightlessness and you have to be quick to catch them'. The toilet is like an aeroplane toilet but you have to wash in a plastic hood because the water behaves in odd ways. I forgot to ask what happens with nature's waste. Valentina says weightlessness feels like turbulence on an ordinary flight, only much worse.

I am nearly moved to tears seeing the charred capsule in which Valentina made her return journey. It reminds me of the continuing courage, combined with a special need for privacy, of other heroes, for example Odette Hallowes, tortured in the war, and how they can somehow survive the strain on even the strongest human minds called upon to endure possibly more than they can carry, provided that their privacy is protected. I believe that is why Valentina conserves her feelings: to keep her identity intact.

The space director returns and says children are right to expect a space village in their lifetime. He says the return to earth travelling through intense heat is the most testing time and the astronauts are cradled in seats which copy the child's position in the womb. 'In Russia we are following nature's laws more and more; the human body is such a marvellous formation.'

Valentina leaves to help Hope cook the lunch. The director of training takes us to see the swimming pool, four times as high and as deep as the ones specially made to protect incarcerated dolphins in aquariums. The cosmonauts wear heavy weighted suits and are trained to move slowly in the supporting water. Then we are shown a short video on the launch, living conditions and docking system. Peter and another astronaut are sitting on either side of me. It feels strange to think they have been through it, blast-off and all, and that they feel at home in space which for me feels so far away.

The Soviet cosmonauts who show me round are Peter Klimuk, Yuri Glaskov and Boris Volynov. At Valentina's small lunch party I meet Anatoly Beresovoi, and two others, Stepanov and Demin, call in to congratulate her. They are all humble, friendly, good-humoured and interested in life outside Russia. They all agree that planet Earth is very beautiful but frighteningly fragile.

Then Peter takes us to see the Space Museum starting with a visit to Gagarin's room. His mother's photograph is in a corner; a fine, good simple face with dreamer's eyes. Peter says: 'She was sad she was uneducated – she felt this let him down.' Gagarin's widow lives in the cosmonaut village. I remember the rumours in the West that his aeroplane was sabotaged because he was becoming too popular. I know he was Valentina's greatest friend. In the museum we see a wall panel dedicated to Peter and one to Valentina, also those of other cosmonauts, including French and Syrian, with the clothes they wore on their flights. Valentina's space suit looks very small.

I ask the director about important progress being achieved by Russian energy research, having read a *Times* article on this. He is very pleased I am interested and says it is a major project which will help humanity. I realise how privileged I am to be made to feel one of the family here in Star City where so many important scientific advances are being made.

Peter is very interested in my visit to Moscow during the Millennium. He says, 'When you are in space you have to have faith.' I wonder if his grandmother baptised him in secret. I also begin to wonder whether being a true believer depends on having the humility not to magnify one's own importance. In this respect the cosmonauts are certainly believers.

We join Valentina for the lunch party. As is usual in Russia, it is a feast of sufficiency: boiled and smoked fish, small pots of red and black caviare, vegetables, sausage-meat, delicious soup, plain sugared buns, cherries. The irritable and elderly favourite, her pug Pepki, is guest of honour. I think she loves him more than anything else. In her modest flat with its pleasant wood furniture, again I saw Valentina as an equal among equals, happy and laughing.

With Natalya translating Valentina tells the four cosmonauts that I like going to church. One said, 'But Valentina, when we were in space didn't you feel another power was upholding us? Perhaps Tony is right.' Valentina's answer is, 'It may be right for some of you.'

The cosmonauts reminded me of many similar loyal servicemen and women I had known in Britain. Their work is their duty, politics seem to be outside this, no matter how politicians govern the world. This made me wonder: how politically indifferent can a soldier be? Valentina has never been an expert in political philosophies. Her mother did not join the Communist Party. Her father was killed in Stalin's ill-conceived Finnish war. She is a Soviet patriot who has served her country as a soldier and a scientist, and patriots are usually ready to defend native soil. In this as in all else she is consistently normal. She loves children and animals. She sometimes annoys the friends around her because she tries endlessly to feed them, often with apples from her garden, which turn yellow when bitten – she explains this only happens because they are full of iron. Obviously she understands political developments – she questioned the Thatcher poll tax – and she remains immensely proud of the USSR she grew up in, hence the motivation not to work only in the cosmonauts' city, but also to accept the opportunity to travel round the world, arranging Soviet-inspired meetings to help people to understand each other and the USSR. I believe this motive is genuinely humanitarian. She is frightened by the prospect of the destruction of the planet and believes cosmonauts have a major part to play to remind terrestrial citizens of the dangers they have seen from space. She hopes that this knowledge will unite humanity. We are all enjoying the celebration party and it confirms my trust in Valentina as a very honest, very brave, and very loving Cosmonaut Colonel in the Soviet Air Force.

Then in comes the birthday cake, chocolate and cream. Valentina is as nervous about us enjoying her party as I was when she had supper with me in London.

Peter is very enthusiastic about glasnost. 'Now we can talk openly about religion – did you admire Patriarch Pimen?' 'Which churches did you like best?' Valentina says she admires Mrs Thatcher. She is genuinely grateful to the Prime Minister for always remembering her when they meet.

Talking to the cosmonauts, I get the impression that although there is satisfaction that glasnost has opened up a new epoch of increased freedom, this is accompanied by anxiety as to how to make it obtain consumer improvements. I say I hope Russia will only get the best out of the West – not the worst.

More cosmonauts come in to congratulate Valentina. The pug is also congratulated. 'The only pug in Russia. Catherine the Great brought them in long ago.'

The table is heavy with brandy and vodka. I resolutely stick to mineral water and explain that I have taken a health pledge. This starts the usual discussion about Gorbachev's determination to clamp down on alcoholic poisoning in Russia. 'It is very unpopular as it is so hard to change the habit of celebrating with vodka.' I answered hopefully that it took me four years to alter a habit and the cosmonauts agree it is the same in their training.

Valentina says she has been asked to go to China, so the next visit to Britain may be cancelled. In October she had planned to visit the Russian Exhibition in Birmingham, and we could have met in London.

Then Valentina remembers she must leave to meet two of the women cosmonauts who trained with her in the space programme. Elizabeth says she is missing every chance to make her Jubilee known; journalists want to interview her in Moscow but she has had to tell them that Valentina is in Star City with an important guest. 'The guest is you.'

We collect ourselves to travel back to Moscow in the car. Suddenly I realise the time. I will catch the flight back to

London with only minutes to spare. To my relief I remember that this aspect of administration in Russia is always efficient. Russians seem to enjoy being in airports and are experts at welcoming or seeing off friends. In any case, as Valentina's guest I would be given special facilities.

Valentina returns from her meeting. She comes down the stairs with us and goes upstairs again to do the washing-up.

I leave Star City with hope and energy renewed. Obviously the future of Soviet space progress depends on the necessary financial support. Funding space research has always proved a problem for both East and West, but since Soviet technology is deservedly successful, from now on funding might be shared with the West. The events I had been involved in confirmed for me that the Soviet Union was now moving positively towards co-operation with the West. Perhaps the world would soon be safe from a nuclear holocaust.

On my return to London I wondered what Valentina would think if she knew the extent of the analysis by which I tried to avoid both Western hypocrisy and Soviet propaganda so as to arrive at objective conclusions. I felt sure she did not analyse the political motives of the West in the same way when she met me. The Soviet approach seemed to be that such studies should be left to the official intelligence service. The job of those who were not part of that service was to carry out instructions, and to concentrate on doing their own work well although, obviously, there was more demanding commitment required from Communist Party officials.

For me, witnessing the revival of Christianity in Russia and my visit to the Soviet space city of the future had been two important milestones along the road on which Valentina and I were travelling together.

But in Britain I found it difficult to persuade people to accept my conclusions, particularly if favourable to the Soviet Union. I was repeatedly asked if I could prove that these were based on facts, and this required evidence.

For example, there was much did I not know about life for average citizens in the Soviet Union. I was meeting servants of the state, administrators and scientists. These seemed comparable to the West's senior civil servants and servicemen. I had also met Valentina's assistants working for the Friendship Societies, which she compared to the British Council, and these included women who worked to end discrimination. I had found these categories in the Soviet structure all reassuringly familiar, even if sometimes inhibited by unquestioning obedience.

But how much did I know about how average Russians lived? I knew very little, first hand, about the day-to-day life of the majority of Soviet citizens. I imagined that they looked up with admiration at the cosmonauts, and with some envy at the civil servants who were made reasonably comfortable by the State, and that they might also be looking up even higher, with fear, at those in power who could allocate or remove comfortable living conditions. I had no notion as to whether the 'middle' class I had met had any experience of Soviet life at the lower levels where, I was told, there was no unemployment and poverty was relieved by standard supplements and the solidarity of Russian family life. I reminded myself again not to be hypocritical about poverty in Russia. In Western society life is not usually austere and poverty is controlled, but there are slum areas near prosperous areas and they are not likely to meet. In the Soviet Union, however, keeping within one's own category seemed to be a rigid rule. The reason given to me for some categories living differently was that promotion was earned by work well done.

Some of my television colleagues who visited Russia to make documentaries had described a world of film producers, artists, dancers and singers, who, if they were successful, enjoyed luxury dachas, cars and swimming pools. This other working world was one with which Valentina did not appear to be familiar, even if it sometimes interacted with her cultural activities, and in any case such privileges would only apply to a minority. I had to admit that I still did not know how the majority lived.

It was a relief to find I could investigate such questions and widen my knowledge with a friend I worked with in Scotland, Meg Luckins. An Edinburgh history teacher married to a medical researcher, she was secretary of the GB–USSR Association and she visited the Soviet Union regularly. She was a fluent Russian speaker and, unlike me, she did travel by bus and train and stay with Russian families in their homes. She knew her Russian friends well, and regretted that the majority could not travel abroad or buy expensive food in the free markets, let alone in the shops restricted to hard currency, which was not available to them.

It was very helpful for objective reporting that Meg gave another side of the picture to the one I was now familiar with, and it was reassuring to find that, after comparing experiences, we both agreed that the whole Soviet system was evolving towards extreme Scandinavian-type socialism rather than towards increased autocracy. As a historian Meg had studied the tragedy inflicted by Stalin when the purges destroyed the best in Soviet intelligence and ability. We both hoped that for the future a new, well-educated generation would replace the lost talents and skills. Life for these young Soviet people was slowly improving, even if they felt deprived of the consumer goods they knew were easily available in the West. They should be able to develop extreme socialism successfully. Why then had the initial demonstration of enthusiasm for perestroika been followed by inertia? Not only were there no signs of the reform process being accelerated, it seemed to be dying. Why?

Valentina often spoke of her conviction that the Soviet genius for craftsmanship, invention and design was unrivalled provided that it was given a proper structure within which to develop. Where were such structures now? Meg and I had both found that many Russians put the blame on Gorbachev's not having sufficient administrative ability to organize the reforms. Others blamed political dinosaurs for their powerful 'conservative' manoeuvres to ensure that the reforms became unworkable. All appeared to agree that a Margaret Thatcher-type leader was needed and many hoped that rebels like Yeltsin would provide action and necessary reform. He had been a capable Party administrator when in Sverdlovsk.

For loyal Communist citizens another depressing explanation of the paralysis was that extreme socialism was being proved not to be possible in practice. In the West many held that socialist attempts at equalization would always fail, because the 'equal shares' ideal inevitably led to corruption.

Now in Russia capitalism was being idealized and self-interest with it. Capitalism indicated that the profit motive could create prosperity, and then those who created riches could share with the poor. For those of us who did not trust readiness to share by the rich this was not convincing. But reality is reality and dreams are dreams. In Gorbachev's Union these were not interacting.

Meg Luckins's impressions of life in Russia in 1988, during the first years of perestroika, gave me a valuable assessment of living conditions. She wrote:

> My frequent visits to Leningrad and Moscow during the 1970s had given me a few good friends but they had always been reluctant to pursue the friendship beyond a certain level and rarely invited me into their homes. These contacts were, by the nature of their work in language schools, from a privileged section of Russian society. To meet ordinary Russians I travelled on public transport and to places not normally visited by foreigners and chatted to the Russians I met on the buses, in the trains and in the cafés. They were always initially very wary and cautious but gradually opened up once they found out that in Scotland I was a teacher of Russian.
>
> Fraternization with Westerners was not approved but despite their apprehension these Russians were always very generous with their gifts and keen to know more about Scotland. I will always remember an old lady in Zagorsk who was breaking up the solid ice on the pavement with a long pole. Tears rolled down her cheeks as she thanked God for bringing me 'to see her beloved motherland'. I

have not forgotten the lady from Saratov who gave me a jar of her own honey in the market in Petrozavodsk. We corresponded for many years. I have not forgotten the lady who gave me her copy of a journal she was reading on the train to Lomonosov because it had a new short story by Chingiz Aitmatov. She later let me use her hot shower when our hostel only had cold water. I was aware that Soviet society had a definite structure with different groupings at different levels. With my limited access to ordinary Russians I felt that they lived on various steps of a ladder, but I did not know how they could go up and down this ladder.

After a long absence I have been back in 1988. I was eager to see what changes perestroika had brought – if any. Very few were evident and I was shocked to see the general shabbiness and economic hardships. What pleased me was the effect of glasnost. There were still steps on the ladder and the official meetings were with those privileged to live on the higher steps, but it was so much easier to talk to ordinary Russians on the lower steps. They were no longer anxious or reticent although then some of the older ones were reluctant to believe that the changes could be permanent. Nonetheless I made many new friends: a glass engraver and his wife in Kiev who gave us a delicious supper in their one room in a large hostel; a grandmother who lives in St Petersburg in a *kommunalka* and shares her small flat with another family; a lady on the train to Maiori from Riga; an oceanographer who has made a startling success as a businessman in Moscow.

Recently in Russia I have found that there is now a great desire amongst many Russians to forge contacts with Westerners. They look to us to provide the goods which they have lacked for so long. But, despite the recent momentous changes in the Soviet Union the ladder is still there and until there is a complete restructuring of Russian society there will always be opportunities, through this ladder, to occupy positions of privilege.

Public transport in Moscow and Leningrad is efficient. The Metro is essential because of the vast distances between various parts of the cities and it offers a cheap, fast and regular service. The cost of public transport has gone up recently more than ten times. Buses, trams and trolley-buses are less efficient now because of frequent breakdowns in the old stock. Driving down the Nevsky Prospekt squeezed into an overcrowded bus is part of daily life – brute force is necessary to extricate oneself from the seething mass and it has happened that I have missed my stop by not being able to get out.

Taxis are notoriously difficult – standing at the edge of the pavement trying to flag one down is hit and miss. If a taxi does stop, you have to open the door next to the driver and tell him your destination. If he does not want to go there, he will shake his head morosely and drive away. If he is interested then you negotiate the fare, in roubles or hard currency, and fix your price. Dollars will get you anywhere. The best way to travel is by private car – and Russians do this, even without dollars. Stand in the road and hold out your arm – low – and wait, as the little Ladas pull up. Speak good Russian and these drivers will take you for roubles (from 100 – 500 roubles) through the rushing traffic. Speak English and they want at least 5 dollars. The alternative is often a long wait until the crowded buses come along or the team has fixed the overhead cables on the broken-down tram which is holding up a whole queue of trams. Car drivers are almost all men – there are few women who can, or want to, drive. Private cars are very expensive to buy and maintain and always dirty outside and inside, with damaged mirrors and frequently broken windscreens. The condition of the roads is often appalling with enormous potholes and irregular surfaces, even in the cities. Main roads are also badly repaired and cars and buses have to zig-zag to avoid holes, sometimes even driving on the pavement! Roadside services are rare and very dirty. Petrol is in short supply and there are enormous queues to fill up. Diesel is even rarer. Toilets at the roadside are dirty and to be avoided.

Train travel is essential, given the size of the country. It is cheap and speedy with frequent and efficient services on the main routes. Local trains to country towns and villages have wooden, slatted seats and move slowly from station to station, taking city dwellers to their dachas. They carry large rucksacks, bags and white enamel buckets to bring back produce grown in the dacha gardens or mushrooms collected in the woods. Inter-city travel is better on night trains; it is comfortable and still reasonably inexpensive for a single in a first-class sleeper with only two berths from Moscow to Leningrad. Ordinary class has four berths and males and females are mixed together. Food is rarely served on trains but tea is available from the lady in charge of each compartment. The toilets are usually very dirty. The stations always bustle with so many people travelling – struggling with vast quantities of luggage in ungainly packages.

Most Russian flats are small, based on the old state allocation of 9 square metres of living space per person. Often a sitting-room doubles as a dining-room and bedroom – the bed settee at the wall, with a carpet hanging above it, and a table in the middle of the room. Balconies are a bonus for storage space, and are often glassed in by DIY methods. Dark paintwork and dull, poor-quality wallpaper have to be enlivened with wall hangings. Curtains are thin and rarely drawn across the net curtains at every window. A small window high up in the double-glazed frame gives good ventilation and the space on the sill and between the glazed windows is a perfect larder for the bottles and jars of pickled and preserved fruit and vegetables – the winter stores.

Fridges and cookers are available but there are very few washing machines. Dishwashers and microwave ovens are rare, and tumble dryers virtually unknown. Detergent liquid and powders are little used and of poor quality. Dishes are mostly washed under a running tap. Clothes and bedding may be sent for cleaning to a laundry, but items are not always returned safely; consequently, bathrooms are cluttered with washing dripping over the bath. The baths are usually poorly enamelled and gritty. Shower mixer taps are popular but poor water pressure makes them inefficient. Gas water heaters, lit by matches, provide good, hot water but often the pressure is reduced in whole regions of blocks of flats and there is only cold water. Toilets will be in separate closets – poor flushing and bad design often make these unpleasant. Not all flats have their own kitchen, bathroom or toilet and often several families have to share these facilities. The public bathhouses – *banya* – are popular and essential.

Food preparation is usually in cramped spaces and hygiene standards are low. Markets are a source of a limited supply of vegetables, fruit, meat, poultry, cheeses, but are exceedingly expensive. The State shops are cheaper, though becoming more expensive and they supply only a narrow range of indifferent-quality food. The diet is generally poor and workers rely on their works canteen for a cooked lunch, always with lots of bread, to save time looking for food to prepare at home after work, late in the evening.

Men very rarely help in the house; the housework is left to the women who, without labour-saving devices – no hoovers, no polishers – have to sweep the uncovered floors with besom-type brushes. Visitors always take their shoes off at the front door and are provided with slippers: *tapochki*. Russians are very hospitable and will take great delight in providing meals for guests – at considerable expense and effort. Many Russians dream of having a dacha in the countryside to escape the dirt and noise of the cities and to have a plot of land to grow much-needed potatoes and other fresh fruit and vegetables. These small, wooden houses provide very basic accommodation, not always with running water. Usually the toilet is in a shed in the garden with a communal well. Gardening is for survival and the West's neatly kept lawns surrounded by colourful flowerbeds are a fantasy – growing food is far more important. The disposable society and consumerism are virtually unknown.

This description of how Meg's friends lived was a sobering contrast to the comfort of the Friendship Society dacha and the hotels we had stayed in. It sounded more like life in Calabria or even perhaps a croft in the Highlands.

It was my only act of unfaithfulness to Valentina that I did not mention my correspondence with Meg to her. I did not want her to feel I was obliged to obtain additional information when she gave me so much, and so truthfully. It was just that I needed to find out how much one category in Russia knew about living conditions in another category, and whether the divisions set by Communism were even more rigid than the divisions imposed by money in Britain or America.

Also I did not want to tell Valentina that both Meg and I had reached a depressing conclusion about telling the truth to the West and how we had both learnt that in the West a customary reaction from many people to reports from Russia was, 'Serve them right' if told of a Soviet setback, and only a grudging, 'Wait and see' if there was Soviet progress. We were surprised that this hostility and caution seemed mainly to be reserved for Russian autocracy and that there was more leniency in Western attitudes to despotic systems in South Africa, South America or even China.

For those of us who wanted reformed Communism to succeed the continuing prejudice was frightening. There could be no recovery without massive Western aid, an option which was being considered but more often than not rejected by the majority of people in power in the West, even if an increasing number saw in Russia's vast resources and prospective customers a good investment for the future.

The question I wanted to ask was why aid could not be given now in a way similar to that of the Marshall Plan, which had enabled European recovery after the Second World War?

There had been no post-war Marshall aid for the Soviet Union because Stalin had decreed that Russians should rebuild from the war ruins on their own, proving that a socialist state could overcome difficulties independently. The Soviet people suffered accordingly, but after Stalin's death and the Khrushchev revision the West had continued to believe that there was nothing but evil in the Soviet system in the second half of the century, and that this did not deserve to be encouraged by financial investment. Now that I had found out what was good in the Soviet system I regretted this point of view.

Trying to get to know about ordinary life in Communist Russia had taught me one more unexpected lesson: conditions were not as unbearable as the West held them to be. Soviet Communism had not entirely failed to create the system which it believed could form a just society. Now from what I could see, seventy years after Lenin's Revolution, some Soviet Communists, and probably the majority of people, were prepared to build on the old system so as to include one man – one vote democracy and private enterprise.

If the Soviet people willed this then the seventy-year-old Soviet structure might improve in this way. But the leaders of the West would also need to transform their thinking if they were ever to assist the development of the Soviet system into democracy. Why were they hesitating? Did the West still too strongly remember how the dispute with Stalin had tarnished the inspired inter-community vision of Marshall aid?

General George Marshall, former chairman of the Joint Chiefs of Staff in World War II, was a particularly impressive thinker. Among many peace projects, he had tried to reconcile Mao Tse-tung and Chiang Kai-shek. President Truman appointed him Secretary of State with Dean Acheson as his chief assistant in 1947, and Marshall described Truman as 'the Captain with the mighty heart'. Marshall, Truman and Acheson were not content to commiserate with the Europeans brought to the brink of collapse by the war; they were resolved to assist renewal. The Truman Doctrine, established and supported by the US Congress, described the policy of the United States:

120

'To support free peoples who are resisting attempted subjugation by armed minorities or by outside pressure'.

It was the opposite of isolationism. America was willing to become involved in a mission to achieve European stabilisation and this could be for mutual benefit, because the American economy needed a healthy Europe for trade.

General Marshall had visited Moscow and seen for himself the vast desolation left by Hitler. In 1947 he made a historic statement in a speech at Harvard: 'Our policy is directed against hunger, poverty, desperation and chaos. Its purpose will be the revival of a working economy in the world so as to permit the emergence of political and social conditions in which free institutions can exist.' It was very necessary because the future of Western Europe was in the balance.

Dean Acheson threw his weight behind the Marshall Plan to initiate an economic recovery in Europe to include the USSR. But then Soviet non-participation changed the scenario. Stalin refused to allow the Soviet Union and its Eastern satellites to accept American aid. So when, in 1948, the Communists took over Czechoslovakia, the Marshall Plan rejected by Stalin came to be seen in America as a measure disliked by Stalin and therefore one which could halt his territorial ambitions. Ironically this made it more acceptable in the USA than the former objective of preventing former allies from starving and, even with the world economy less stable than at any time since the depression, Congress voted to send thirteen billion dollars to fund the 'free European reconstruction programme'. Then the rebuilding of Western Europe began.

The Marshall Plan was probably the most inspired policy of mutual aid ever envisaged and executed. It was administered with particular sensibility by a small group of American officials in Paris who approved the applications made to them. Once approved, dollars were exchanged for European currencies and with the dollars Europeans could purchase what was urgently needed. The direct link with American aid was hidden in this way so there was no hurt to European pride. The Americans benefited from so-named 'Counterpart Funds'.

These were substantial holdings in European currencies held by America and spent on investments in Europe by American businessmen. Thus the Marshall Plan solidified the Western alliance while it emphasised the separation of the West from the Soviet Union.

The original vision of the Plan had been to unite the whole of Europe and America. It was never envisaged that it would bring about the division which then developed so dangerously that East and West separated into apparently irreconcilable military alliances, the Warsaw Pact and NATO. This in turn led to a revival of the House Committee on Un-American Activities, which had first been set up in 1938, and which now initiated a series of often irresponsible anti-Communist investigations, which demoralised many Americans and heightened US-Soviet antagonism.

That General George Marshall's inspired concept developed into this antagonism and even the possibility of atomic war between East and West was tragic; he deserved a better accolade. He had taught the international community how to save itself. It worked well once. I kept thinking it could work again, this time to build East-West partnership. But where was another George Marshall to ensure stability in the East in 1988?

On my return to Britain I found more evidence that I had not misjudged the lack of sympathy for Communist reform. My optimistic reports on how the Orthodox Church, the women's representatives and even the cosmonauts all supported perestroika were again dismissed as Soviet propaganda. It was frustrating for a messenger with good news.

Only history will confirm whether the West should have supported Gorbachev more strongly in the years before the 1991 August coup. The negative response to his appeal for financial support ended all hope that the Soviet Union could survive within his system of reconstructed Communism. In the event, his attempted reforms in Russia were watched, not carried forward, by the West, and for better or worse this resulted in the collapse of Pax Sovietica.

In our attitude to the USA Valentina and I did not agree. She admired the love of homeland she had seen in America and she wanted to understand and trust the Americans. I remained worried that America would only live dangerously in the cause of its own interests, although I did withdraw this misjudgement when the USA risked American lives to save the starving in Yugoslavia and Somalia in 1993.

The contrast in our opinions illustrated how different our personal attitudes could be, and that this did not diminish our trust in each other was probably the most positive proof that there could be unity in diversity, because we never disagreed where measures to protect the planet were concerned.

At the end of the eighties I found it difficult, living in London, to understand whether what was happening in Eastern Europe increased or decreased progress for peace. In any case I did not want to appear to have pretensions to becoming an expert on Soviet affairs. My purpose remained to know enough to encourage the understanding on both sides which was needed to prevent atomic war.

In a way it was a relief to face the fact that I should not in any case try to reach a Western conclusion on political developments which were integral to the Soviet Union, and could only be properly understood and commented on by Russians.

But I looked forward to knowing more about Soviet co-operation with Europe after my next meeting with Valentina when, as a UK delegate, I was due to attend a conference to study the Helsinki agreements, to be held in Moscow in 1990.

The Fifth Milestone

The Russian Road to Democracy

As I expected, in the autumn of 1989 confirmation c a m e through Gennadi Fedosov in London that the Union of Friendship Societies was organizing a symposium to prepare for the official top-level Helsinki conference to be held in Moscow two years later. A delegate was needed from a voluntary organization in Britain to speak on voluntary work because such work was new to Russia, where the State had governed all social assistance. Gennadi wrote to ask could I go on behalf of the UK National Council of Women as I was the Patron? Madame Mitterrand was to speak on youth projects in France; a former President of Rotary International would speak for the voluntary American services. It would be a large assembly. My fellow British delegates would be the Labour MP Giles Radice, Malcolm Harper of the UK United Nations Association, and Dr Morgan, President of the European Regional Confederation. We were expected in Moscow early in the New Year.

I rang Ros Preston, President of the National Council of Women and she said she would consult the next Council meeting. The answer came back: 'Agreed – but we cannot cover travel expenses.' I contacted Giles Radice. He said that we must find a cheap flight and he hoped that if he wrote a press article after the event this would reimburse him. He had been told we would stay at the Academy of Sciences, which assisted the Friendship Societies with accommodation.

So in January 1990 I was flying into Moscow again to attend a conference on 'The Human Dimension of the European Process and the Role of the Public'. Out of the porthole I could see dark woods, snow fields, ice on the roads, leaden skies and a glimmer of sun. This was the landscape from which both Napoleon and Hitler had retreated. Fortunately the representatives of Security and Co-operation in Europe were in a mood to advance. The participants included leaders from the non-governmental organizations of twenty CSCE nations and many Soviet delegates. It felt very different from the time, three years ago, when friends had warned that it was not only foolhardy to travel to Moscow, it was not even worthwhile. Now the Berlin Wall had been ground into gravel, and the Iron Lady had led the West towards a new era of co-operation with the East. Only the Bamboo Curtain remained rigidly Communist and ideologically intact. The movement for freedom had progressed so rapidly that it still seemed difficult to believe that in five years out of seventy there had been events which changed the twentieth century beyond recognition. Those who worked for peace not only wanted to be in Moscow, they actually were in Moscow.

A year previously in 1989 Sir Geoffrey Howe, the British Foreign Secretary, had stated in Vienna at the closing ceremony of the Conference on Security and Co-operation in Europe: 'Between now and 1991, the year of the Moscow conference, we shall be watching carefully for reassurance that the Soviet commitment extends beyond the personal effort and determination of a single Soviet leader or leaders. More than that, the freedom and reforms, of which President Gorbachev has spoken so eloquently, need to be accepted and absorbed into his society and no longer be regarded as an alien and unwelcome virus.'

Sitting in the House of Friendship conference hall in Moscow this statement appeared to underline how little the leaders of the West knew about how rapidly reform was already accepted in the USSR, and that now it might be the freedom that the West was determined to impose which would develop into a dangerous virus of discontent for the Russian people if the West did not assist its implementation.

It was becoming increasingly clear to me that if East-West co-operation was to be firmly cemented, then accurate information was a vital element in the cement. Without it more dangerous mistakes might be made. Bridges must be built, but those building needed to know enough to be able to separate the strong stones from the weak, otherwise the bridge was likely to collapse.

The conference was a triumph for the new Soviet era of free speech. Valentina in the chair was very much in control, and she gave an inspiring opening address on the need for humanity to share in true global democratic progress. In the subsequent sessions she encouraged hours of time for dissident Russians to make speeches pouring out their grievances. We were taken in coaches for a series of interviews with the head of the KGB, and the Minister of External Affairs found time to attend while dealing with the crisis in Armenia. We also met the Minister of Culture and the chairman of the Supreme Soviet. These were important Soviet leaders and we interviewed them as if they were in the dock, guilty men obliged to give an account to the West of their sins.

It always made me feel uncomfortable that the delegates from the West so often gave the impression that democracy had no flaws. I wondered if the Russian self-accusations served a positive purpose. 'I wish they would forget and just look to the future,' one of the Italian delegates remarked, 'also because when the Slav opens his soul it takes an hour each time.'

It reminded me of the fifties for Britain. In 1956 I had been in New York with my husband who was a member of the UK United Nations delegation at the time of Suez. The traditional concept of the British Empire as indispensable for the protection of international justice had been discredited. I had always been proud of the Commonwealth with the Queen at its centre, but in New York British intellectuals were openly prepared to admit guilt about the Gallic complicity combined with American duplicity which had encouraged Britain in the Suez offensive. Fortunately the British public's indifference to the end of their Empire avoided useless national self-immolation. It had already seemed a high enough price to pay that the 'we stood alone' moral superiority earned after the Second World War was never regained. Pax Britannica died with Suez, but Everyman in Britain hardly noticed. Now Pax Sovietica was dying under the burden of past Communist malpractices exposed, but the contrast was that the Russians seemed to be sinking in a sea of guilt.

German friends told me that they had also felt devastated confronting the evil which had grown in the Nazi night which had seemed like day. But listening to the Soviet dissidents I asked myself if the Saxon psyche was more resilient than the Slav. I respected the Russians' sense of shame, but wished they could now hope for the future, not sink in the past. A few months earlier, at a literary forum in Edinburgh, when a succession of Soviet authors including the poet Yevtushenko had poured out their humiliation at creativity being controlled by the state, I had felt compelled to intervene, pointing out that freedom in the West had its press barons and advertising controllers.

My speech at the conference on the work of Britain's voluntary organizations did not last long. It made me feel nervous thinking that I was being heard by so many distinguished world delegates and I wondered what I sounded like translated into their varied languages. I genuinely believed in the ideal of voluntary work and hoped I managed to convey this. Alyona who had joined me approved, and *Pravda* reported it, emphasizing my statement that without Russia and her culture Europe would be breathing with only one lung. It was also reassuring that the caterer, who was serving coffee and had come out to hear me 'because I was Valentina's friend', asked how she could find similar voluntary services in Moscow. She wanted to help the disabled. I told her that I believed the British war hero, Leonard Cheshire, would soon be opening a home to rehabilitate Russian ex-servicemen.

Alyona told me that Valentina was pleased that I was there in the conference hall. In private we only met on our own for an hour in her office. She wanted to know if the vitamins had helped Donald's illness and she was happy to hear he was stable. Nearer to home she was worried about the ever-increasing financial crisis and the ethnic troubles.

At the conference I heard many of the foreign delegates discussing the possibility of civil war. The Romanian delegates – Communist and anti-Communist – commented cynically on their own experiences of frying pan into fire. It seemed possible that to chair the conference would be the last of Valentina's contributions as an official Soviet spokeswoman. She still represented all that remained most sound in the disintegrating Soviet system. She spoke with quiet authority from the platform, Madame Mitterrand beside her, and above her the picture of planet Earth as she had seen it from space. A tall Lutheran woman pastor from Denmark enfolded in a red cloak confided, 'I would follow that woman all the way.'

Not for the first time I wondered, 'Does Valentina have special power over people?' As I have observed it, charisma is a sort of light which transforms the shape it surrounds and makes it immensely attractive to the imagination. But often the shape thus created dissolves when exposed to reality, and it is then easily replaced and forgotten, particularly if it has been over-exposed. Valentina's power over people is not that sort of power. She is a very impressive person who can truly claim solid skill and courage, but these enduring assets are not charismatic. A member of the original space training team at preparing for Valentina's flight, Tatyana Kuznetsova, told me that her first impression of Valentina had been: 'Obviously a leader because of real knowledge of the work she undertakes, and the gift of communicating with people mainly because they trust her.'

With every new meeting I saw another side to Valentina's character. At this Helsinki conference I saw the woman soldier who might be as powerful a political figure as de Gaulle, controlling an audience of international leaders. They were all drawn to her not only by her personal integrity, but also because all knew beyond doubt that while de Gaulle had primarily earned respect for opposing Petain and Hitler, Valentina's achievement would light a flame of interest and sympathy among almost all peoples in the globe transcending race, religion and creed. The very poor were as impressed by the way a woman had first represented humanity in space as were the very rich. No one anywhere could ignore her and all respected her, not only as a Hero of the Soviet Union, but also of humanity.

In recent times, Elizabeth said, Valentina had worked hard to be elected to Parliament but she certainly did not intend to become a Russian de Gaulle. She was happy to continue combining her work for international understanding with research work at the Cosmonaut Centre, and to represent both in Parliament.

We now seemed to meet at times of chilling political crisis, but with some reasons for optimism. In the Soviet Union Gorbachev was increasingly blamed not only for the short supply of food and consumer goods but also the increasing administrative chaos. The young and old I met longed for order, combined with freedom of worship and expression, but it seemed to me that if there had to be a choice, order was the priority. At the same time, like the Italians, the Russians seemed capable of overcoming official incompetence by organizing basic food supplies through a variety of outlets. For those with money the morning subsidized air flight was still coming in from Georgia, jammed with the best of everything for sale which they could buy. Was anyone really hungry – yet?

The many Russians I spoke to had been encouraged that, after both Chernobyl and the Armenian earthquake, the international community had shown solidarity and support for the victims, sending aid to the Soviet Union. There was a firm feeling of fraternalism with the West.

Elizabeth Zolina was sad about her native Armenia. I sensed it was the first time she had been forced to think of it outside the disciplined embrace of the Soviet Union, with her family now vulnerable to violence. The former orderly Armenia had now become an inflamed independent area fighting out a racist conflict between Islam and Christianity. Militant sectarian divisions within the same State had reached Russia later than Ireland. Another anxiety for Elizabeth was that statues of both Lenin and Valentina in Armenia had been vandalised. For the first time Valentina as a Soviet symbol of courage had been challenged.

In her opening speech Valentina welcomed delegates from nineteen nations as well as from the UN and UNESCO, saying: 'Perhaps only now on the eve of the Millennium can we begin to understand that the sense of the meaning of international politics is above all a sense of attitudes between people, and the main thing today is that the attitudes of the people of the world are different. There is an awareness of the integrity of our common earthly destiny, and a growing understanding that the world is indivisible and interdependent. A Europe of peace and co-operation is developing before our eyes. The "Iron Curtain" is being pulled down, the walls of alienation are being pulled down.' It was a clarion call for the hope that the Soviet Union could find a home in Europe.

During our week in Moscow the British Ambassador and Lady Braithwaite gave a lunch for members of the British delegation. For the first time in my visits to Russia I felt part of the UK establishment. The Russian guests included dissidents and Gorbachev supporters. They spoke of a demonstration opposing Communism which was planned for the next day and which they believed would prove that the Soviet people now rejected Communist ideology. They described fringe groups forming, some likely to become disproportionately influential and dangerous, the monarchists, the neo-fascists and the anti-Semitic *Pamyat*, and also a major assembly of 'conservatives', party members and officials fearful of losing power. The main question seemed to be how these would influence the first democratic vote. After seventy years of totalitarianism, the people of the Soviet Union would be using the ballot box to decide on a matter of national policy. Would they vote for Gorbachev's reforms? Would he remain in power? Lunch at the Embassy had been both pleasant and interesting but it had not been reassuring about future stability in the Soviet Union.

Back in the conference hall the dissidents were still exposing Communist crimes. I watched Valentina's reaction. She seemed to approve criticism of past misdeeds. I respected the Russians for being so truly hurt remembering Stalin's holocausts, but I hoped they would arrive at a balanced perspective for the future. There had been other holocausts imposed by man's inhumanity to man: Cambodia, Hiroshima, Hitler's holocaust, genocide in Africa and, undoubtedly, Stalin's holocaust. All holocausts seemed equally evil to me and those responsible should be equally repentant.

I found relief when, submerged by one of my monotonously-recurring viral infections on one of the conference evenings, I could not go out with the other delegates to an official dinner. I had supper and watched television with the Russian conference organizers in the canteen instead. I sat at a table with young civil servants – some probably KGB. They were not impressed with Madame Mitterrand's plans for a student exchange. 'All the First Ladies bring us their welfare toys.' They respected Bush. But the only politician they were interested in was Margaret Thatcher. 'Does she really only sleep for four hours – that is what she told us on television.' Then one asked, 'Has she got a Swiss bank account?' I unhesitatingly replied, 'I am sure not,' and I was surprised by my certainty. They all seemed reassured, as if the Leninist image of a responsible leader which they had been taught to admire was true of at least one world politician.

I took myself early to bed and to sleep, until Valentina, Alyona and Elizabeth knocked on the door. With typical Russian faith in natural rather than synthetic medicine, they had brought tea and honey to cure me.

Before flying back to London next morning I tried to write my report for the National Council of Women. Giles Radice and Malcolm Harper were also working to set out their conclusions. Malcolm voiced my feelings when, in the February UNA-UK newsletter he described the new Soviet openness to the West as being exemplified by the many official leaders we had been allowed to question. In his report Malcolm asked a relevant question: 'When have as many Western ministers and senior officials last made themselves available to the scrutiny of NGO and other representatives from the CSCE countries?'

He also reminded his readers of the problem which remained a priority for me when he referred to the polarisation of too many resources in the North and too few in the South: 'Any all-European process which fails adequately to consider the needs and rights of the South and Europe's responsibility in helping to enhance them is doomed to failure.'

On a different level I also agreed with Giles Radice when he wrote in the *Times* after our return to England, recommending international backing to underwrite the Soviet currency: 'In the long term the benefits of such an initiative would be considerable. Not only is the Soviet Union rich in resources, it is a potentially vast market. It could be the motor for continued world growth well into the next century. The costs of standing aside have also to be taken into account. The risks of watching from the sidelines while the Soviet Union slides into chaos with all that could mean for the new European settlement are too great to be contemplated.'

The British delegation had concluded that for the sake of world stability the Soviet Union should urgently be saved.

To prepare myself for the conference I had been fortunate in obtaining information on the Helsinki Agreement from the former British Prime Minister, Lord Home. He had been present at the initial meetings which he described to me as 'the first breakthrough in the cold war'. Three areas or 'baskets' for East-West co-operation had been identified. These were military security, economic and scientific issues and humanitarian freedom. He hoped the time had come when the West could trust the East. The week in Moscow had proved that the Helsinki baskets might now be filled and some economists in the West were advising a positive response to new circumstances by increasing investment from the West.

But in my view a major problem persisted which the Soviet Union must face up to: a psychological revolution was necessary among the Russians themselves to prove that they were determined to work for order on democratic lines. The realization of this aim did not seem to have yet begun, there seemed to be no will to work for it, perhaps because there were insufficient incentives.

On my return to London I was to give a lecture on the choices for Russia's new democratic voters. The question I was required to answer was: 'Who are the voters in Russia and who will they want to vote for?' In the lecture this is how I tried to reply:

I see ten different streams running into the Russian river. Everyman's helm is directed towards a democratic sea, but the rivers create whirlpools and cross-currents in which many boats may sink before reaching a hoped-for harbour for Russia in the EEC.

River One.
The committed Communist Party members aged between 30–50, trained to be as disciplined and self-sacrificing as Britain's Commandos. They respect moderate leaders such as Gorbachev, Shervardnadze, Sobchak and Ryzhkov. They are surprisingly open to change. They disagree with older Party members who support Ligachev, who could fix a take-over bid from Gorbachev within the Party, to return to old-style control.

River Two.
The Army energized by angry young generals humiliated by the withdrawal from Afghanistan and resolute to restore Russia's self-respect. Some blame current problems on

Gorbachev's revolutionary changes. Would they support a Ligachev-type leader? Or possibly rule themselves with control of nuclear weapons? They are proud of USSR law and order.

River Three.

Two types of extremists. On the one hand the dissidents who have crusaded for human rights, and on the other the new Revolutionaries. These could form a lesser lunatic fringe. The dissidents demand more resignations, more apologies, more retribution, even if now there are only 20 political prisoners. They are reminiscent of Irish patriots who can never forget the undoubted injustice inflicted on Ireland by England in the past, but who remain too deep in recrimination to construct, positively, a present and a future where the old injuries no longer exist.

The new Revolutionaries are fierce. They are different from the idealists who followed Sakharov. On the far left a few believe in eliminating anyone who undermines the USSR and its Marxist mission. On the far right extremists shout, 'faster, faster,' for financial reform. To preserve their freedom to be extreme, such minority groups may all support Gorbachev.

River Four.

The cool sophisticated young professionals, only nominally, not ideologically, Party members, who observe, often cynically, the often-hypocritical motivations of self-advancement in both East and West. They are pragmatic, moderate, and want to keep their jobs and security. They like the look of the EEC. They would probably all vote for Gorbachev. They are 'yuppies', and already enjoy Western-style rewards.

River Five.

The skilled workers whose salary is augmented by a generous food box every week; who are used to subsidized food prices and rents and full employment. Are they for Ligachev and the Army? Most have learnt Leninist orthodoxy and it is part of their chemistry to equate it with security. How much do they want change? They still believe in Lenin's dream to make the poor powerful. They could be enraged by corruption exposed and then support Gorbachev.

River Six. The Women.

To find out what it was like for women I went 'shopping' in Moscow and found three alternatives. I saw these for myself.

(a) *The subsidised shop*

On the shelves bread, milk, spaghetti, carrots, onions, potatoes, jam, honey, butter, soft cheese and low-grade frozen meat and fish. Prices amazingly low but goods of poor quality. The *magazin* was in Lenin Avenue and middle-aged women and students were putting a few items in their trolley baskets.

(b) *The co-operative counters*

Much the same as the shop, but more expensive with better quality and more variety.

(c) *The market*

A Russian equivalent of the best Western country markets. Rows of country women with firm faces – very dignified – having travelled up with their produce by lorry, car or even aeroplane, standing steadfastly behind expensive and extensive variety. First-class fruit, cakes, fish, cheese, vegetables, guinea fowl, baby pigs, every cut of meat – you name it – all there at a price. Some Russian customers are able to afford it and payment is in roubles.

(d) *The* beriozkas

These are nearest to Western-style shops but payment is only in Western cash or credit cards. Few Russian customers, the aim being to raise foreign currency from foreign visitors.

In Moscow these are the shopping choices for the home refrigerator, and can gain or alienate women voters.

Most women live in low-rent flats and shop at the Co-op and their children are well educated. No one looks hungry, and they put up patiently with shortages hoping for more consumer goods soon. Every home has a TV. Who will win the support of these women? Someone who controls violence, does not allow children and grandchildren to become TV and computer zombies, and above all anyone who prevents husbands and sons being killed in a war. Lower-income category women are unlike their counterparts in the USA or UK; in Russia, with far fewer consumer goods available, they are more like the poorest European women who also cannot afford quality clothes or electric kettles.

Moscow is a city desperate to control violence. This partly succeeded when sales of alcohol were discouraged. The prospect of Islamic violence is a new terror. The women I met were not comforted when I said we had to live with IRA terrorism: the Armenian sectarian crisis means they are only just beginning to understand why we have not yet solved Ulster. They might vote for a benevolent dictatorship with order maintained by the Army. I doubt if the majority of women worry about human rights or the EEC, although the younger ones are highly educated and resemble their counterparts in the West. At present there are few women with top level influence – among these is Valentina Tereshkova.

River Seven. The Older Women.
The majority are deeply religious and have had to worship in fear. They see Gorbachev as the champion of the new religious freedom, which despite in-fighting within the Orthodox Church is undoubtedly increasing. But they too fear disorder and any prospect of their beloved grandsons being involved in war. They are indivisible from the Russian Orthodox Church which is indivisible from allegiance to Holy Russia. They could prove to be the silent majority which turns the voting tide because they are the most

similarly-minded force in Russia. Nearly all babies are baptized because of their babushkas. They form a very powerful national network not least because they influence all ages in their families. Who would they vote for? Probably Gorbachev but they might prefer someone with less revolutionary ideas, someone who would keep the security of the past dispensation whilst eliminating the imposition of atheism and other 'Stalinist' injustices along with Russian military ambitions. I doubt if they give much thought to the EEC. Like most orthodox nuns and priests they prefer to remain 'Holy Russian', steeped in the immense spiritual and cultural heritage of the Orthodox discipline.

River Eight. The Experts.
These resemble those in any Western country: highly-qualified scientists, economists, doctors, lawyers, writers, artists. They are an intellectual meritocracy which is highly valued and adequately rewarded. Probably all would vote for Gorbachev with a few still hoping eventually to find a leader like him who was also an economic wizard. All are in favour of the EEC. They express controversial opinions openly. Some speak of 'Purification Communism' and 'Consensus Communism'. All agree that effective economic reforms are the key to political stability.

River Nine. Youth.
Moscow's modern youth is well educated, idealistic, and sometimes spoilt. Many are only children and the result is a mixture of apathy and an ache for superficial Western symbols like rock music, jeans and McDonald's hamburgers. They take their fine libraries and museums for granted. Who would they vote for in a few years time? The majority admire Gorbachev. A minority might become patriots attracted by a leader determined to heighten national pride. All would probably feel at home in the EEC. Their greatest concern, shared with all Russians, is for ecological protection. Their Russian light is no longer red – it is green.

River Ten. Disorientated Citizens.

The Russians are a proud and patriotic people. In all the current whirlpool of self-analysis and self-accusation and being urged to dismantle what is good as well as bad in past history, they could become so disorientated as to seek national identification in a strong leader. Who could it be?

I have not identified human rights as an electoral issue, because mainstream Russians do not single it out as important except as part of improved living conditions which should provide a surer system of justice and the right for citizens to complain, with more varied opinions expressed in press, radio and TV. They want more freedom to travel, to buy foreign books and products, and more choice in food. They also want more individual influence. These are the 'human rights' promised by Gorbachev and his New Communists.

On the subject of human rights I was reminded that the USA infringed human rights in Panama without being castigated, and that Israel, while condemning Russian treatment of Jews, does not apply the same principles to Palestinians. Such anomalies suggest to Russians that the words 'human rights' are often only used as a weapon to diminish Russia in the eyes of the world.

This is not the same as the Russians now realizing the extent to which past tyrannies removed their essential freedoms. It seems to me that there is still a prevailing wish for control, but purified of all the worst aspects of totalitarianism. Russian self-respect needs to be sustained and Russian pride needs to be satisfied.

As Russia sails towards the devious cross-currents of democracy, and Soviet citizens leave the stagnant but familiar waters of the autocratic State behind them, which river will allow their boat to sail on, which could alter the course of the onward journey, and which could halt it entirely? For observers in the West it has to be a case of 'wait and see'.

138

I ended the analysis by saying,

> The outcome will affect the future for us all, so my summing-up is that the West should give the exceptionally civilised, kind and brilliant Russian people the support they deserve to reach harbour in the EEC.

This was how I saw the voting situation in Russia in 1990. I did not have sufficient knowledge of the Republics in the Soviet Union to attempt to include these but I was pleased that subsequent developments proved my Russian analysis to be sound. Increasing revulsion against Gorbachev in Russia had been the only factor I could not quantify. Perhaps mistrust of his wife was a strong contributory component? Russians expect women either to prove their own merit or help husbands of merit. I also underestimated Yeltsin's popular support, particularly among young people.

The lecture was given in London on my return but meanwhile, in Moscow, a main preoccupation remained for me. How would the result of the forthcoming vote for the Presidency affect Valentina's future? If the Soviet Union disintegrated, could she continue her work? I knew it was an anxious time for her, but she was always positive when faced by a challenge. She often reminded me that her mother had taught her to overcome difficulties.

As it happened there was no immediate crisis. Gorbachev was elected President by the Congress of People's Deputies which had been voted into power on March 26th 1989. The spectre of civil war receded.

Meanwhile the CSCE conference in January had proved that East-West confrontation was now radically changed to collaboration. Having read my analysis, Alec Home wrote: 'It sounds as if you were there for the turning of the tide.'

But usually my friendship with Valentina did not involve politics, and she now proposed another congenial plan for the future. Before I left Moscow she asked me if I would like to bring out a party of family and friends, so that her newly-formed travel organization could give us a really unforgettable week's insight into 'the best in Moscow'. The work of the Soviet Friendship Societies had never been commercially orientated but now Elena Loschenkova, Valentina's aide and a professor of physics, was in charge of the independent tourist arrangements which the Gorbachev administration insisted must replace free entertainment for VIPs. It was a mirror of the new move into the open market that Elena did not know precisely how much to charge and that she was appalled by the high prices required by hotels in comparison to the lower prices charged by the subsidized Intourist monopoly. That a scientist like Elena should become involved in travel problems showed how Valentina could inspire her friends to work for her.

The proposed visit of one week in Moscow seemed to offer a unique opportunity to share what I had loved with people who would appreciate it. I began to make a list of friends to fit the criteria. It was an exciting prospect but I could not help wondering if it would ever materialise. It was a time of more questions than answers and many of the questioners were pessimistic, anticipating not only the break-up of the Soviet Union but also again the fear of civil war.

I opted for optimism and having returned to London I pursued Valentina's offer and looked for a group of people who would love what she loved in Moscow. We were to be the first recipients of Elena's competence in the field of travel to enable visitors to stay as paying guests.

I had felt part of Valentina's family on many previous visits to the Soviet Union. This time I was bringing a group of friends. The travel agent who made our arrangements in the UK worked from Glasgow, and sometimes helped Elizabeth Smith and the GB-USSR Association. I had first met Elizabeth at the Women's Congress and we saw each other in Edinburgh. She had agreed to act as co-ordinator for our group jointly with Sir Fitzroy Maclean, one of the most knowledgeable experts in the West on Eastern European political developments, also the author of numerous books on Russian literature and art, and a fluent Russian speaker.

The Glasgow agent had never before attempted a business deal with Russia, let alone the new Russia plunged into the mysteries of capitalism. He did not find it easy. The seats booked on the aeroplane could not be definitely confirmed until the day before the flight and Elizabeth and Elena struggled to work out prices which would leave neither side out of pocket.

However, as with all similar Russian invitations, on our arrival the welcome and the comfort we found in Moscow were beyond expectations.

The group which travelled out in June 1990 was made up of a remarkable collection of experts in different fields, who hoped to see an aspect of each field of interest during the week of our stay. When the party left London, it consisted, in alphabetical order, of: Floella Benjamin, actress, and pied piper for Britain's children through the television show *Play School*. Jane Buccleuch, expert on art treasures and their conservation. Our daughter Cecil Cameron, a graduate historian writing a novel about the Decembrist Revolutionaries. Our son-in-law Richard Dalkeith, particularly interested in Soviet media communications because of his own work in the same field in Britain and also hoping to compare agricultural and forestry developments in West and East. His wife, our daughter Elizabeth, Chairman of Scottish Ballet and a graduate of the London School of Economics and a radio presenter for the BBC. Barbara Hosking OBE, secretary to two Prime Ministers, and Director of Yorkshire Television. Our son Ralph Kerr, representative for Sothebys, the firm whose link-up with Moscow dealers was already bearing fruit in the sale of Russian pictures. His wife Marie Claire, a professional artist with portraits widely exhibited including the Royal Society of Portrait Painters, who wanted to see modern Russian pictures. My husband Peter Lothian, a former government minister who had served in the Foreign Office. Diana Makgill CVO, who had just retired from a distinguished career at the Foreign Office as Chief

Ceremonial Officer, remembered with affection by the diplomats who had served their Embassies in London from all over the world, including the Soviet Union. The youngest member of the group was Charlotte Anne Scott who had recently passed entry exams into both the Home Office and the Foreign Office.

On arrival we stayed in the Academy of Sciences, reminiscent of Edinburgh University Halls of Residence when the students are away. We were all friends, happy to be in Moscow to appreciate and to learn.

Valentina was, as always, true to her word. She had said we would see the most interesting aspects of the capital city of her beloved homeland, and no one was disappointed. In fact the week proved to be overwhelmingly the reverse because almost too many cultural riches were available.

We also saw how much remained admirable in the now failing attempt by Soviet supporters to keep the Union intact whilst gradually developing freedom. A slow advance towards capitalism had been Khrushchev's way; now Yeltsin urged haste, and Gorbachev appeared unable to decide whether to stand still or to move forward fast. As onlookers it was hard for us to know what solution, long term, would be best for Russia, the Republics and the regions.

Meanwhile our party experienced pre-Yeltsin Communist reform and we valued much that was positive in the interim regime. A number of thoughtful, tolerant, efficient young professionals were with us throughout the week to interpret and to ensure we had all we wanted. We heard unforgettable music, including *The Queen of Spades* at the Bolshoi, we saw art galleries, and we exchanged dialogue, dialogue, dialogue. Our companions seemed similar to the bourgeois Russians that Lenin had feared, but they did not seem fear-deserving; only worried, well-informed and seeking new freedoms within socialism. For us they lit a candle of integrity in the midst of political uncertainty. They represented the Soviet youth which had never known Stalin, but, having been trained by disciplined principles, was full of promise, well-educated, modest in its material needs and very stable in its family outlook and love of small children and grandparents. We often asked ourselves: 'What would this generation gain from the West?' Obviously the answer was 'freedom', but at what price?

We called our group 'The Moscow Fellowship'. We were appreciative but not easily taken in, and we all obtained incomparable benefit from the innumerable gifts Russia can give the world.

For me the week still runs like a film reel of impressions. The silver and gold in the Kremlin; the visit to television and radio centres; the midnight changing of the guard in Red Square, with the flag flying like red silk in the wind, not yet taken down to be replaced by the tricolour. The great cathedral in Zagorsk with a question and answer session with the impressive Rector of students. Music, concerts and musicians; the Bolshoi Opera backstage; our group drinking, talking and singing; lighting candles in dark shrines with glowing icons of the Mother of God and of Russia. The museums of modern art; Tolstoy's house; and perhaps the most memorable experience of all: the welcome given to us in Star City by Alexei Leonov, the first man to walk alone in space above our planet: 'Attention, attention, Man has entered open space.' Throughout our stay Floella Benjamin had brought the laughter, love and vitality of 'black is beautiful' to every occasion. When Leonov saw her he opened his arms and said, 'Welcome blondie.' Then the two greats hugged each other. It was a privilege to be shown the mechanics of space exploration by the human who, walking alone, had experienced 'very black sky with many stars – blue stars – big stars – very bright sun.'

Returning to our rooms in the evenings we discussed the day. We were increasingly impressed by our four young Communist companions and by their sense of humour. Why did they seem admirable? Had Lenin's formation for life been similar to living in a monastery: hard rules and hard conditions, but also a sense of security within shared obedience? If so, what benefits would they obtain from Western-type freedom? The obvious advantage of democracy was freedom of choice. To remain a Communist Party member, obedience was obligatory.

Nevertheless Communist training had resulted in kind, clever, capable people. Did Western youth compare favourably? Russian youth was so anxious to learn from the West.

There were many exchanges to make us laugh. Alexander, Valentina's organiser responsible for the smooth running of our daily timetable, was an expert in making VIPs happy. So was Diana. They were both experienced in protocol problems, and Alexander told us of the time when, having hooked a fish beforehand so that the honoured guest could proudly reel it in believing he had caught it, the special fish brought from Moscow had disintegrated before delivery. Diana told matching stories to describe the hazards inherent in providing the best for honoured guests.

Alyona was with us whenever she could be free of hospital work. She seemed to me to be like a young niece, or even a daughter. She enjoyed everything we were shown as much as we did. I wondered if her disciplined professional life allowed her enough time to enjoy leisure. She was immensely proud of her mother as she knew that Valentina was trying to master difficult problems at world level. Alyona was a skilled orthopaedic surgeon and a loyal Soviet citizen but her mind was open to accept all the best the world could offer. She had always put family duties first, whether in caring for her grandmother or cooking for her mother, and she looked forward to the added fulfilment of being a wife with children of her own. But for the time being helping Valentina to work for Russia and the world was her main preoccupation. In a different way Elizabeth seemed to feel the same. Valentina's work was vital. Personal wishes and problems were not as important as commitment to helping her to succeed in the work of the Friendship Societies to build international bridges.

We only saw Valentina on the last night after a brilliant final concert and supper she gave for us all. She had been kept informed of our doings hour by hour, but she had been working in the Kremlin Parliament throughout the week and could not get away. Her presence at the party caused the customary impact. Fitzroy said he felt like bowing as if to royalty. She and

I spoke together for half an hour on our own – we exchanged family news and we also talked about how best she could serve her homeland and world peace in rapidly changing circumstances. Meeting our friends and knowing how much they had enjoyed her hospitality was a source of special satisfaction to her. She was expecting to come to Edinburgh in the autumn to receive an honorary doctorate from the University and she hoped that we would all meet again then. I told her, and I meant it, that she and I now shared one family. It did not surprise her.

Fitzroy's royal comparison struck our group as valid. Valentina never failed to work tirelessly when on public duty but in private she chose whom she wished to be with and I had been told that she could be ruthless, ignoring the many who wanted to attract her attention. She was acutely aware of ulterior motives.

Talking to Valentina, even if only for a short time, confirmed for me again how exceptionally well-informed she was about international developments and that she was an expert on ecological problems. My life had enabled me to meet many men and women who were thinkers of outstanding calibre and she was second to none. Indeed, she proved how the assumption that great thinkers are usually men is patently discriminatory. She remained an unswerving patriot but her supra-terrestrial experience had formed into her into a world statesman for peace.

I kept wishing that the other members of our group could talk to her properly. We had all been discussing many problems building up for humanity, such as the possibility of ecological disasters including asteroids destroying the Earth; and how to solve the social challenge of finding employment for those who would become unemployed when the armament industry was reduced. They were all questions on which Valentina would have made a valuable contribution, particularly because she was a pragmatic idealist. She never recommended or undertook anything she was not sure was workable in practice. Her advice would have been of immense interest to our group representing different fields of expertise. But as usual there had not been enough time to expand beyond exchange of family news and discussion of a few immediate international events. As we parted she said we would have more time – next time.

Our Moscow Fellowship felt sad when the week ended. The hope that Valentina and I shared, which was that from the West and East there should be a genuine exchange of cultures so as to establish trust, appreciation and co-operation, had been realized. Falling in love with Russia had also happened again. So it made us particularly uneasy that we left fearing that civil war might endanger the USSR. But I remembered that such wars usually only happen when rival tribes fanatically hate each other. It did not appear that this was true of Russia, whose people only seemed obsessed by two objectives: to live better and to live in peace. We all drew comfort from the hope that Valentina's honorary degree from Edinburgh University, only a few months ahead, would bring her to Britain so that we could give her our own genuine welcome from the West.

The Sixth Milestone

Honorary Doctorate, Edinburgh University

I n the event, fears of civil war in the Soviet Union were proved to be unwarranted and in November 1990 Valentina travelled to the UK. We met first in London and then in Edinburgh, where the University was to confer an honorary doctorate in recognition of her work for peace through the 'Edinburgh Conversations'. These had encouraged moves for disarmament at the time of the cold war through an influential USSR-Scottish committee mainly composed of scientists and academics. In the new climate of co-operation, future plans included discussions on environmental problems, and the City Council of Edinburgh had agreed to support these.

Valentina was to be in Britain for five days. In London, the Moscow Fellowship had devised a great welcome. Having been Valentina's guests, all were anxious to do something special for her. We made plans with Vladimir Molchanov who had replaced Gennadi Fedosov as Valentina's Embassy represent-ative. Elizabeth and Richard Dalkeith were in Japan but organized a supper party for her which they gave in their house in London on their return. Diana Makgill worked tirelessly arranging an interesting programme which included a VIP invitation to Covent Garden, where Valentina found Benjamin Britten very modern and his music gave Elizabeth Zolina a headache. Alyona was also in London with a Soviet medical delegation on its way to Washington. She was childlike in her excitement at being in Covent Garden. Valentina was invited by the Science Museum to see her achievement inscribed on a painted ceiling, and by the Royal Academy to see the Monet exhibition. They were all anxious to honour the first woman in space.

There had been an inexplicable and almost libellous article about Valentina, first printed in a French paper and reprinted by the *Daily Mail*, describing her as a tragic has-been. It was good to prove by her presence that nothing was further from the truth. Concurrently I was given the chance by Susan Raven, Assistant Editor of the *Sunday Times Magazine*, to write 'A Life in the Day of' to be published the following year. It meant my having proper professional interviews with Valentina, but she agreed and she was prepared to talk to this journalist – for once!

Peter gave a small reception in the House of Lords with twenty guests, as widely representative as possible, including former Chancellor Denis Healey, and his wife, the author Edna Healey, and Heather Couper, past President of the British Astronomical Association. The impressions were surprisingly similar: 'Straight – kind – disciplined – really nice - obviously very intelligent.' My respect increased seeing her capacity never to change, no matter the circumstances. I wondered if it was her soldier's training always to appear calm. Did she actually feel vulnerable?

It was disappointing that Britain's former Prime Minister Lord Home, an expert on East-West diplomacy, was unable to be at the party because he was ill in hospital. Valentina immediately volunteered to drive miles to see him and was only dissuaded when I suggested a cosmonaut in the ward might cause an unhelpful commotion.

Two months previously we had invited the Prime Minister but Mrs Thatcher replied that she might not be free: 'It is an exceptionally busy time of the year.' As it happened, it was the night she lost the vote for the leadership. Few inside and outside Britain could believe it when she was removed by a sophisticated coup. A year later, in December 1991, the 'riches to rags' experience felled Gorbachev in the same democratic way. When he said: 'My work is done,' it matched Thatcher's comment: 'It's a funny old world.' After that the two radical reformers were left for history to redeem. Valentina was always loyal. She continued to respect Margaret Thatcher.

During Valentina's stay in London Alyona joined us intermittently. She had never left Russia before. Valentina now accepted that Alyona was increasingly an independent woman. When I first met Alyona she was finding her surgeon's training hard and she persevered to please her mother. Now it gave her great self-respect. Valentina did not expect Alyona to come to Scotland. She believed that if her daughter was going to travel abroad it must be under the same conditions as other young Russian professionals, and after two days in London Alyona and her colleagues travelled on to America for another medical conference.

Valentina, however, was in Britain on official business and this allowed her to come to stay with us in our home in Scotland, having first attended the ceremony in Edinburgh. Throughout the time I have known her she has never deviated from her obligation not to accept personal privileges. She is basically a Puritan, only really enjoying permissible occasions within the limits set by her sincerely-held socialist principles. Veniality does not attract her. Her concern is never for money, but always to safeguard her integrity. This became clear when we considered possible fees for publications or lectures. She smiled when I reported on the substantial sums being received by fellow Soviets for their published revelations. 'We need to protect the truth,' was her regular reply.

The occasion of the degree ceremony in Edinburgh was very fine. The University Hall was full to capacity. Peter and I had been invited. We sat not far from the platform. Three others received degrees with Valentina: Neal Ascherson, William Brown, and Professor Heikki Raisanen.

The Principal of Edinburgh University, Sir David Smith, read the citation.

> *VALENTINA TERESHKOVA: A person of prodigious courage who has not been content to rest on her laurels. Her energy, commitment and skills have contributed significantly to exercises in mutual understanding for East-West relations long before the end of the cold war.*

Valentina wore her red gown with magnificent dignity, the only woman among many men. The ovation she received from the students was enthusiastic.

During her day in Edinburgh she called on the Lord Provost, Eleanor McLaughlin, and the GB-USSR Association gave a lunch in her honour arranged by Meg Luckins and Elizabeth Smith. It was sad that John Smith, who was then Labour Shadow Chan-cellor, could not be there. The Scottish Labour MP Tam Dalyell and his wife were among the guests to congratulate Valentina.

We drove down from Edinburgh to our home in the Scottish Borders, with Elizabeth Zolina and Vladimir Molchanov, for a visit of one night and two days. On the drive down we had to stop at the Edinburgh Woollen Mill for the inevitable explosion of Russian shopping. Valentina accepted Margaret Thatcher's resignation as Prime Minister but she was puzzled by a 'coup' happening in England. She bought a shawl as a gift for her. I dreaded these Thatcher gifts in case I was appointed to deliver them. Life with Valentina always involved a near-obsession to find the right gift, no matter whether it was in Moscow, London or Edinburgh.

The gift she brought from Moscow for me was the picture of a small isolated white church on a hill with the cross on its dome etched against the sunset. On the reverse she had written: 'To remind you of the land you have learned to love.' This was true, even if I realised I had only visited Valentina's native Russia; Yaroslavl, Vladimir Suzdal, Moscow, the Golden Ring, the heart of Russia and Valentina's homeland. I knew very little about the Republics or of the varied vast territories contained by the Soviet Union. 'You must visit Georgia,' Valentina always recommended, and she was sad that I had not done so. But my travelling plans were not encouraged by historic happenings: currently Georgia was on the brink of civil war. Still, it was true I had learned to love all I had seen and met in Russia and I hoped she would love Scotland in the same way.

Vladimir had asked for a programme of her stay, and suggested that it might include a 'cultural evening'. We arranged an informal supper with the Maxwell Scotts of Abbotsford as guests, because Sir Walter Scott's work was well known in Russia. After supper Dr Rosalind Marshall, a distinguished Scottish historian, gave a short address on Mary Queen of Scots, where I suspect Valentina found a comparison with the Thatcher drama. The music was provided by the Hawick Fiddler, Bob Hobkirk, and we danced reels led by Betty McLeish, an Elder of the Church of Scotland and our family administrator. The next day on a visit to Abbotsford Valentina was inspired to find her romantic reading of Sir Walter Scott becoming reality in the house he created, and lived and worked in. Afterwards we drove on to lunch at Bowhill, where the Duke and Duchess of Buccleuch gave her a special insight into Scotland's history, its art and its music; and also into how well artistic treasures are preserved in Britain's private collections. Valentina enjoyed it all and appeared, superficially, to forget the problems she had left in Russia.

When I had last been in Moscow a young journalist had said to me: 'Ideals of democracy are not what we need to solve our economic crisis. Gorbachev is not intelligent enough to adjust his reforms into a structure which will deliver food and consumer goods. That is what his success or failure will depend on. He could redirect efficiency at providing armaments into the same efficiency to provide food. But he is not capable of such leadership. In any case just distribution will never be achieved in Russia by a democratic free-for-all. In the West you provide it through competitive prices, in the East we need to provide it through controls.'

This was not the voice of Yeltsin and his plans for a democratic open market, nor of Gorbachev's Swedish-style socialism. It was the voice of the Communist conservatives now seeking to regain power in the USSR.

I did not discuss politics with Valentina but during her visit we read of fierce forces which might yet pull the USSR apart and leave a vast area of the world, with atomic weapons, under diverse and possibly irresponsible control. This was of serious concern to Valentina. Remembering the release of religion, I remained on the side of the perestroika reforms and I relied on the Soviet people to achieve stability.

Valentina being with us was like having a close relative to stay. We listened to Pavarotti singing while Valentina flipped the record over again and again until she found 'O Sole Mio'. She was always watching the sheep in the field which we call our garden. She insisted on stopping to call on horses, whenever we saw any, and she and Elizabeth were always laughing, sometimes teasing us about imaginary love-affairs.

There was still a lot to learn about each other. One night at supper Valentina asked me, 'Why are you called Tony?' I explained that my mother was convinced it would help me to have an Italian name, so I was christened Antonella. 'Anto... what?' my schoolfriends had asked me incredulously at my first army school. So, humiliated, I quickly switched to Tony. Later, to be more formal, I used the single initial 'A' which was becoming normal practice for men and women alike. Valentina accepted this explanation, not least because I still had not completely understood the intricacies of Russian name terminology.

Ferniehirst, our home in Scotland, is a fifteenth-century fortified former farmhouse, with a long room where we eat, sit by the fire and play the piano. Old portraits hang on the rough stone walls. Each tells a story of frontier warfare between Scots and English. Valentina said it reminded her of Russian history in the same century; turbulent, often cruel, but passionately defending a much-loved land.

When our granddaughters came to meet her it was obvious that she was in tune with children and that for them she brought to life a universe which they wanted to understand; a sky with spinning asteroids, planets and stars and the mysteries beyond. They also instinctively related to her plans to protect planet Earth and the dream of a future world without nuclear war. For them man on Mars had been science fiction. Now they were actually meeting a space expert who was planning for man to live on Mars in reality.

This was the first time I had seen Valentina off duty and it did not last long. She had allowed herself two days so that we could work on the *Sunday Times* interview. 'We must start again,' would be her reminder, even in the middle of a meal, that time was difficult for her to spare. During our interviews she gave me the trust she did not give others. She was totally accessible, not least about the trivialities on the edge of the day which the *Sunday Times* format for the 'A Life in the Day of' series requires. I had to ask about her hairdresser, dressmaker, breakfast, bath and bedtime, and her favourite foreign films which included *Gone with the Wind*. She reacted favourably to these first sessions and promised to give me a final interview before she left London.

But I was stunned by what happened next. Just before leaving to be driven to Edinburgh the following morning she said she had a great favour to ask me. Would I write her biography? As Alyona had often remarked, 'What happens to us is like a dream.' This was no dream. Valentina had made her request simply and she expected a similar response from me. Obviously

I felt inadequate, but my journalistic training responded to the challenge. The world's first space heroine, probably one of the most interesting women in the world in her own right and with the intention to use the rest of her life to protect the planet, trusted me to record her life story. She wanted to speak about her past and the present, and her hopes for the future. 'I want to tell you the truth; there have been so many lies.'

Elizabeth Zolina was relentlessly encouraging. 'If you don't do it she will not do it at all. You have seen how she avoids all publicity. Please say yes. I will help you. I will translate everything.' She was pleased when I said that I could not refuse and indeed that I was inspired by the prospect. But I added that to be sensible we must first see whether Valentina approved of the *Sunday Times* article. Valentina agreed, and I promised I would send the draft to Moscow for her to authorise. 'After that we will meet in Russia, and we can spend time together to begin our book,' she said.

During the *Sunday Times* interviews I had found one more side to Valentina, clear and open and with inspiring insight into the questions I raised about human love, the new attitudes of youth, spiritual and moral values, women's work, ecology, peace, space research. It was very interesting to hear her answers, always original, always positive, always reflecting the common sense she had inherited from her mother yet adding her own expertise in technology and space research including plans for new energy supplies. Elizabeth was right, her life story was long overdue. I could only hope I would do it justice.

Vladimir and Elizabeth seemed genuinely to enjoy being in Scotland. We all felt proud of the honour Valentina had deservedly received. We had been happy celebrating it as a family, at home. It had been another example of our exchange of genuine personal experiences that I had been able to share with Valentina in Scotland our way of family living just as in Russia she had shared hers with me. At the end of the short Scottish stay it was depressing seeing Valentina and her two companions drive away.

A day later I rejoined her in London for a lunch at the Soviet Embassy in her honour. I expected her to be preparing for two television interviews arranged by Floella Benjamin and Barbara Hosking, but the side of her character which can never promote itself had become apparent. Her way out is always the same: 'Recalled to Moscow'. She left two days earlier than planned, proving that in public relations she is her own worst enemy; not least in Russia, where the public knows very little about her, only that she is one of their most courageous women and that when she was Chairman of the Women's Committee she became an active counsellor, receiving hundreds of letters from women every week asking for her help on many varied problems and that she did all she could to help when she was a member of the Central Committee with responsibility for women's issues.

On the day of her departure from London she came to our small cottage near the Thames and we talked over the content of the magazine interview I had prepared. She was pleased with what I had written, but embarrassed because the editor had asked for a photograph of her with Alyona. So far we had felt secure combining our work together. Would it be the same for the life story? She was enthusiastic about our small London galley kitchen which she recognised as a hallmark of my way of living. She said, 'I could be really happy here.' But I doubted whether the next interviews would take place in London. Then Diana Makgill came to collect her for an official lunch at the Science Museum and to see her off on the flight to Moscow.

We parted, as usual, preparing for the next meeting; but as always the place where it could happen was uncertain. Valentina's organization was involved in the main Helsinki conference planned in Moscow for 1991. She asked if I would attend a seminar on 'Culture and Peace'. It now also seemed certain that she would be in Britain again in 1992 as guest of honour at the celebration in Edinburgh organized by the International Science Festival for the United Nations Year of Space. She would be speaking with Helen Sharman, the only British woman cosmonaut. Valentina said that we might meet again after the conference to discuss the account of her experiences. Elizabeth was very anxious that it should be published to commemorate the thirtieth anniversary of her flight in June 1993. But I wondered if she would find the necessary time, and I was worried that she might not like the *Sunday Times Magazine* article, the first interview she had ever given. Elizabeth reassured me: 'She really has faith in you. She likes what you have written already.' Nevertheless, the uncertainty as to where we could meet for interviews did not give me confidence that work on our commemorative book would soon begin.

Believing that in the future Valentina would be interested to read it, I continued to record the major events which were happening during the East-West journey on which we were still travelling. In this chronicle it was already very encouraging for me to find evidence of how, year by year, the former black wall of hostility had been mainly demolished, and that our friendship had endured through many crucial social and political upheavals. The experiences Valentina and I had shared seemed indivisible from the world's journey from the darkness of the cold war towards a new world order which appeared to have overcome the danger of nuclear destruction. If there was to be a biography, my personal impressions of the events I had observed from the West during a dramatic decade could provide an important part of the story. Valentina agreed, and looked forward to reading it before we began our *Conversations*.

After she had returned to Moscow she felt far away again. I could not know what she was thinking. The world was holding its breath watching the aggressive intentions of Iraq toward Kuwait. What did she hope for or fear? Even while she had been in Britain there had not been enough time for a wide-ranging exchange of views. Perhaps we could talk at length when we met to start work on her life story. Valentina had asked if I would travel to Moscow early in the New Year of 1991, and I was ready to do so unless it was prevented by the mounting Middle East crisis with its probable ending in war.

The Seventh Milestone

The United Nations Alliance

The alliance of the USA and the USSR during the Gulf War seemed to me to be the final milestone on my East-West perestroika road, because it proved that the fear which dominated most of the twentieth century, that the superpowers would eventually obliterate each other and put the whole world at risk, was no longer valid. As talks with Saddam Hussein failed to find a solution and the crisis escalated into armed intervention, Russia and America held together within the United Nations. After the war, President Bush promised a new world order based on the continuing co-operation of the international community.

The rebuilding ideal of perestroika had succeeded in replacing East-West confrontation with collaboration. The previously hostile worlds Valentina and I had lived in were now allied instead of threatening each other with fatal nuclear weapons.

Due to the political uncertainty, my visit to Moscow was postponed. But the 'A Life in the Day of' had been published.

It gave the first ever description of what Valentina's daily life was like, and Valentina was pleased with it. The message from Elizabeth – with another small present – was: 'She is ready now to start the book with you. But for her this is not the best time to travel.' That also applied to me.

To oppose the Iraqi invasion of Kuwait, the UN was building up for the armed intervention of Desert Storm. It was astounding to reflect that at this time if the Soviet Union had opposed rather than supported UN policy, the situation would almost certainly have escalated into widespread nuclear conflagration.

Some years before, Alec Home had given me a best-selling novel by Morris West, *The Clowns of God*, published in 1981. I had discussed the plot with his wife Elizabeth, one of the most discerning minds I have ever known, and we both wished we could ignore the implications. The story describes a Pope forced to abdicate because of his vision of atomic annihilation. The critical question was, 'Would the USA or the USSR operate the red button first?' Until 1985, when Gorbachev and Reagan met in Iceland to investigate positive disarmament, this crisis was not a possibility, it was a probability. But now, even with the uncertain alignment in the Middle East, neither superpower looked likely to end the world.

Many Russian friends tell me I am wrong because they believe that reforms were wanted by the Russian people and not by one man, but my view remains that it was due to Mikhail Gorbachev that the novel's missing answer was given in a way which for nearly a century had seemed impossible. Speaking for the Soviet people, he had been empowered to halt the increasing stampede towards the war to end all wars. The Soviet people's wish for peace was a factor which Morris West had foreseen in fiction, but in reality it had seemed too much to hope for, and so a lethal atomic arsenal was piling up more and more dangerously. Now, in 1991, mentally atrophied television viewers watching air assaults in the Gulf War saw the lifting of the curtain on what could have become planetary extermination if there had been US-USSR confrontation. But the Morris West scenario had been altered. Even if thousands of victims like the Kurds were killed as part of the Gulf War, it remained only a horrific revelation of what might have been.

The real-life answer to Morris West's challenge was due to the Soviet people's determination, spoken for by Gorbachev when he surprised President Reagan with radical Soviet proposals for disarmament and when, after that, Soviet deeds spoke louder than words.

It was the journey's end I had hoped for and believed to be possible.

It was all the more dispiriting that, even with evidence to the contrary, people in power in the West still retained ingrained suspicion of Soviet intentions. Whenever I had returned to Britain from the USSR I had tried to convey how dangerous it could be if Soviet proposals for peace continued to be misinterpreted. I had sounded out my impressions on two wise friends: Ian Haig, a former Australian Ambassador; and Davidson Nicol, a former Under-Secretary General at the UN. They appeared to believe that what I reported was true, but their advice had been, 'Wait and see.'

That has never been my way. When I was writing for the *Scottish Daily Express* as a current affairs columnist, a colleague told me: 'You can become a fine investigative journalist, but you will never be a popular journalist because you write ahead of opinion. Public approval or disapproval only develops after an event. Popular journalists answer the questions which are already being asked. No matter how valid your exposures may be they will not make any impression while the public is happy not to be disturbed.'

My reports had been disturbing because I had evidence to prove that in Russia there was a genuine will for disarmament, at a time when in the West the NATO versus Warsaw Pact confrontation had become almost comfortably established. Was it easier to live with the possibility of calamity than act to prevent it? As the philosopher Herbert Marcuse had reminded humanity, modern means of persuasion can make almost any form of anti-social behaviour acceptable – until too late when the deception is unmasked. Top-level indifference to the radical Soviet change of attitude struck me as a dangerous lack of discernment because it prevented the Soviet people from receiving the assistance that their stabilizing reforms deserved. The Marshall Plan-type aid needed was not forthcoming from nations which could spend millions on protecting oil resources.

I had no way of knowing Valentina's views but I had been reading an account of Soviet attitudes to disarmament in the years from Khrushchev's first *détente* up to Gorbachev's appointment to the Soviet leadership, given by Arkady Shevchenko, a Soviet official who had been adviser to Gromyko when he was Soviet Foreign Minister and who had eventually served him in the UN as Under-Secretary General until Shevchenko defected to the West in 1973. He had no motive other than telling the truth in his book, *Breaking with Moscow*, where he described how genuine Khrushchev and the USSR had been in wishing first to limit the arms race, and then to proceed to complete disarmament. The Shevchenko story of Soviet intentions, even if he finally repudiated the system, is a story of true attempts by the East to achieve peaceful co-existence being blocked by rigid disbelief from the West.

The same story, from a different angle, involved the years in which Valentina served the Soviet system with unfailing patriotism. Shevchenko had lived as a very dissimilar servant of the same State, but his revelations do prove that the Russian people's wish for peace was not propaganda. It was sincere and it was not sufficiently encouraged. Those who work for peace cannot but see this as a serious misjudgement which might have resulted in the ultimate tragedy happening by default.

Shevchenko's defection can be compared with those of Burgess and Maclean. Defectors usually claim that they can only work for their ideals in the system which embodies these ideals. In contrast to this view, Valentina and I never wavered in our conviction that shared ideals were best served by working loyally within and not without our own national systems and that this was the right way by which patriots would achieve progress for human survival together. We did not trust defectors. But we had tried not to miss opportunities to achieve peace, and in this context at the end of the eighties so much seemed to be for the better, not least because of global response to a series of disasters in the Third World when the international community united to provide aid for earthquake, flood, cyclone and famine.

At the time of the Gulf War I did not know what Valentina thought of Allied military intervention. My own feelings were that everything possible should be done to prevent innocent civilian casualties. I felt certain that she hoped, as I did, that the new world order proclaimed by Bush heralded the beginning of genuine disarmament moves, and that at last the international community would unite for real human progress in the future.

Now there was no longer any need for me to give Valentina my personal impressions on the Allied side of developments as agreed on by both East and West. For my own interest, however, I was reading American, Italian, French and British press accounts on how the joint strategies were proceeding. I continued to keep a record of the major events, not least because this could be useful as a background for the *Conversations* I hoped to achieve with Valentina before the end of the year.

The press accounts provided conflicting conclusions, including reports from the East which were now widely available. Certainly the last decade of the century had become a difficult time for reliable reporting on international affairs. There was little optimism about a stable future for the USSR. Despite perestroika, or perhaps because of it, after the Gulf War Western media saw the Soviet empire freezing into immobility. One writer described its citizens as moving slowly inside the iceberg, waiting for a monumental crack.

Obviously the financial situation was crucial and commentators highlighted the traumatic task of making the Soviet Union change from centralized control to the open market. Professor

JK Galbraith had written: 'There has been a world of experience in moving from pure capitalism to the mixed system which now prevails in the West and Pacific lands. But there is no experience of moving back from pure socialism to Western-type mixed economy.'

I knew how anxious Valentina was to secure funds to save her inter-cultural work and that there were increasing cutbacks on her budget. But I certainly did not understand the problems of open and command economies in East or West. Financial affairs had always been a closed book for me, not least the reasons why in the West a philanthropist economist like George Soros lost 650 million on Black Monday in 1987 and gained 2 billion on Black Wednesday in 1992. The welcome news was that he intended to invest millions to stabilize the Russian economy. I wondered if Valentina understood instability in the open market, but I doubted it.

Meanwhile political developments did not stand still. Professor Gordon Smith of the Chair of International Studies at the University of South Carolina, and author of the definitive analysis for American students, *Soviet Politics Struggling with Change*, described his revision for the 1992 edition as being 'like changing a tire on a car when it is moving'.

Gorbachev still appeared convincing outside Soviet confines, but political analysts reported that the citizens most needed to save the Soviet Union – the young middle-class; modest, disciplined, and intellectually well informed – were becoming the most materially deprived. They had seen the EEC as the oasis ahead, but the European bureaucrats postponed action. I certainly regretted that at the time there were not enough visionaries to encourage Soviet hopes for integration with Europe.

In August 1991 the whole world watched the attempted coup to replace Gorbachev so as to return to autocracy, and how this then became a call for Yeltsin to take command. He was seen standing on the armoured car surrounded by soldiers who had refused to open fire. They were sick of bloodshed, just as British pilots had refused earlier to open fire on the Basra Road 'turkey shoot'. Yeltsin was the new symbol of freedom. Now the universal question for a watching world was whether or not the democratic changes in the Soviet Union were irreversible or, indeed, capable of realization.

I continued to hope for Marshall Plan-type aid for the East.

In London I found it difficult to assess which Western media views about Russia were false and which were true. Few were sympathetic. Delegates from my own independent Institute of Journalists Union, describing a conference of the new Yeltsin Confederation of Independent Mining Unions, reported: 'a cauldron of noise, interruptions, criticisms; no idea of how to conduct a discussion. The old unions rejected as transmission belts for Communist ideas are still staffed by old party nominees and are well resourced with buses, offices, typewriters; every help that bureaucrats need.' A Russian parliamentary delegate had been cynical: 'Come back yesterday – we Russians will quickly know when we are hungry under the new system.' But the old system was beyond recall. The coup which failed was the beginning of the end of the Soviet Union.

This raised another critical question. Were we all watching the collapse of the Soviet version of Communism worldwide? I had always felt genuine respect for some of Lenin's aims and in talks with Valentina I had meant it when I said I thought the immense misery of half the world could only be rescued by 'Christian Communism'. A combination of Lenin and St Francis might oblige the very rich to share with the very poor, and create a spiritual fraternal revolution to save the Third World. As I have never been a fair-weather friend I could not forget that Communist ideals had restored hope and pride to many exploited men and women. Was capitalism now the only way to do so?

The reports I was reading asked questions but gave no positive answers. In December 1991 the leaders of Russia, Ukraine, Byelorussia and Kazakhstan had met in a central base in Minsk to support the new Commonwealth of Independent States.

This represented seventy per cent of the Soviet Union's 270 million people.

In January 1992, Yeltsin met John Major in London and President Bush in the USA. He also addressed the United Nations Security Council in New York. James Baker, US Secretary of State, recommended support for Yeltsin's revolution: 'aid for a proud and exhausted people in their hour of despair while dark political forces lurk in the wings to exploit frustration.' John Major advised the European Community to take in Russia: 'What a prize if the whole of Europe could be drawn into the same economic structure. It would make it inconceivable that the Western nations would ever again have armed conflicts.' Perhaps at long last a safe future for East and West could be built on this hope.

I had no news of Valentina and no direct contact with Russia at this time. My own view from the West seemed to have lost its bearings. Press reports said that the August coup leaders claimed that their motive had been patriotism. I remembered the French friends who were willing to die for Algerie Française, and young Englishmen for Rhodesia to remain British. It had come under the umbrella of patriotism, but in the final analysis fierce and insular patriotism could become a contradiction of individual rights. The only safeguard for the democratic ideal was 'one man – one vote' and this right was now being established in Russia.

The 1990s had begun as a depressing new decade. It was forecast that the transnational plague of Aids would decimate both prosperous and poor countries, while famine continued to destroy the latter. The Rio Earth Summit, called to unite all nations to protect the planet, revealed deep divisions between the needs of the poor and rich worlds. Discord was putting European unity in peril and tribalism inflamed the Balkans in a horrific civil war which condoned 'ethnic cleansing'.

In comparison the disintegration of the Soviet Union caused less international concern, and appeals from the Third World for financial support had little hope of being heard at a time when a serious recession was overtaking the rich nations of the world. The former stated aim of the international community – improving the quality of life for all peoples – seemed now to be downgraded.

I kept wishing I could ask Valentina what she thought. But I doubted if she would want to give political opinions. Here our attitudes had always been dissimilar. Before marriage I had dreamt of becoming a war correspondent and my work as a journalist had been to report on current affairs. I was interested in politics even if I could not believe in any political party enough to become a member. Valentina, on the other hand, surveyed political changes without wanting to become personally involved. Whatever happened in Russia I was sure she would continue to serve the government legitimately in control. Politicians could come and go; for her what mattered most was to work for her homeland in the discipline for which she was trained. When we had been together, living as a family, it was noticeable that although she was an exceptionally warm and responsive companion, interested in details such as family photograph albums, and talking enthusiastically about history, art and music, she was only transformed with a particular kind of energy when she was discussing space with its discoveries and potential. 'I am a cosmonaut. It is my profession.' That thought made her happy and she welcomed a chance to leave us so as to complete an essay on the Russian project to land on Mars. For Valentina this made the best use of her time. Her vision for the future was to 'use science well' and in our interviews she wanted to give a detailed description of the technical requirements for a Mars landing. But when?

It was eventually reassuring for me to hear from Vladimir Molchanov, her representative at the Russian Embassy in London, that she was regularly speaking for the Friendship Societies outside Russia as part of her continuing official duties, and that she had spoken on global morality at the United Nations and, at a university in Spain, on Russian projects to land on Mars. She was also meeting her colleagues in cosmonautics as a member of the Association of Space Explorers.

The week after the coup Duncan Shaw had attended the long-awaited Helsinki conference in Moscow which had been adversely affected by delegates' reluctance to attend at a time of political uncertainty. Valentina's organization had arranged international discussions on the 'human dimension of the Helsinki process'. She had given an inspiring introduction to the conference: 'We citizens from twenty CSCE countries are here to share our concerns with each other. We seek to find solutions for the pressing problems facing humankind. We believe that the well-being of all members of the human family is the goal of life.'

This was not official Soviet-speak. It was Valentina saying what she believed to be true. It reminded me of how in 1980 I had heard two other reliable scientific thinkers – Barbara Ward and Professor Margaret Gowing – warning that the planet might not survive. Subsequent atomic war anxiety had started me on my perestroika journey. Valentina had been the guide I had trusted and looked for, and she had not failed me.

The Helsinki conference in Moscow heard Valentina's last call as a Soviet citizen proclaiming a European vision for world security. I met Duncan Shaw when he returned to London and asked him what could happen to Valentina's organization following the end of Communist rule. He did not know, but he was sure that she would continue to serve her homeland.

Increasingly, I looked to the time when Valentina and I together could consider how fast and far history had travelled since we first met. So much had happened and was happening now. I needed to hear her views, not least because she was always more optimistic than I was. For example, I remained as worried about global survival as I had been at the time of our first meeting. But when I discussed frightening ecological reports from the Rio Earth Summit with Valentina, her answer was reassuring: 'I do not want to believe that some terrible catastrophe will destroy our planet. It is so beautiful and it is unprotected, but it can be protected by human intellectual potential based on the eternal principles of morality.' Her view was founded on scientific research which did unravel the mysteries of the Universe and this put the problems of planet Earth into a much less limited perspective than mine.

Now, in the nineties, I often asked myself: why had I become so involved in what happened in Russia? It reminded me of how far I had travelled beyond the barriers of prejudice which for most of my life had prevented me from learning anything about the land which Valentina rightly said I now loved. It amazed me to think back to the time when, before I met Valentina, Russia had been totally unknown to me.

For example, in the seventies Mikki Doyle, a Communist, was my greatest friend but for me that did not involve Russia – we both worked for the feminist movement. Other friends belonged to CND, but that was not Russia – it was concern about the atomic hazard. I studied Marx, Lenin and Gramsci, but that was not Russia – it was the worldwide challenge of how best to help the disinherited and whether Communist ideology could advance equality. I knew something of Russian literature, art and music, but these belonged to world cultural heritage and did not seem relevant to Communist Russia. Admittedly the time when I knew nothing of Russia had been a time when it was impossible for average women in Britain or in Russia to know the truth about each other's lives. Certainly, if I had not met Valentina I would never have travelled to Russia where I found so many aspects of misinformation disproved.

It surprised me to find that, even after perestroika, there was little change in the critical attitude of the Western media towards what was happening in the USSR. Reports were either unintentionally or intentionally misleading, and often abysmally ignorant, for example, of the way Russians like Valentina and her colleagues really lived. The Russians I met were annoyed that the West could be so wrong about Russia. That is why real-life experience, such as Valentina made possible for me, was a sharp surprise. I found so much kindness, generosity and security, whereas I had been conditioned to expect the reverse. Now, friends from Moscow called to see us when they were in London or Scotland: students, artists and lecturers on cultural exchanges, and we always found interests we could share.

Then, because we had agreed to learn about each other's lives, I had tried to give Valentina the personal view of a woman living in the West, a view I saw as true. For example, I described the sad sides to democratic life: the homeless sleeping on city pavements; the rejected grandparents ending lonely lives in overcrowded mental hospitals; the sectarian fundamentalism which caused the weekly deaths of innocent citizens in Ireland; young people on suicidal exploits in stolen cars; increasing crimes of rape and violence; the collapse of family life. Democratic living was not always admirable. And, in contrast, I described free Social Security in Britain, and how many in the West, from all ages and conditions, gave up comfortable homes to work voluntarily for the disinherited. I wrote as friend to friend as I tried to tell her about the so-called free world – good and bad.

But dialogue obviously depends on an exchange of diverse opinions; without these it becomes a monologue. It worried me that my account of the shared experiences with Valentina was becoming unbalanced, with my views being heard too often and Valentina's too rarely. My reassurance remained that in the conversations which would shortly take place between us to record her life story, she would be giving me her views from the East, openly and at length. Meanwhile we had crossed the frontier of fear which existed at our first meeting and we both believed that our honest exchange had brought warmth to a corner of the cold war.

Now the cold war had ended, even if permanent peace had not yet been secured.

In March 1990 Lord Home had initiated a debate in the House of Lords on 'Eastern Europe and the Soviet Union'. It was a timely review and he had concluded: 'What kind of Russia shall we have to deal with? That is of course for the Russians to decide. However, the danger of fragmentation of the Soviet Union is one to which we might have to face up. I have been hoping that Mr Gorbachev would move towards a Confederal system or a Commonwealth structure. That will be vital because when we come to the negotiations which are so serious for the future of Europe and the world it will be important that we find a country expressing its wishes with one voice.' The Soviet Union had spoken with one voice during the Gulf War, but now the Soviet Union no longer existed. In 1991 there were many fragmented voices. In fact the United Nations was facing fragmentation instead of integration all over the world.

When I began my journey East in 1984 it had been the mission of the West to cause the end of Communism in Russia and the end of the Soviet Union as an equal superpower, proclaiming that if this was achieved there would be a new epoch of peace. In the event, after the Soviet dissolution world peace was exploding, with the fireworks of more and more national hostilities lighting flames in a darkening sky.

Meanwhile the question remained. When would I see Valentina to start work on her life story? I was relieved when in the autumn of 1991, Elizabeth Zolina sent a message: 'When are you coming?' I decided not to delay and so in mid-November Peter and I were in Moscow again.

At long last it seemed hopeful that I could conclude the interviews. We discussed the options again, and Valentina repeated that, at fifty-four, she was not ready for a formal biography. She wanted to give an account of her life to me, separating it into its most important stages. She would speak openly, breaking her long silence by describing the pioneer space flight and then the other major events she had experienced. We agreed that I could begin with the chronicle I had recorded of the dramatic changes we had been involved in since our first meeting, and then Valentina's voice would be heard in twelve 'Conversations'.

I had my bag of tapes and my tape recorder with me. I found Valentina's office changed by the uncertain future. There was little money for projects available from Yeltsin's beleaguered administration. The Academy of Social Sciences had been closed. The toppled statues of former Communist leaders had been laid carefully side by side in a Moscow park.

I hoped that the cultural exchanges achieved by the Soviet Friendship Societies in so many countries all over the world, including Scotland, would not now run down. Could a chapter of international friendship be closing or would a similar organization continue the work for Russia and the world? Would there be a new and different role for Valentina? So many uncertainties.

During the time of the coup and Gorbachev's replacement by Yeltsin, Valentina had been in Moscow. As always she was reluctant to make political comments but she was obviously overwhelmingly relieved that there had been little bloodshed. She hoped that the new reform programme would succeed. 'All progress which helps people and brings stability deserves support.' We were taken to see the graves of the three heroes of the resistance to totalitarianism at the time of the coup. All young. One Christian. One Muslim. One Jew. It was a symbolic tragedy and everyone in Valentina's office shared in it.

Valentina had just returned from an international conference held by the Association of Space Explorers in Berlin, where she had contributed to discussions on the protection of the planet, the monitoring of pollution, the provision of new sources of energy and the proposed mission to Mars in 1994.

The motto of the Association of Space Explorers explained the vision of its members: 'Space has no frontiers.' An observer at the Seventh Planetary Congress held on October 4th 1991, which Valentina had attended, wrote down its objectives for me:

The Association of Space Explorers (ASE) is a non-profit-making international organisation of professonals who have flown in space. Established in 1985 ASE unites the efforts of

its members to enhance education, strengthen the environmental stewardship, encourage international co-operation
and promote space exploration.

The same observer reported that from eighteen countries the
Congress had concluded with a general statement agreed by the
space explorers. It appealed for action to protect the Earth: 'a
fragile and endangered planet.' Future projects being investigated included human journeys to other planets in the solar
system.

The combination of Valentina's international work with her
scientific expertise obviously made her participation valuable.
Added to this, in the new Russia she was continuing her work
for international understanding. It made me see her life story as
more important than ever. Not only would it tell the truth for
the first time about her flight and the first women's involvement in space research but also explain why and how she had
become a bridge-builder for peace. It was an added incentive
for me to record her views.

In Moscow we stayed in the Friendship House dacha – a
yellow-brick six-bedroomed villa built by a Mongolian
president half-an-hour's taxi drive from Moscow. The housekeepers were a mother and daughter team, with everything
spotlessly clean and plentiful plain food. The mother mended
my rosary.

The first meeting to review our conversation about the space
flight took place in Valentina's office. But there was never a
quiet moment; friends arrived, including Alyona. My tape
machine was turned off and then on again. It seemed impossible
to start the next question. Valentina kept tidying her store
cupboard. She wanted us to eat and drink to 'stay strong' and
she was busy organizing a day's drive to her native city of
Yaroslavl for me to see the house she was born in, and her
grandmother's wooden log house, which she is restoring. I gave
up hope of a serious interview. Valentina said 'We can talk in
the car.'

Fortunately her colleague Tatyana Kuznetsova was working in the office, and she gave me an interesting account of the difficulties faced by the first Soviet women in the space programme.

Valentina left us to it. She had to attend a reception by the Women's Committee and then meet an industrial delegation. As I was obviously in despair, she promised to come for another interview on the space programme the next morning at the dacha. 'We will sit by the fire, talk and record, without interruptions.'

I had my doubts about there being no interruptions. The Russians had waited for free speech for so long but now that they had achieved it there was a great deal of speaking. Elizabeth drove us back to the dacha in the dark for another welcome (and, by Valentina's standards, 'healthy') meal by the log fire.

The next morning I made an early start to be ready. But Elizabeth Zolina arrived by car with her husband Paul. Paul's family belonged to the old Orthodox Church which was expelled to Siberia by Peter the Great. They do not drink or smoke. It was Peter the Great's church reforms which made the Russian Orthodox a State Church – 'diamond-encrusted' – as reviled by Tolstoy. Paul worked in an office but was willing to help us as a driver in his spare time.

Elizabeth had come to say that the interview had to be postponed. Valentina had arranged a meeting with Metropolitan Juvenaly, whom I had previously met during the Millennium with Duncan Shaw and who had given me the message for Mrs Thatcher.

My reaction was one of irritation at the change of plan, but I was wrong to be irritated. The hoped-for space interview was replaced by one of the most moving experiences of my life, which brought another insight into the shared chemistry with Valentina: the mystery of spiritual hopes and fears.

We arrived at the Novodevichy Convent at 11.30. We were an assorted group – Valentina, Lisa, my husband Peter and Colonel Vladimir Zakharov his interpreter, Tatyana Kuznetsova and me.

The Metropolitan was at the great door to welcome us. I remembered this door: on our family visit in June 1990 it was firmly locked for the summer and was only opened by the stern young soldier on guard in order to commiserate with us, when we told him that Scotland had been knocked out of the World Cup Finals!

The Metropolitan looked older, his former black beard was now grey. We sat in the same room where Duncan Shaw and I had first met him and, as he did then, he took us to his newly-restored private chapel, with the restoration almost too vivid for me, like the strong colours of Italian religious paintings.

He knelt before the Sacrament and I also knelt and prayed. Then he took us to his study where on a desk I noticed a particularly beautiful, small and very old icon – pale green and orange and brown. So kind the face of the Mother of God, so loving her divine baby Son. I noticed that Juvenaly watched me as I looked at the icon.

Tea was ready and Valentina, the Metropolitan and I, with Elizabeth interpreting, sat at one table. Peter and the rest of our group sat at another. Just beforehand Juvenaly had shown us the icon of an aunt of the last Tsar. He hoped she would be beatified and then be confirmed as a saint. I asked, 'Was she a lover of poverty like St Seraphim?' His face lit up and he told us of the reburial that year of St Seraphim in Kiev. He found a medal of the holy monk, who lived almost naked, gave everything he loved away, and believed in prayer, suffering and fasting to save Russia. He pinned it on my coat, then blessed me, and said, 'St Seraphim will take care of you.'

Then the Metropolitan and Valentina talked about their youth in Yaroslavl. They had been at school together. I told him how kind and understanding Valentina had been to me ever since I first met her in London, and how, when I had told her of my hope in eternal life and that I trusted God to save the world from atomic fire, she had replied, 'I am not a believer but

I hope you are right.' I also said that even then, in London in 1984, Elizabeth had been the interpreter.

Valentina described how years ago when her mother was ill, she and her sister had gone to church on impulse to pray. She added, 'My grandmother was a believer and I was baptized.' Juvenaly said, 'I believe Valentina will see her mother again.' The whole room was silent.

To change the subject I told him how I took his gifts and the personal message to Margaret Thatcher and how she seemed happy to receive them. He said he hoped to meet Mrs Thatcher soon. I gave him a little booklet with a speech by Professor Tom Torrance, winner of the Templeton Prize for Theology, in which he had explained that there should be one Creed for all Christianity. The Metropolitan looked thoughtful. Suddenly he got up, went into his study and came back with a carrier bag which he gave me. Inside was the icon I had seen on his desk – so ancient, so beautiful, so holy. 'I want you to have it,' he said. 'When I was a boy I visited a priest who knew I liked one small object in his study. He loved it too but he wanted me to have it. I have never forgotten him.'

I will never forget Metropolitan Juvenaly and the icon now has pride of place on the altar of our small sixteenth-century chapel in Scotland. As we left he stood at the door, waving.

The next day we drove to Yaroslavl. It had been Valentina's unswerving resolve that we must go. 'It will explain to you what I love most.'

Her friend, a distinguished surgeon, drove one car with Valentina, Elizabeth and me in it. She put Peter in another car with Tatyana. She said, 'I expect they will fall in love.'

The landscape was like Scotland and Valentina said, 'I drink my native land like pure water to refresh me. It is this land which inspired me to attempt difficulties and overcome.'

The roads were rough: 'Not improved since Napoleon's time,' according to Elizabeth, 'and they defeated Napoleon.' The car jolted so much I could not even scribble my notes. Elizabeth had forgotten her tape machine. It was a pity because

174

the comments Valentina was making should have been written down. For example, her assessment of the supra-national threats to the planet from pollution semed prophetic. We drove past flat green fields, bare after haymaking, lined with plantations of elder and birch. I was fascinated by the ingenuity with which Russians paint their wooden houses, all different designs and colours, not unlike Romany caravans.

On our way to Yaroslavl, Valentina's celestial city, she explained that it was founded in the eleventh century as a Christian fortress by Yaroslav, Prince of Kiev, at the juncture where the river Kotorosl flows into the Volga, the longest river in Europe, on its way to the sea. In the fifteenth century it had briefly been Russia's capital after Moscow. The city's architectural reconstruction had been on Catherine the Great's initiative, and the cathedral was built by Ivan the Terrible.

In the car we had carried on talking and I continued to be fascinated by the acuteness of Valentina's views on human affairs combined with sturdy common sense. I said to Elizabeth that this awareness and realism was like that of some ancient of the forests we were passing. Then, carved into the roadside, we saw the symbol of Yaroslavl – the bear.

Valentina quoted a poem by Nikolai Nekrasov:

O Volga! O my cradle
No one could love you more than I do
At sunrise when nature is sleeping
I come back to the banks of my mother river
To admire the scarlet of the sun on the dark blue
    of the waves.

Her need for poetry, art, literature and classical music was another side to Valentina's character. Now I asked myself, was she part-prophet, part-poet, as well as technical engineer? Valentina was really happy in her home territory. We stopped in the village of Nikulskoye to see an exact copy of the actual house Valentina was born in, now a sort of shrine. It is very small – three windows, a door, only one room with a store and a loft. Her mother's kingdom. It stands beside a modest white-washed building, the Tereshkova Space Museum, full of documents, drawings and replicas connected with the flight. There were no tourists but an old woman looking after her cows was happy to see Valentina.

In Yaroslavl, the sun was shining, the skies were blue, the river Volga gleamed. We saw a bridge from which she had practised for her first parachute jump. For Valentina this was home, and she was proud to show it to us. At the same time she followed her brief of matters to attend to – one being an exchange between German and Russian orphanages.

In Valentina's honour we were all then welcomed to an official lunch by the Mayor – robust and keen to extend business abroad. It was like being in Milan or in any European city based on trade. He proposed a toast to Valentina. After the Mayor's lunch Valentina took us to see 'my beautiful Volga river'. Then we drove back into the country again where another large lunch had been prepared for the daughter of Yaroslavl in the local collective farm. Everyone was proud of her. The woman director and all her family made up the party, including the sturdy eight-year-old daughter, Olga, who showed me the gold chain given on her birthday with a crucifix hanging from it. I told Valentina that the future depended on Olga and how much she could learn about the new open-market administration. That meant a decade before the ways of the West would work normally. 'I am too old to go to school again,' a middle-aged woman told me sadly.

Communal farming had always been an essential practice for successful results throughout Russian history, but current collectivism appeared dangerously disorganized. The farm director described how it had been a marvellous harvest but transport had not been well provided. Valentina was proud of the food which was obviously plentiful on the farm. 'That is the healthiest soup you will ever eat; look, all fresh vegetables.'

Then we drove on to her grandmother's house; a fine old log house, two rooms, windows painted in traditional colours, the eaves carved with fretwork on the wooden boards. It was larger than her mother's house. Very isolated by a pond, miles from the main road and only reached by an intrepid Land Rover, driven with some difficulty. Valentina told us enthusiastically, 'It was all alive when I was young – music – games – the family together and sheep and cows and goats and ponies for me to ride. Now it is dead I must restore it and give this wonderful place life again.'

It all reminded Valentina of her father and later she read me a poem, 'Cranes', by Rasul Gamzatov.

> I believe that my fellow soldiers
> Killed at the war
> Have become white cranes
> Looking at us from the heights of clouds and
> Calling us with their own songs.
> That is why we want to watch the sky and the clouds.
> One day I'll join the flock of cranes
> And then I'll call all of you I left on earth.

The Land Rover took us back to the car, and the Surgeon-General said he would find a better road back to Moscow. I took out my notebook and started asking Valentina questions about her childhood. I really thought I could write at last; the road was smoother, the light had not yet gone. Suddenly Valentina saw two cassettes of Pavarotti's songs which she always kept in the car. 'You will love this,' she said triumphantly and for the next half-hour, before the darkness made any attempt to begin writing impossible, the car was filled with soaring music and we were all singing: 'Non ti scordar di me'. I should have felt frustrated. I had come all the way from London for interviews – but unreasonably, overwhelmingly, I really loved her. Ground Control had called her 'Seagull' in space, and she had sung to them. Perhaps her biography could be called *Song from Space*.

The day before we left, in the dacha, we achieved two satisfactory interviews on tape about the space flight. I could hardly believe I was actually sitting there listening to and transcribing the details of how this one woman, the only woman to do it alone, had withstood a test of such fearsome magnitude. Valentina was calm, matter-of-fact, as though she was describing a journey by road. Elizabeth said she had never heard her give an account of her flight before. When my husband heard the recording he was staggered by such supreme courage in the face of the unknown, 'when anything might have gone wrong.'

When we left Moscow Valentina said, 'It was only a try-out; now we know that at our next meeting we can finish our work.' But when would the next meeting be? 'Come in January,' she suggested. Not easy for me. I hoped for February. Valentina was preparing to travel to New York to speak at a United Nations conference of non-governmental organizations. She wanted to tell me about the assessment made by the UN Secretary General, Javier Perez de Cuellar, on four major world areas for action and hope. She read these to me from a published speech.

First. There are growing signs that international relations may be entering a new and more positive era. As rarely before, nations are now recognizing that they must address international problems multilaterally, through consultation and compromise. And, increasingly, they are turning to the United Nations.

Second. The dangers of the new generation of global problems, such as the degradation of the environment and drug abuse, have compelled all nations to realize that solutions can only be found through collective action.

Third. There is, however, no reason for complacency. Conflicts still persist in many parts of the globe. The build-up of arms has not ceased. Far too many people still live in absolute poverty without adequate food or shelter and face discrimination on grounds of race, religion, sex or political belief. We are a long way from achieving universal respect for human rights.

Fourth. We have the immense responsibility and also the possibility of ensuring that future generations live in a peaceful and secure planet. I see signs of a new commitment on the part of the people of the world to act together towards this goal. The United Nations can and will make a vital contribution to this common endeavour.

Valentina said that she shared Perez de Cuellar's hopes and took the warnings seriously. She remained second to none in hoping that the United Nations could act to provide positive solutions. She had attended several meetings of the United Nations: in October 1963, as guest of the UN General Assembly; in 1975 and 1977 to discuss some of the activities of the Soviet Women's Committee. She had been Deputy Chair of the International Democratic Federation of Women, within the framework of the UN Women's Year and the UN Decade on Women (1975 – 1985). Now, at the end of 1991, she would be addressing the annual conference of non-governmental organizations, held by the UN Department of Public Information on 'A New World Order'.

I was relieved that a beginning on the *Conversations* had been made. Valentina wanted us to meet again in Moscow for more interviews as soon as possible, and she hoped to be in Scotland in April for the International Science Festival. But how could anyone know what might happen, month by month? The news we heard on our return to London was grim. Yugoslavia riven by hatred was not an optimistic omen for the newly-fractured USSR. I dared to believe that Russian people were different. As one of the most attractive civilizations the world has ever known they have always been acutely aware of the inevitability of death, which strips away false ambitions and promises. Russia today is bombarded by both.

Before Christmas Elizabeth rang me in London to ask if we could travel to Moscow in February. Valentina hoped that

Peter would come with me again. She is really fond of him and it is reciprocated; Peter loves music and so does Valentina.

So in February 1992 I was in Moscow once more. Valentina had met us at the airport and insisted on carrying the heavy luggage. This time there was no official car; we were driven in a taxi to the dacha we had stayed in two months before. Again we found a delicious supper prepared. 'It is ecological food,' Valentina announced proudly, 'brought from my village.' There was honey, potatoes, home-made bread, cottage cheese, chicken broth, apple fruit drink and salads of every kind. We shared this with the new caretakers, an elderly married couple who joined us regularly to watch the television news. I was pleased to be back in the dacha with a study to work in.

Outside we could see snow-covered fir trees in a small surrounding garden. 'It is a beautiful season,' Valentina said, 'very sweet to the eyes.'

She was wearing the familiar blue and white check suit, which I had seen her in so often that I wondered if she had it copied regularly. What was it that always made her so attractive? Was it the strong bone structure of a face without make-up, or was it most of all the humour and acute awareness of the blue, blue eyes?

Despite my protestations about having plenty of warm woollen underwear, she was worried that my clothes were too thin for the freezing Moscow winter. The next morning she arrived with her own sheepskin coat and boots which she insisted on lending me. She studied my tape recorder with a technical eye and laughed at my apprehension about using it properly. We sat near the friendly log fire. Hanging on the wall beside us I could see an interplanetary guide to the solar system, a space dance of planets circling round the sun. Within the dance, distinct from the other planets because of its pattern of colours, was planet Earth.

It was typical of Valentina that although she was constantly involved in negotiations to solve severe financial cutbacks for her organization, she used all her spare time to think of every detail to make her guests content. Life with Valentina was always full of home comforts, lovingly provided.

Suddenly my mind registered a minor shock. I was sitting comfortably talking to a friend I sincerely respected, but she had also been a major protagonist in the space race between East and West which had been taken to dramatic degrees of brinkmanship, suspicion and fear. The mastermind of the Soviet space programme, Sergei Korolev, known as the 'Chief Designer', had been thought by the Americans to be an evil genius. He must not get there first – 'there' being a global platform from which to drop atomic bombs on America.

Valentina, sitting beside me, had been his friend and colleague and she had been in the forefront of Soviet space progress. Admittedly, the American fear of being destroyed by the Soviets had diminished almost immediately after her flight. Then the Nuclear Test Ban Treaty had been signed and Khrushchev initiated a further ban on weapons in space, a safeguard for humanity to which, it could be said, Valentina's achievement had contributed because it emphasized space parity and thus reduced superpower rivalry. I told her that at one time it had been feared that, like a dark angel, she might drop bombs on New York. 'What a horrible accusation!' she had replied. She had never seen herself as a possible exterminator. I quickly added that from our first meeting I had not only been inspired personally by her work for peace, I had also come to believe that because she was universally known and admired she could inspire human unity in the new epoch which demanded co-operation to ensure survival. She was reassured.

Certainly, as we were speaking, developments in East-West relations were encouraging. The American-Russian alliance on disarmament, a dramatic reversal of previous antagonism, was actually happening as Valentina was telling me her life story. She had been a hero of the Soviet Union; now she could equally be acclaimed as a hero in the USA for being the first woman in space. It was an exciting time to be working on

Conversations with a Cosmonaut, to be published in June 1993 to commemorate the thirtieth anniversary of her flight.

We started by reviewing the interviews we had made in November and Valentina made amendments. Then I switched on my tape recorder. Valentina was ready to answer my questions, 'To tell the truth,' as she had so often said she wanted to do.

I asked the questions, Elizabeth translated and Valentina answered directly; thoughtfully, with inherent self-discipline, but always with spontaneous and very Russian reactions; constant humour, poetry readings and historical information. I had warned Valentina that to cover the full spectrum of her life I might be raising issues she might find sensitive. It was typical of her that she accepted this.

After the twelve conversations had been transcribed one more working session was needed so that Valentina could approve the text for the publisher. When and where would this be possible? Could it be in April when Valentina was to be guest of honour at the International Science Festival to be held in Edinburgh? I hoped for this, otherwise I would go to Moscow again.

As we left to fly back to London Elizabeth said: 'At long last, even if no one else is allowed to hear it, you will know her life story. Valentina has broken her silence because she trusts you.'

The Edinburgh International Science Festival held in April 1992, during the United Nations Year of Space, was heralded by a fanfare of publicity. The promoters proclaimed: 'Teachers, students, postgraduates and scientists rub shoulders with the general public and businessmen, sharing the events which cover the whole spectrum of scientific disciplines from astrophysics to zoology.'

The chief executive, Brian Gamble, had written to me to give advance information for my press work. There was to be a meeting of international scientists, a debate on science and religion, a seminar on pollution and then, as the high point, a discussion on space research, the speakers being Dr Heather

Couper, first woman President of the British Astronomical Association; Helen Sharman, the only British cosmonaut; and Valentina Tereshkova, the first woman in space.

Valentina had not been sure if uncertainties about her work in Russia would allow her to come to Britain. But her home problems were resolved. President Yeltsin had appointed her to chair a newly-formed umbrella organization for voluntary work in Russia, and she could now attend the Festival.

She arrived in London accompanied by Elizabeth and was present at receptions arranged by the Science Festival. She also gave a lecture on cosmonautics at the Science Museum.

The many who admired her in Britain, including members of the Moscow Fellowship and the Women of the Year Association, agreed with me that the occasion of her important new appointment in Moscow should be recognized. Barbara Hosking and I planned a lunch at the Reform Club, of which we were both members. The guests represented the many areas of influence with which Valentina was connected. Fitzroy Maclean agreed to speak and propose a toast of good wishes for Valentina's future work for international understanding. The guest list was drawn up with Vladimir Molchanov, and it included members of the newly-established Russian Embassy as well as scientists, trade unionists, educationalists and journalists; for example, Kate Adie. The lunch took place on the day before the General Election, not a good time for politicians but we had not asked any. Valentina replied to Fitzroy with her usual modesty and sincerity and said how happy she was to be meeting so many old and new friends again.

That night she attended a performance of Russian opera at Covent Garden, where she met and talked to the Princess of Wales. The next day she travelled on to Edinburgh for the Science Festival.

When we were in Moscow Valentina had said that she hoped to try to come and stay at our home in Scotland after the Science Festival, so as to authorize the text I had prepared from the Moscow interviews. She had been giving more thought to the conversation on the need for global morality. It was becoming a project of great importance to her and she hoped to organize a global morality conference in Moscow for the fiftieth anniversary of the founding of the United Nations. She wanted to finalize her thoughts. If she did come to stay at Ferniehirst it would be on the strict understanding that we would work with no distractions, because time was not on our side. Valentina was urgently expected back in Moscow as she might be going to India, Australia, and New York on behalf of her new organization.

The Science Festival lecture on April 11th was a once-only occasion. The three women who took part in the discussion, Helen Sharman, Dr Heather Couper and Valentina, were all leading scientists and pioneers. The standard of speeches reflected this. Helen's contribution was accompanied by brilliant American-style videos and slides to illustrate her successful flight with the first Anglo-Soviet space mission, for which she was continuing to work. The film brought home the difficult aspects of being a pioneer in space, such as painful medical tests. Valentina had always discounted these as routine, and when she spoke it was mainly about the planned Mars space programme she was involved in. The illustrations she chose were precise black-and-white diagrams and drawings. A scientist sitting next to me commented, 'It is that sort of lack of hype which always gets the Russians there first.'

It was very memorable to be taken into the vast dimension of space by three women who were exceptional astronautical experts and, although there were a few children in the audience, as Jane Buccleuch said afterwards, 'There should have been thousands.' The children had asked the most pertinent questions.

The next day was the Sunday before Easter. We all attended a Science Service in St Giles' Kirk in Edinburgh. The address was given by Dr Heinz Wolff. The minister, the Very Rev Gilleasbuig Macmillan, had proposed that Valentina should read the Easter Lesson from the New Testament. But Valentina took religious affirmations seriously and she did not feel she could speak the words of Jesus with conviction. I had hoped the minister would ask her to end the service reading poems by Pushkin, but he thought it would not be appropriate.

After the service we drove down to the Borders so that we could work in my office. In the car we discussed the chronicle I had written about our journey from misunderstanding to understanding, which I had left in Moscow for Valentina to read. Why had I kept the chronicle so carefully? Obviously to achieve genuine exchange, to end the ignorance which led to enmity among nations, we had agreed that it was necessary for us to know each other's thoughts and reactions to the momentous events which had taken place during the years of our friendship. That is why I had written an account as seen from the West of our experiences and of the exchanges of views on them which Valentina and I had shared. It had become, for me, a Western woman's portrait of an apocalyptic period. But I had wondered; what would Valentina think of my impressions? Would she find them irrelevant, or even controversial?

Certainly now in 1992 superpower enmity had ended, and our continuing co-operation reflected the new alliance of East and West. But we had been pioneers in 1983, remembering that Gorbachev's election as General Secretary had been in 1985, followed by his promotion of glasnost in 1987 and of perestroika in 1988. Our shared hopes for planetary protection from nuclear disaster had started earlier. We had crossed frontiers to work for peace with no loss of patriotic allegiance when the prevailing mood had been hostile and obstructive. Of course we could not presume to claim that we were the only ones to work for peace at that time. From East and West there had been many who felt and acted as we did. President Carter and Billy Graham had been two outstanding American examples of world leaders who looked for international understanding. The story I had tried to record of our journey was not exclusive. But my meeting with Valentina and Russia was very personal for me. Would she find the account of my Journey as genuine as I meant it to be?

185

As I had expected, having read my account, Valentina had been surprised by some of my observations and had not always agreed with my political conclusions. She felt that I had sometimes been ill-informed about what was happening in the East. She repeatedly emphasised that the true voice of glasnost was the voice of the Russian people. It was their contribution which would finally govern present, past and future, and it was their will and genius which achieved all that was good. She thought I gave too much importance to the part played in perestroika by individual leaders in both East and West. What pleased her most was that, having come to know the Russian people, I myself had travelled far from much earlier misinformation.

She had written her own thoughts on the journal she had read and she wished these to be included:

In the first part of the book Tony describes the journey we made from the West to the East and from the East to the West. Reading the manuscript I came to know much more about an unusual woman, my faithful friend Tony Lothian. When we met in 1984 we had only begun the process of understanding which we have not yet finished. While we are still alive we will increase our knowledge of each other and we will enjoy this process until we die.

'Of course I realise that Tony gives her own independent impressions and that there were possibly many in the West who thought differently.

'Turning over the pages of the manuscript I was often surprised, always interested. I asked myself, "Was this really Tony's reaction to this event? Did Tony think this?" I kept admiring her boldness. She set out on a difficult journey without any suspicion and her only luggage was goodwill and striving for understanding. Here was a woman who had lived a very interesting life which mirrored many crucial events of the twentieth century. Thanks to the chronicle she kept of the ten years we shared I understand better how strong and generous Tony is, how determined she is to get at the truth and defend justice. Tony will always be – for me

– the example of harmony in a woman's many-sided character. This year she received the Templeton Award for her contribution to promoting Christian unity. She has earned recognition for her journalistic activities. Each page of the manuscript brought me proof of her sensitivity. While expressing some opinions which I cannot share, and this is quite natural for two people born into and educated in two absolutely different cultures, she has always tried not to hurt me, not to impose her opinions or her convictions on me. Mutual respect for each other's opinions, traditions and way of life has always been the basis of our friendship.

Valentina's continuing trust gave me great encouragement.

That evening we started reading the transcript of her life story as she had told it to me in Moscow. Valentina's English had improved and I had taken a few lessons in Russian. Valentina worked as an academic, studied every word with her customary critical attitude. She also brought to the different stages of our readings typical Valentina side-effects. She sang sad Russian war songs when we were reading about her youth; she did exercises on the floor if she was getting stiff and she went to the window regularly to look at the new black lambs with their pensive Hebridean mother. One morning in a downpour, Valentina ran out to herd the sheep under the shelter of a tree 'as I did on my grandmother's farm'.

To my relief the twelve conversations as I had transcribed them were acceptable to Valentina. I felt the fact that it all read well was mainly due to her always telling the truth as she saw it, facts not fancy.

We worked in a small office adjacent to the house. Hanging on the wall we could see a picture of Philip Lothian, my husband's cousin. He died as Ambassador to Washington in the war, after a lifetime of political involvement, beginning as secretary to Lloyd George at the time of the Versailles Treaty, when he had supported the Bullitt Mission to make contact with Lenin. This had been cancelled by President Wilson. Towards the end of his life he had become convinced that world peace would only be possible if there was a central world government which could control federations of nations in the various continents. His portrait now presided over our discussions on many of the same problems fifty years later, all still far from being solved. He looked down as if in sympathy with Valentina's call for global morality at a time when planetary hazards had joined those of the divisive nationalism which had overshadowed the thirties he lived in.

Valentina wanted to construct her proposals for global morality carefully. She intended to obtain a consensus on the basic needs for human survival, agreed to by world-wide religious, educational and scientific leaders. She hoped their proposals could be discussed at a Moscow conference which she planned to arrange in 1995 as part of the United Nations fiftieth anniversary celebrations. The objective would be not to supersede the ideals which already helped humanity but to strengthen what she called 'the eternal principles of morality.' She believed in a new advance in human unity. She hoped that the urgent actions which had been agreed on as necessary to save the environment would be undertaken by the people of the world, not separately, but together; so as to answer the cosmonauts' challenge – 'peace or perish'. Above all she hoped that educationalists would teach children which actions would either protect or destroy the planet. Her fundamental proposal was that all should ask themselves: 'What hurts – what helps the planet?' and then guidance could be found in the basic priorities set out in a Global Morality Charter. But she continued to be concerned to act only on logic and practical possibilities.

It was a concept I found particularly helpful as later in the year I was to be awarded the UK Templeton Prize in recognition of 'inter-faith endeavour' for human unity. A part of the sum was to be kept for my own use, but I could give the rest to a deserving charity. I was always sceptical as to which fundraisers put the money raised to positive use, and I wanted to ensure direct assistance. So I asked our daughter, one of the organizers of Save the Children, for her advice. She recommended the positive aid being given to protect street children from being murdered in Brazil. I duly made the donation. But afterwards I wondered – why did a Christian country with so many millionaires, who probably attended church regularly, allow its poor children to be killed? Why did I have to protect the poor at the heart of capitalism? Were conditions better in Communist Cuba? Probably there was little difference. How could I know for certain? Global morality seemed to be essential so that all nations could first agree and then act on measures to provide equal justice.

I had come full circle at the end of my journey which had included capitalism and Communism, and I was still asking the same unanswered question: which political philosophy was most likely to bring relief to destitution? For centuries man's inhumanity to man, usually based on self-interest, had been stronger than any philosophy seeking social reform. In the new century could humanity build compassionate structures within which assistance for the poor and helpless would be globally provided?

I wished that my own view from the West at the end of 1992 could be more optimistic. During the years of our journey from West to East many of the dangers which had threatened human survival had been overcome, above all the superpower antagonism with its threat of atomic annihilation. The new glasnost openness now provided evidence which confirmed that in the seventies and eighties, fuelled by mutual fear, brinkmanship to achieve what was called 'nuclear capability' had led Israel, China and South Africa to arm themselves with atomic deterrents. At the same time NATO had its Cruise missiles, and the Warsaw Pact devised strategies which included nuclear weapons. Devastation could have happened, but when both West and East shared perestroika it had been prevented. In the ten years which changed the world the journey had brought us from darkness to light. So why the growing fear that in the new century the next destination could be back to darkness again?

In 1992, events reflected both darkness and light with death as the equalizer. Marlene Dietrich, Alexander Dubcek and Israel's peace award winner Menachem Begin died, also Petra Kelly, founder of the Green movement in Germany and Sunnie

Mann, heroine of the Beirut hostages, and with the death of Willy Brandt, the world had lost an outstanding champion for justice and peace. Space continued to provide surprises. The Second Australian Space Conference was told that a comet might hit the Earth in August 2116. It had been named Swift-Tuttle and it was estimated as being between three and six miles wide with an impact force 1.6 million times greater than the bomb dropped on Hiroshima.

In Asia the boat people preferred death to being denied the home they felt was their due. Human suffering had increased in the Third World and the agonies of wide-eyed skeletal children continued. Religious differences persisted. Islamic fundamentalism was heightening worldwide with its adherents believing that they could offer mankind an alternative social, political and moral philosophy which would provide solutions where capitalism and socialism had failed. Political differences were mirrored by the Danish vote against the Maastricht Treaty to unify Europe. Ethnic enmities were assuming monstrous proportions in many nations. The most encouraging examples of human unity in 1992 had been provided by the end of apartheid in South Africa and by the world's Olympic athletes excelling together in Barcelona.

I could not help thinking that the arms dealers must be feeling happier about their future prospects and that it was like an Aesop's fable that people on earth were still quarrelling with atomic weapons, forgetting the cosmic danger they were in.

For those of us who believed in Valentina's wise proposals, there was one encouraging aspect. The punitive result of the continuing struggle between the builders and the breakers of human unity might yet oblige potential victims to listen to Valentina's appeal for a global morality which would unite the human family and preserve all its members, both rich and poor, from destruction by some environmental catastrophe. Her call for global common sense was not an impracticable ideal. It was urgent and rational.

The day before Valentina flew back to Moscow we allowed ourselves a short break from work. Lord Home came to tea. It was a unique occasion, with one of the world's most respected statesmen, whose career had mainly been spent guarding the West against Soviet Communism, communicating his hopes for peace based on democracy to the Soviet cosmonaut who hoped to find solutions for the new dangers which threatened the planet and its inhabitants. As he got into his car he drew down the window. 'Remember,' he said to Valentina, 'democracy depends on multiple political parties.'

After he left she referred repeatedly to his advice, not least because he had counselled caution about instant solutions. This was always her view. Again and again she curbed my tendency to call for immediate action. 'It needs to be thought out carefully and based on facts,' was her consistent reaction to new ideas. This was also evident in her international cultural work which she believed should enrich but not diminish individual identity and patriotism. Love of homeland would always remain a priority for Valentina.

Now I had heard her view from the East, when for so long she had listened to mine from the West. I had no illusions about which was the most important, and I was happy that through the *Conversations with a Cosmonaut* Valentina's views at long last could be widely known.

As I watched her drive away from Ferniehirst, the car disappearing round the bend of the long lane with its tall Scots pines on either side, I wondered if this was the last time I would ask, 'When will we meet again?'

Our shared experiences had now fallen back into history and the future belonged to Valentina's interplanetary expectations and her vision of a new human epoch in space. I hoped that destiny would lead us on so that we could continue to encourage each other to defend the women who should not see their children die unnecessarily, and who rightly wanted a better, safer life for them in the new century.

Valentina had said of our friendship that a shared understanding of the need for international co-operation to protect the planet and prevent nuclear war had united us to the extent that we had become two halves of one whole. Certainly we had shown that, even when it is difficult for nation to speak to nation through political leaders, individuals can meet, exchange independent opinions and still prove that there is more to unite than to divide humanity. Our journey could be repeated by all those who seek to end dangerous ignorance.

Although we valued the mutual understanding which had developed between us, neither Valentina nor I would claim to have made an earth-shattering discovery because of it. We had merely confirmed the simple, reassuring truth that, to assure security for themselves and their families, it is not necessary for human beings to remain within tribal confines without ever looking over the fence. It is possible to remain faithful to one's own homeland without believing that this obliges us to refuse to see, hear or speak to those on the other side of the divide. The reverse, in fact, is true. The more we find out about the lives of those in other communities, the less likely it is that there will be conflicts resulting in the unnecessary suffering of war.

As friends Valentina and I had crossed the barriers between West and East, capitalism and Communism, democracy and dictatorship; and we had proved that genuine co-operation is possible even in supposedly impossible circumstances. We had tried and we had succeeded in building a bridge between like minds, with the added good that what had been described as a 'destined friendship' now inspired the first woman in space to speak for the first time on what mattered most to her and to the world.

THIS ENDS THE JOURNAL OF A WEST TO EAST JOURNEY

PART II

Conversations with a Cosmonaut

Contents

Prologue

We were sitting by a log fire in the dacha near Moscow belonging to Valentina Tereshkova's inter-cultural organization. The thirtieth anniversary of the first flight by a woman in space was only a few months ahead. Valentina and I had hoped that it would be at a time which confirmed a new epoch of peace and prosperity for humanity, but now preparation for the next century was not so optimistic; there were wars and rumours of wars. This made Valentina's answers to my questions, giving her advice on how to prevent ecological and planetary catastrophes, particularly important. Thirty years ago the world had been united in respect for Valentina. It was possible that again she could unite humanity to avoid global dangers, because now, for the first time, she was ready to break her self-imposed silence, not only giving a first–ever personal account of her life and her pioneer flight, but also to speak about her fears for the present and her hopes for the future, including plans for man to land on Mars.

Hanging on the wall beside us we could see a guide to the solar system, a cosmic dance of planets circling round the sun. Within the dance was planet Earth, small, fragile and unique, a multi-coloured jewel with its continents and seas, a reminder for us both of the other world of space, a vast new ocean of opportunity which was familiar to cosmonauts and to Valentina.

I read out a summary of the questions I would be asking. Valentina nodded assent. I switched on the tape recorder.

The First Conversation

Valentina Speaks

on

Childhood in the Soviet Union

A.L. *We have worked together in the years of East-West conflict. Now West and East are allies for peace, and proving it by dramatic defence cuts.*

I know that you have hidden the contribution you yourself have made to this astounding change of direction. You have always shunned publicity. That is why I feel privileged that you are prepared to answer my questions now, not only because you have confronted what has been described as the 'greatest unknown except death itself' but also because I know you have proposals which can help our human family to overcome the many dangers ahead of us.

V.T. You say that people are interested in my experiences and that my advice on the dangers increasingly faced by our planet could be useful. I am ready to speak the truth and to

197

answer with real sincerity. But I base this on the trust I have in you that you will only ask what is important for those who are truly interested in our questions and answers.

A.L.   *I have heard you speak on many subjects and I know how sincere and straightforward you are. Women are not always expected to be thinkers and philosophers, but you are both, as well as being a space pioneer. It is important to know about your life and hopes and fears.*

V.T.   The discipline of my profession is to consider evidence carefully and to study facts. This means not only being prepared to take the necessary action but also to weigh up the consequences. I will try to answer your questions according to this attitude. I feel the time is right now for me to tell the truth as I know it and above all about my beloved motherland, its people, and the country of the Volga where I was born.

A.L.   *For a start can you tell me about your childhood? Then can you tell me about your youth training, your work in the factory; all the influences which prepared you as a cosmonaut for the crucible day, your test in space?*

V.T.   Why do you call it a crucible? I do not see it like that. Cosmonauts in training did not think of death, danger or pain in the way you seem to think we did.

But you ask about the influences and memories of my childhood and I will try to remember this very special time for me. I want to describe how much goodness there was in the Yaroslavl region in the years after the war and how many important human ideals were upheld. There was joy in the spiritual arts like music and theatre, and pride in local history. We enjoyed sport, swimming and parachute jumping. I remember above all how upright and kind most people were. Political decisions and struggles took place very far from our lives. We did suffer enormously trying to rebuild our country after the devastation of war. Life was very hard and many political schemes seemed to fail. But we were proud to hear of how we had been allies of the West, fighting against Hitler in the Great Patriotic War.

I grew up some way from Moscow and I knew nothing about how people in power lived. I loved my own region, the Volga river, the countryside, the dogs, horses and other animals and my family, friends and neighbours. My schoolteachers influenced me, but above all my mother. She was my childhood. She protected us from suffering shortages during and after the war. She taught us songs and stories from all over the world. She gave us ideals and pride in being morally strong. That was nothing to do with ambition. Moral strength and the love of one's neighbour meant much more to her than money.

I was born in 1937 and Stalin died in 1953. I grew up when Khrushchev was in power. By the time of my flight in 1963 Khrushchev's term as First Secretary of the Communist Party was nearly finished. I worked as a cosmonaut under Brezhnev. Then understanding between East and West was growing and the cold war was ending.

From what you have said and because of our previous honest exchange of opinions I know you are one of those in the West who hope to remain open-minded about the developments in the Soviet Union since Stalin, and also since Khrushchev after he exposed Stalin's crimes. But even you do not seem to understand what we Russians endured in the war against Hitler.

My childhood was completely involved in what happened during the war. Hitler had reached the gates of Moscow and our parents and relatives would have done anything to save our beloved Mother Russia. Millions were killed. When we had defeated Hitler we faced terrible poverty and shortages of every material kind. This meant that we had to make sacrifices to make life better again. We trusted our political leaders to show us the right way. My family were country people in the Stalin and Khrushchev eras. Their moral strength helped them to rebuild their lives after the war.

That is why those of us who were lucky enough to be selected for space training, and at a time when it was new to include women, did not think of it as a crucible. We saw it as a marvellous chance to be pioneers in the most exciting adventure and development of our generation.

But first of all you have asked me to remember where and how I was born. As you will understand I can only recall what my mother has told me.

I am not quite sure about my mother, but my father wanted me badly. My mother was tired as she had lost twins before me, but my father was so proud of a new baby that he was determined to give me the name he wanted: 'Valentina'. It was not the name my mother had chosen and this was one of the few times in their short but happy married life when their opinions were divided. My mother told me how delivery started at four o'clock in the morning. There was no midwife to attend. My father was alone with my mother and he felt very lost. He said to my mother, 'Yelena, wait a little. I will go and bring my mother here.' He ran to the other end of the village, to my grandmother's house. But while he was away bringing back his mother to our small wooden house, I was born. When my grandmother Matryona arrived running she clasped her hands in dismay and said to my father, 'Good gracious, how could you possibly have left her absolutely alone to give birth to your child?' But my father was young. He was only 25 years old and my mother was 24.

That was in 1937, the most difficult year for the whole country. It was the time of Stalin's purges, which Russian people referred to as 'the repressions'. The best representatives of our intelligentsia, military men and professional people, were put in prison, without trial, and then they disappeared. We found this out much later during the 20th Congress of the Communist Party in 1956 when Khrushchev was in power. My father's cousin Ivan was arrested in the purges of 1937 and was imprisoned. He was a factory worker in Yaroslavl with a wife and three children. As children we heard nothing about why he was arrested but only that he was in prison. He was freed at the beginning of the war and was killed before it ended. His family still live in Yaroslavl.

A.L.   *Did the victims of the Soviet system see you as*
         an image of the system, when you later became
         a Party member?

V.T.   I do not think so. They saw me as a cosmonaut, working for cosmonautics. Ours was a typical Russian family and, as children, we heard our grandmothers speak Byelorussian and Ukrainian. We were proud not only of our Yaroslavl region, but also of the whole Soviet Union.

But, to return to my childhood, as a much-wished-for child by my father and by my grandmother, I was born at a very happy period in my parents' short married life. Of course, my mother loved me too, as every mother loves her child. But my father had a very special love for me.

He was a tractor operator by profession, an amateur accordion player and musically gifted. He was young and handsome and was loved, not only by my mother and grandmother, but by all our neighbours in the village. Russian people call this type of young man, one who is a popular and hard-working family man, 'the first guy of the village'. Even now people who knew my father, though few are still alive, say that he was very special, kind and generous.

No-one at the time of my birth could possibly have known that three years later my father would be killed on 25th January 1940 during the Soviet-Finnish War. He had been drafted on 15th September 1939, as a tankman. So I was only my father's darling for the first two years of my life although I have preserved throughout my life a very special love for my father.

The Finnish War was Stalin's whim. The dispute could have been settled by negotiation. Our soldiers were not prepared, not even properly clothed for the bitter winter. I resent very much what Stalin did to my father and other young Russian soldiers like him. I believe that Stalin took my father from me.

201

My most important childhood impression is still about my father. I often think of him even now and look at his photograph and remember the descriptions my mother and grandmother gave me of him. They spoke a lot about him and I took in all their remembrances. Perhaps I am being too romantic but it seemed to me that those two women loved him with an extra-special love and I had to explain this for myself. He was blue-eyed and fair-haired. I mentally understand his existence even if I cannot picture him. I don't remember him physically but when I close my eyes I remember him as a long, warm shadow. My mother's and my grandmother's memories were very eloquent for me. For example, he was fond of bicycles and my mother remembered me sitting on his shoulders as he rode a bicycle. My mother's memories made a great impression on me. She said I had a favourite red dress and when she looked for my father bicycling back from the fields she saw the red dress on his shoulders. He played the accordion really well and I still imagine him playing and singing with my mother and grandmother. They told me I always sat close to him and hugged him when he was playing, hugged him more than anyone else. Why did he love me specially? I don't know. Perhaps because my eldest sister Ludmila, the first child in the family, was brought up by my mother's parents and she was often with them in their house. I stayed with my father and mother. It was simple. My maternal grandparents loved Ludmila, while I was the special love of my father and mother and my paternal grandmother. She taught me to ride horses and I took my love of horses from her. She was tall with a fine stature and lovely grey hair which was always neat and beautifully kept. After marriage, Russian women in villages wear shawls, and my grandmother wore beautifully coloured shawls covered with small flowers. She loved all colours.

My brother Volodya was born five months after my father had been reported as missing. He was born at a very unhappy time for my mother, when she would not admit that my father was dead. Volodya is short for Vladimir, like my father. My mother lived through a tragedy and for many years she would

202

not accept the catastrophe. She nearly died of sorrow after being told the news about my father.

A.L.   Did someone knock at the door?

V.T.   The War Ministry sent my mother a letter of notification saying that our father had been killed. I know the text by heart. 'Your husband, Vladimir Tereshkov, has given his life as a Hero in defence of the Socialist Motherland and has been buried with full military honours.' It did not state exactly where he was buried. This led my mother to believe that he was not dead. Millions of women received the same letters, '*pokhoroniki*' in Russian. Years later, General Yazov helped me to trace the documents in the military archives which proved where my father was buried. But at the time we were given very little information on the Soviet-Finnish War. It was kept a secret.

My mother devoted all her time to bringing up her children. We just saw her crying. At the time of the notification we lived in the village and our life was easier. We had food. We were warm. We had sheep, a cow, butter and milk. Later, in the city it was different although even in the city our grandmother Matryona sent us food from the country.

A.L.   What was your city grandmother like?

V.T.   My mother's mother, *babushka* Sophia, was a very special beauty – small with lovely dark eyes and olive-coloured skin. My mother was just like her, a small woman with bright eyes and dark hair. I had two very different looking grandmothers but both were beautiful; one tall, one small. I was fondest of my father's mother, perhaps because she lived in the countryside I loved.

Both grandmothers originally came from country villages thirty kilometres apart. My mother's family lived on a small farm with two houses, four horses and sheep. My mother always wore nice dresses. There was beautiful furniture in their house, and carpets. I can remember my mother's silk dresses –

navy blue, dark red, lilac, and always with lace. She loved underskirts with lace. I was especially impressed by this. My mother's family owned a sewing machine and my mother loved sewing and knitting. Our house in the village of Maslennikovo was full of lace curtains and mats made by my mother. The Russian bed in a village is usually decorated with these laces and covers. The huge brass bed is a great tradition. Everything is decorated with lace.

The village where I was born will always be special for me. It is not far from the old Russian city of Yaroslavl near the Volga river. The landscape is marvellous and many local places are closely connected with the history of the Russian State. It became natural for me to listen to my mother and my grand-mother telling me about important events in Russian history. My native region is well-known as the birthplace of Nikolai Nekrasov, the leading nineteenth-century Russian poet often compared with Pushkin. In his poems he described the beauty of Russian meadows, fields, forests and the Volga river. He was the first to sing about the beauty of the ordinary, hard-working and industrious Russian woman. The poems of Nekrasov have always been my favourites. They first taught me to appreciate the beauty of nature in Russia.

As a child I envied children who had fathers and I longed to be like them. But my sister, my brother and myself worshipped our mother, who became both father and mother to us. Al-though she did not have a diploma in education, she gave us so much knowledge. She knew Pushkin's poems by heart and she inspired in us children a deep love for Pushkin, Lermontov and Tolstoy. She was interested in literature, and it was my mother who first began my appreciation of music, not only folk music, but classical music too. We lived in the centre of Russia and our Russian countryside was closely connected with the Rus-sian music of Tchaikovsky and Glinka. My mother also loved Beethoven and other great world music. In our family, music was always welcome. My mother sang Neapolitan songs and she had a special love for Italian composers and singers. She was quite a good singer herself. She was the first person in my life who taught me to combine love for Russian culture, art, music and literature with love for the culture of other countries and peoples.

For me, the image of my childhood is very sunny, with a blue, clear sky just like the Russian landscape we are looking at out of the window now.

However, thinking back, I know that not everything was happy at that time. We were children of the war and saw my mother's tears even if we could not understand the scope of the misfortune our country was living through. We felt intuitively, in our children's hearts, that something dramatic was happening, mirrored in our mother's unhappiness. But we could not understand the real dimension of the drama.

It was difficult for my mother to live in the village, without an income and with three children to feed. That is why my mother's mother, who now lived in Yaroslavl, advised our family to move from the village to the city, so that we could go to school and my mother could find paid work.

I was very sad to leave my beloved horses and dogs, but my grandmother convinced my mother to move.

Now you cannot see the village where I was born. It is a dying place, although nature's landscape is still beautiful. I want so much to give it life again. It was a shining village full of children, very joyful. My grandmother's house was a loving home, happy with music. Now the pond is empty and the ducks have gone. The house my mother lived in was very small. You must remember that although she educated herself so widely she was a Russian countrywoman.

A.L.   *It is important to see Stalin's Soviet Union*
       through the eyes of your mother.

V.T.   It was her motherland. She did not think of it as belonging to Stalin. I think my mother only thought of her daily difficulties, as a widow with three children. It was a period of near-starvation, and she had a really miserable life. She tried not to cry openly so as not to hurt us. But even if we were materially poor we were not miserable, because people helped each other. Our neighbours came to our house to sit round the stove with its blue flower-pattern tiles. It was the centre for our friends to come and share simple food, just bread and potatoes.

Life in Yaroslavl, the city, was very different. There was very little food there. My mother found work in a textile factory where the pay was very low. She only received the state allocation for a single mother, not a soldier's widow, and had 50 roubles for each of us. A loaf of bread at that time cost 180 roubles in the market.

After the war the whole country had ration books. We could only get basic foodstuffs in the shops with these coupons. My mother could not afford to pay for anything in addition to official rations. My village grandmother helped and sent potatoes and occasionally meat. But all the time it was my mother's moral standards which gave us strength. She lived far from the political centre and never became involved in politics. When Stalin died in 1953, as children we knew nothing of his crimes. He had been an ally of the West and we were told he was the Father Saviour of our country. At the news of his death some cried. Others did not cry; somehow we understood that they knew something. At the 20th Party Congress in 1956 Khrushchev told us about Stalin's crimes.

My mother never joined the Communist Party. She felt deeply about many matters but not about politics. She knew that it was my own decision when I joined the Communist Party in 1962 and she trusted me. Now, after her death, I still ask myself, 'What would she think of what is happening and of what I am doing?' She was always against injustice.

Even in my school-days, whenever I did something my mother did not approve of I later concluded she was right. But sometimes she was not. She feared for me when I began parachute jumping, but I do not regret having done that.

At my marriage she said, 'You must get your own life experience.' But she was not happy. She lived with us always. Later she came to Star City, the Cosmonaut Training Centre, when a flat was allocated to me there.

A.L.   Did your mother know about Stalin's purges?

V.T.   Yes, she did. She knew because some of our relatives suffered in the purges. This caused my mother great hurt, but trying to survive with her small children, what could she do? She was one of the many ordinary Russian women who dreaded war and wanted peace. In the West would you have called her longing for peace Soviet propaganda?

A.L.   What were you like as a little girl?

V.T.   My mother would say to me, 'You should have been born a boy.' I wanted to do everything that boys were doing. But I liked dolls, although we did not have any. It was sad for us that there were no toys. I started school in 1945, the year we moved to Yaroslavl from the village. My sister had begun to go to the school in the village but she had had to walk two kilometres. We were proud of our village schools, with wonderful teachers, and even now the old teachers still uphold tradition and culture.

*A.L.   Were you kind to your little brother or did you
        bully him?*

V.T.   As my mother was working when we moved to the city my sister and I took care of Vladimir. We did everything we could think of to throw him away. My mother was so cross with us. But I was only eight. How could I be a good educator? Now my sister has three children and six grandchildren. She works in a research institute. Her husband is in the Navy.

A.L.   Poor Vladimir! Who loved him?

V.T.   My mother. He was her favourite child and his grandmother also loved him. Both women felt he had come to replace my father. That is perhaps why, when he grew up, he was not anxious to study. That was our fault. We did not want him to know that life was tough. He is a very kind person, very musical, and plays the accordion like my father. After he gave up his studies he worked as a driver. Now he is the deputy manager of a car building workshop in a town on the outskirts of Moscow and a deputy in the City Council. He grows the best tomatoes, carrots and potatoes on his small dacha near Star City.

A.L.   Some men are spoilt all their lives. Why?

V.T.   I think it is predestined. Some people work hard and they take care of the others who do not work hard.

A.L.   A teacher once remarked on my always wanting to work. He said, 'The world is divided up into lifters and leaners.' Your mother was obviously a lifter, but how did she get the books which influenced you all? She did grow up in Stalin's time. How did she get the foreign music?

V.T.   In my grandparents' small farmhouse there was a personal library with many books, and as a child living with them she met members of what might now be called *intelligentsia* – doctors and school teachers. Their aspirations were always not only to extend their own culture but to pass it on and develop the interest of the country workers. She wanted more knowledge, and friends who were well-educated helped her. Books were shared and my mother took a lot of books with her when she married my father. Still, she always remained a countrywoman who worked with her hands. Her family were farmers, not intelligentsia, but they wanted their daughter, as a young widow of twenty-six and a favourite child, to have everything they could manage to give her. In fact she had had a typical peasant education for a country girl, even if her parents could buy her dresses and pay for extra lessons. She lived in the same way as the other village girls. She just wanted to learn more and become better educated and she got what she wanted.

A.L. *Did you look at the Moon when you were a child and think you might fly near to it one day?*

V.T. As a child I never had any idea of reaching the Moon. What I liked best, once we moved to the city, was sitting near the railway station watching the passing trains. You can't imagine what a delight it was for me. I envied the engine drivers having an opportunity to drive them. I wished I could be in their place. I wished I could drive locomotives throughout the world. These were my dreams when I was little. Later when I started parachute jumping and flying planes, I realized that nothing could be better than to be a pilot.

But back to the Moon; as the permanent satellite of the Earth it cannot but attract one's thoughts. I often now say to my daughter Alyona, 'Look at this beautiful full moon.' Yesterday, for example, it appeared so red, so huge, so surprising. It rose high and became brilliant.

A.L. *You said that you liked dolls.*

V.T. As a child I wanted dolls, but I had no dolls in my childhood. Perhaps because of this I brought my daughter dolls from everywhere I went, inside the country and abroad. As an adult I tried to fulfil the need for toys, unsatisfied since my childhood, by giving these to the children I met. I was one of the generation of war children without toys.

A.L. *Do you remember your first years under Stalin as well-ordered and protected?*

V.T. Stalin was a long way from our family. Protection came from our parents, relations, neighbours. For example, I remember my mother did not like storms and rushed round trying to save everything that might be damaged by the strong winds. I did not mind storms. When I was playing with boys they thought I was brave. I loved riding horses bareback. It is a wonderful feeling, to be racing along with the wind whistling in one's ears. In the village it was a healthy life; when there was deep snow in winter and early darkness it was safe inside the house. We were comfortable.

We had to learn poems about Stalin in school. But that was in school, not in the family. And then, you see, in the provinces political problems seemed to be far away. We did not feel close to these. We were influenced by some of the propaganda, saw films about Stalin, read history books glorifying him. But the propaganda only stressed for us that he was very high and we were very low. I can't say that he left any special traces in my thinking. All the same, it has to be admitted that he was not an ordinary man. Whatever the opinions of journalists and scholars may be now, our people, our army, together with Stalin brought us victory in the Great Patriotic War against Hitler. At that time the West accepted Stalin's point of view and many of our people went to their death believing in Stalin's name. This, for me, was the worst treachery by Stalin. He betrayed those who trusted him. The feelings of common people towards him were sincere and he betrayed them.

A.L. *In your family did you ever feel unhappy about the excesses of the Communist system – the way it controlled everything that happened to you? Did you mind that churches were closed and people frightened by anti-religious laws? In the West we heard of cruel purges.*

V.T. We were not told about Church purges. My city grandmother was a believer and I was baptized. My mother did not go to church but she was very tolerant of all religions. In my village grandmother's house there were icons. But we were not a religious family and we accepted that we should live according to State laws. I agreed to oppose religious activities when I

210

joined the Communist Youth League, the *Komsomol*. But when my mother was seriously ill my sister and I went to church to pray.

You ask if we approved of the Communist system. There were people who approved but also many who disapproved, and there were different ways of showing disapproval even if demonstrations or strikes were not permitted. I was not always satisfied. My family lived very modestly, too modestly, and I wanted to earn more money for my work. I have always worked hard and I believed my work should have been evaluated higher: more money, more material rewards, better clothes, a more comfortable flat. We were living only on the little money we received, and it was not enough in comparison with our hard work.

At the same time, even if it is difficult to believe, what I am trying to say is that the moral outlook of our society was higher than it is now. The hardships we faced and lived through were balanced by our strong belief in a better future. We hoped we were working together and harder for a better life. At least, that is how I saw it. I cannot agree with those who now denigrate everything in our past and who want to paint it all black. The inspiration in my mother's heart and in mine was that we were working for an improved life. This was absolutely sincere, and such sincerity gave moral strength to many ordinary Russian families. People were human, compassionate, sympathetic and more ready to help others. Of course there were those who were motivated by self-interest, but people were less aggressive, less cruel, less desirous of having everything for themselves at the expense of others, as seems to be the case now.

Now we seem to want to stamp out everything from the past, even if it means depriving our youngsters of the good moral structure built up by previous generations. Good traditions could still provide a basis for educating the next generation to make the best moral choices.

Of course Stalin's epoch was a black period, dark years when innocent people were executed without trial for the sole crime of daring to express their own opinions and raise their voice against what they thought was wrong. That was awful. Nonetheless the spirit which helped us to hold out through a terrible war when we had little food and few clothes was high, and we had achieved progress in science and technology. We used our skills well, as when we launched the first man into space only sixteen years after the war ended. Do we have to focus on Stalin's time? After his death many skilled and talented Soviets worked together inspired by enthusiasm for socialism. Look at the Japanese, they have adopted aspects of socialism for their progress, and used socialism's good sides. The point is to know how to use what is good and reject what is wrong. Of course now we are all grateful to have become more free. We can now say what we really think. This is a great advance for us, but it doesn't mean that we have the right to destroy what was built well by previous generations. When in 1961 we heard that Yuri Gagarin was the first man in space, we were right to be proud of this Soviet achievement.

*A.L.   Did you hear news of the world outside Russia
in your youth?*

V.T.   I have read what you have written about the fear of the USSR felt by the West at the time of our first meeting in 1984. It taught me how little we knew about each other's cultures. It seems to me that the West knew even less about us than we knew about the West. Did you really believe we were an 'evil empire', as Reagan called us? At that time a lot of people in the West believed that everything Russian was bad and in Russia official propaganda portrayed everything in the West as bad. I am really thankful this wall of ignorance has now been pulled down, like the Berlin Wall, and that at last we are trying to understand more between East and West.

Still I wonder: in the past, which side was in fact most isolated? In our Soviet schools we learnt about the West. I remember the first teacher who taught me French. I have always been very lazy at learning languages, but she showed me pictures of Paris and read translations of Victor Hugo. Through books, music and history we learnt something about other countries in the world. What we could not do was see for ourselves how people lived abroad and what their day-to-day life was like, because we were not allowed to travel. But we saw some famous foreign films, and had access to the classics of foreign literature, history and music which were available to us at school. We could also go to the local library and borrow books.

After leaving school, those who wanted to know more about foreign culture and languages had opportunities to study these. Soviet youth was well educated. Of course much depended on personal abilities and family attitudes. In my family, my mother read not only Tolstoy, Pushkin, Nekrasov and Lermontov, but also Jack London, John Galsworthy and Mark Twain, Shakespeare and Cervantes. I couldn't imagine my youth without those names. We would have thought it impossible, unthinkable to develop our personality without reading these classics of Western literature. Many were published in our country in translation. We always published more translations of foreign literature in my country than translations of Russian and Soviet literature were published abroad. When I say Soviet I mean Ukrainian, Central Asian, Caucasian; for example works by Nizami, Omar Khayyám, Shota Rustaveli and others.

Another advantage for us was the rich mixture of national cultures within the many different Soviet republics. People living inside the Soviet Union learned a lot from each other. But we could not travel freely abroad and see foreign countries for ourselves. I think this was the main reason why East and West did not learn the truth about how ordinary people lived. There was a shortage of people-to-people contact. We couldn't see the personal lives of people abroad: family ties, everyday life, traditions. We did not see this but neither did you until now.

You must also realise that Soviets had a serious inferiority complex. Even those who lived well were reluctant to invite foreigners to their homes. We felt awkward; a sort of false shame for having a smaller flat, less furniture, no Western domestic appliances. There was nothing to be ashamed of in showing foreigners our homes, even if ours were poorer and less comfortable than homes abroad. But you must believe this sense of inferiority was a real obstacle.

A.L.   *You have opened a window on a Russia the*
       West never knew and even now does not know.
       Not one with the rigid rules of a police state,
       but a Russia of upright patient people working
       to rebuild a system shattered by a dreadful
       despot and a destructive defensive war.

V.T.   You asked me to remember my childhood. I have tried to give you all sides of the picture, sorrows as well as joys, the light and the dark. Throughout it all my mother shone like a star. Without her I wonder what would have happened to me?

The Second Conversation

Valentina Speaks
on
Youth, School and Work

A.L. After your school-days, at sixteen you became more independent of your family. How do you remember your life as a factory worker, a parachute jumping champion and, finally, a cosmonaut in training? What are your memories of those ten years: your friends, interests and loves? Did you have any special friends?

V.T. I still see the friends of my youth and visit them in Yaroslavl. These friendships are important. I used to keep a journal and I wrote about them in this diary. I don't know where it is now. At the time of my flight many of my family documents were given to journalists by my mother. She was very confused when they came to our home, and they took almost everything away. My diary was one of the documents taken and they also removed many photographs.

A.L.   *Was it an emotional, adolescent diary? Did*
       you write about love-affairs?

V.T.   I wrote a lot about my everyday life, about parachute
jumping, and my enthusiasm for the Volga river. I had the
impression that every inhabitant of Yaroslavl would want to
watch our parachute jumping!

My adolescent life was so full of events, I did not have time
for a special love. I had one boyfriend my mother liked. He was
what you in the West call my 'steady' for two years. My mother
knew his family. He was an engineer, his father was a chief
engineer and his mother was a teacher. He was good-looking.
He was called Leonid. He brought me flowers. I liked his
manners. He invited me to the theatre. The first ever drama
theatre in Russia was set up in Yaroslavl. We both liked
Chekhov's *The Cherry Orchard* and *The Seagull*. There was so
much to see and enjoy, like *Swan Lake, Prince Igor, The Queen of
Spades, Iolanthe*. All these classics were part of our culture and
we grew up knowing them well.

Leonid had serious intentions, and he told my mother about
his love. I was furious. I said, 'Why did you speak to her
without consulting me? I am too busy to marry anyone.' It was
a great shock for him. When he realised that I had no time to
marry he gave up.

But I have just remembered. He was Yuli – not Leonid!

A.L.   *Who was Leonid?*

V.T.   There was no Leonid. But I had many friends, including
Yuli.

When I left school I went straight to work at the tyre factory.
There were evening classes as well as work during the day. I
had had nine years of school from the age of eight to sixteen,
and I did not want to continue at school. So I transferred to a
technical institute where my sister was studying. She did not
think I would succeed. I managed all the exams and showed her
what I could do. Finally in 1960 I graduated from the Textile

Technical Institute with a diploma as an engineer. I loved everything to do with machines.

I have very good memories of this time. I believed my fellow-workers liked me. After my theatre visits I used to describe these to them. I explained *Rigoletto* very enthusiastically.

A.L.   Did they think you came from a more intellectual background than they did?

V.T.   I did not come from a different background. If you are intellectual and you underline it, that annoys. But if you have interesting knowledge and share it, your friends enjoy that with you. We all liked Chekhov's *Three Sisters* and *Ivanov*. We learnt about Italian operas together. Every summer artists from other cities came to perform. We heard *Carmen*, *Lucia di Lammermoor*, Glinka's opera *Ivan Susanin*, *Prince Igor* by Borodin, *Iolanthe*, *Sleeping Beauty*, *The Queen of Spades*. My favourite opera is still *La Traviata*. There was ballet too. Going to the theatre was not expensive. My mother had very little money but whenever she could she bought records of Verdi and Tchaikovsky. We were all working then and had salaries.

I persuaded some of my friends to try parachute jumping with me. That was in 1958. Then we made up a folk music group. I played the *domra*, a Russian stringed instrument. We also made up an orchestra at home. I preferred playing as my mother was the good singer. She sang a romance called 'Nightingale'.

I will sing you 'Nightingale' but my voice is not as good as my mother's.

> Nightingale, my nightingale
> Where were you singing last night?
> Where were you flying last night?
> Stay with me, my lovely song-bird.

We also loved Neapolitan songs, and I still do. I can still remember the words of *Non ti scordar di me*.

217

The main memory of my youth is music. Despite all the difficulties there was music every minute in our family. My mother's spirit rose with music and it made her optimistic. When, after the war, relatives came back from the front without my father she still managed to be happy if she could sing at family gatherings. A favourite song was 'Hazbulat'. It is a very old song. I will sing you 'Hazbulat'.

> Tell me, Hazbulat
> Do you agree to give me your wife
> If I give you plenty of gold?
> Do you agree to give me your wife
> If I give you a good horse and a good sword?
> You are too old to make a young woman
>   happy, Hazbulat
> No – says Hazbulat
> When we are together, me and my wife
> We are happy and young
> We don't need any gold.

A.L. *You also know Italian songs, and you almost seem obsessed by admiration for Pavarotti.*

V.T. Of course. I deeply esteem this hard-working singer, a true son of Italy. His art brings great joy to people. All my difficulties vanish when I listen to his beautiful voice.

A.L. *Was there a song which girls your age liked best and you all sang in the factory?*

V.T. We sang so many songs, some from films with marvellous music. There was a favourite singer, Orlova, but there were many more of them. One of the best actors was Alexei Batalov. We are still good friends. He acted in Chekhov's *The Lady with the Dog*, a wonderful film. Batalov is still acting and not long ago I saw him in the Russian version of a British play. He was very good in the role of an intellectual. He gives readings of beautiful Russian texts, from our classics. My favourites are by the famous Russian poet Anna Akhmatova. There are many poems on love written by women. I will tell two of these by Akhmatova for you from memory.

> It is the 21st. The night. Monday.
> My city is in shadows
> My soul is in shadows, asking myself whether
>   Love is a reality
> What is Love? Poems and songs?
> Rendez-vous? Separations?
> Or mystery?
> I have discovered this mystery by chance and
>   since then I feel as if I were ill.

She wrote that in 1917. I will try to remember the words of another of Akhmatova's poems written in 1912.

> I have known how to live humbly and worse
> To look at the sky and to pray to my God
> To walk a lot, soothing my pain
> Creating poems on a perishable and wonderful life
> Back to my home I enjoy
> The crackling of the fire
> The purring of the cat
> The cry of the stork
> I am quiet and well
> I will not hear you
> Even if you are knocking at my door.

A.L.   *These are heart-lifting memories but do you have any unpleasant memories from your time at the factory? Was there anything you particularly disliked; for instance, the smell?*

V.T.   The dust. I was allergic to this. I don't want to be reminded of it. My skin suffered, especially my face. Usually the factory doctors were good. We had a good health centre. Unfortunately the standard depended on the personnel and some medical centres were not good. When my mother became ill she was not well looked after to begin with. The doctor was not honest about her illness and did not treat her properly. Fortunately she was eventually given very good treatment and slowly recovered from the strokes which paralysed her.

Our medical centres were not short of doctors and nurses but they were short of equipment. The post-war period was very difficult; 1,700 cities had been devastated and we had to rebuild them. So many villages were also destroyed. Practically the whole European area of our country was devastated by the war and we had no help from abroad. We had to do all the rebuilding ourselves and we took pride in doing so. We were not dramatic about it, we just got on with rebuilding. You have reminded me of the hardship by asking me to recall the sad songs of war. So many people had perished in my country and there were thousands of widows and orphans. Cultural, material and personal treasures had been destroyed. It was unhappiness for our whole continent. One of the saddest songs was about a husband who was thinking of his wife's love just before he died.

You have asked me what my mother thought of the war leaders in my country. I am sure that the people involved in war should be divided into politicians, widows and children. My mother was a widow. My opinion is that war is never unleashed by the common people. I know that not only Soviet people suffered in the war but also many others. After the war my generation was told about Coventry and we felt real solidarity with the people there. Russians appreciated the support of the British, the French and the Americans during the war. It contributed to our high moral spirit. We were lifted up by a new mentality. We were sure that during the Second World War we had all suffered together to defeat evil.

A.L.   What non-Russian war heroes can you remember? Eisenhower? Churchill?

V.T.   Yes, Eisenhower, Churchill, de Gaulle, Tito, Sikorski and the heroic French pilots in the Franco-Russian 'Normandie-Niemen' air regiment. But I was only four when they were war heroes. My mother did not speak about politicians. Her concern was family problems, and I remember hearing very little about any national leaders in the post-war period.

We heard stories on the radio after the war. And I saw films about the war and listened to my mother commenting on her sad memories. Twenty million Russians were killed, and among these many of our own relatives: in my family two of my father's brothers were killed in the war and there were relatives of my mother in Byelorussia who were shot. They were among the civilian losses, and they were shot by the Nazis.

Our *Komsomol* youth group visited hospitals to help the war disabled, and we read them poems and heard their songs. That is why so many songs of the war period remain in my memory. They were Russian songs, and I still remember the one about a soldier who sends a message to his wife: '...the night is dark, I am risking my life for your life and for the life of my son. My beloved, this night will not divide us even if I die.'

Another song brings back more sorrow: 'My beloved wife, you are very far from me and death is very close; only your love is saving me.'

> A.L.   *Poor human beings. An Italian friend of mine was told that the Russians were barbarians but when her husband was missing in Russia she received only one postcard from him saying: 'My Russian friends are happy if I give them holy pictures. Send me "Imagini".' She said to me: 'Why can't people know more about each other?' She had learnt that the Russians were like her mother in the mountains in Italy who loved holy pictures.*

V.T.   Yes. So many human tragedies. Even though I grew up after the war period, I heard stories of husbands and wives divided, the passion, sorrow and broken lives. But by then my life was mostly taken up with my own hopes and disappointments.

After school I wanted to go to Leningrad to be trained as an engine driver. But my elder sister had married and had her own family when my mother became ill. So I stayed at home and first worked in the local tyre factory and then in the textile factory. My sister could not stay at home. She is called Ludmila, a beautiful name which means 'sympathetic to other people'. My mother chose it after the heroine of a Pushkin fairy tale, *Ruslan and Ludmila*. She was born in 1934.

My mother had her first stroke in 1956, when she was only forty-three. She was very ill. Her whole right side was paralysed for four months. Afterwards she made a partial recovery, because she was well looked after. Yaroslavl had a reliable hospital and medical training institute. A neurosurgeon, a neurologist and therapists helped my mother to recover. Later she came to live with me in Star City when I was working there.

A.L.   *So it is not true to say that only the nomen-*
       klatura could benefit from good hospitals?
       Were there good hospitals for everyone?

V.T.   Ours was a good hospital for workers of the textile factory, *Red Perekop*. The factory made fabrics for industrial purposes. We called these 'technical fabrics'.

I enjoyed working in the factory but at the same time I was looking for something else. My hopes flew higher than life on the ground.

A.L.   *What led to the dramatic change from work in*
       the factory to your seeking a future in space
       training?

V.T.   I have always been fascinated by the sky and I wanted to experience a feeling of achievement in the air. My first parachute jump was in May 1959, after I joined the local airclub. In 1961 I was inspired by Gagarin's flight in space. I kept thinking about new developments in space research and I became determined to try and join the space programme. It would mean leaving my childhood home, and the work near my mother and family. But nothing was going to stop me in my resolve to reach the sky.

The Third Conversation

Valentina Speaks

on

Space Training and the Flight

A.L.   *It is remarkable that in the thirty years since your first woman pioneer flight no other woman has flown in space solo. Also that you have never given a personal, detailed description of your flight.*

   Now at long last you say you will speak, so I can ask.

   How did you prepare for the three pioneer days 'up there'?

   Also, did you prove that women were equal to men in space?

V.T.   Let me tell you how it really was.

My passion for flying began with my first parachute jump on 21st May 1959. I was in a small, green aeroplane driving along the airstrip, bouncing over the bumps, and suddenly it hung in the air. The ground below me grew distant. Afraid of missing the signal because of the noise of the engine I strained to hear the command 'Go!'. Jumping into nothingness my heart turned over and I was very happy. I was reminded of how, years ago, my friends had dared me to jump from a high bridge into the Kotorosl which flows into the Volga and I had done so. Several seconds passed, but then with a jolt, a white dome opened up above me. The ground came towards me. I began to work the ropes which guided me down to the wet grass below. The parachute billowed out on either side of me. My first parachute jump was over. I felt I wanted to do it every day.

I spent more and more time at the airclub and in April 1961 all of us in the club followed Gagarin's flight in space with excitement and pride.

I described this to my mother and I will always remember her words, 'Now a man has flown in space, it is a woman's turn next.'

Her reaction had a strong effect on me. When I found that Gagarin was also a member of an airclub, it led me to think that there was a possibility that I could join the Soviet space programme. Photographs of Gagarin were everywhere and his story *The Road to Space* was serialised in *Pravda*. I studied it carefully. Watching the film *First Flight to the Stars* showed me the extensive preparations which had preceded Gagarin's experience and this did not deter me. I was sure a woman could endure the forces of the centrifuge, the silence of the isolation chamber and the roar of the rocket launch. I wrote a letter to the Central Committee of DOSAAF (Voluntary Organisation for Co-operation with the Army, Air Force and Navy) in which I requested to be considered for the training course in new technology.

In December 1961 I was called upon to appear before a special medical committee in Moscow, and after this I was informed that I had been chosen to go to the Training Centre as one of five women selected to undergo the intensive training programme. Considerable secrecy was still necessary and I was not allowed to tell anyone, not even my mother, of the real purpose behind my subsequent departure for Moscow. The family and friends who saw me off at the station believed I was going to join a parachute team. I left Yaroslavl in December. It was the most significant journey of my life.

My first meeting in Moscow was with General Kamanin, Hero of the Soviet Union, who, in 1934, had rescued Soviet sailors trapped on an iceberg in the Arctic. He was a senior figure in the Soviet space programme. He told me that the medical tests were satisfactory and that, so far, I was the only woman in the training team, although other women would join me in the Centre. I found the atmosphere in the Cosmonaut Training Centre, on the Saturday I arrived, very congenial. I did wonder how the men would accept a woman in the team, but immediately their camaraderie extended to include me as I awaited the arrival of the other young women.

My only great anxiety was how to keep my mother from being worried. I had told her I must be away from Yaroslavl for some time to complete my training in advanced parachute jumping. She accepted this because she wanted me to do well in this activity. But I could not tell her I was on a top secret mission and would be unable to contact her. So I wrote regularly to my mother and on two occasions I briefly visited her in Yaroslavl. Before the flight I wrote ten letters to her and in each one I described how I was well and happy and fully occupied. I asked a friend to post one each day to my mother. But one of the later letters was delayed in the post and it arrived on the day of the flight. When friends told her they had seen a woman in space on television and that they thought it was me, my mother replied very energetically that it could not be me as she had just received a letter saying I was on the last stage of my parachute training and would soon be home again. But then she heard that I was indeed the first woman in space and also received the message I sent her while I was in orbit. She was very upset that I had deceived her and it took a long time for her to forgive me. But discipline was all part of the expectations I was determined to fulfil by accepting every necessary development on my road to space.

A.L.   *When I met one of the women selected with*
you, Tatyana Kuznetsova, she told me that
her first impression of you was that of a gifted
communicator with leadership qualities and
that this enabled you to settle easily into the
all-male community of the cosmonauts. She
told me of the strict programme you all shared,
and that it was both physically demanding and
mentally tiring. She said that the joy of selec-
tion soon wore off as the rigorous realities, such
as the thermal chamber and the centrifuge
vestibular tests with constant medical checks,
filled the days. She remembered classes and
lectures on subjects including astronomy, geo-
physics, rocket technology and radio com-
munication, all new to the women's team.

V.T.   That is true. Our five-woman team was soon introduced to the strict training regime and then learnt day by day
about the hard work that the many months ahead had in store
for us.

There is so much work done on Earth before a space flight. It
took nearly two years to prepare the team of five women for
space. First the demanding training programme to equip the
cosmonaut to deal with technological demands, such as the
problems of navigation and the engineering demands of a
spacecraft, which is a sophisticated technical vehicle.

We were also trained to deal with emergencies, and were
equipped with what was required in case we landed in an area
of Soviet territory where we would not be found quickly. In
the first pioneer experiments it was not possible to know to the
exact kilometre where the landing would be.

There was constant testing on board ship and on the ground.
We were trained continuously in radio communication, space
navigation and orientation which included knowledge of astronomy to navigate by the stars. The human body had to be
trained for conditions in space – especially acclimatization to

weightlessness. The training was on board an aeroplane and centrifuge training exposed us to *g*-forces.

The *surdokamera* (sound chamber) was another experience for which training was required. Here we learned to cope with working in solitude and isolation on the spacecraft. Nowadays there are space crews but then there was a tremendous sense of responsibility knowing that you would be alone.

A.L.   *You have told me that as a group of women*
       you worked well with the male cosmonauts.
       You were treated as equals from the start.

V.T.   We were equals also in physical training which included sport where we were integrated into the various men's teams.

Meanwhile, doctors and biologists carefully monitored our progress to see if the female body was in any way different to the male in undergoing tests and training exercises. Menstruation in space was obviously a problem and the women were not required to undertake centrifuge training at this time of the month. My space flight took place between periods.

A.L.   *Tatyana recalls that the training programme*
       was developed by scientific experts based on
       data from previous space flights.

V.T.   One way this was achieved was by the training programme which prepared us for space being carried out in a mock-up of the real spacecraft, to get us used to it. It would be our house during the flight and as such we had to know all the possible problems which could arise. This was a constant component of our period of training.

As the months passed our expertise in handling the equipment increased and we coped well with the strenuous regime. Not only did we have to learn how to navigate the spaceship but also to learn to deal with the engineering demands of a space flight, since the solo-pilot would be the only person available to repair the spaceship if a problem arose. The first

generation of spacecraft involved a complicated return procedure of catapulting from the capsule and landing by parachute.
That is why our previous parachute training was useful during
the training programme, and we shared our expertise with the
men. The programme included parachute jumping in a spacesuit into the Black Sea and on land. Our spacesuits, which
contained life-support systems, were naturally very heavy.
Specialists were responsible for dressing the cosmonaut in the
spacesuit, which became not only the cosmonaut's clothing but
had to be an autonomous house to enable the cosmonaut to
survive outside the capsule. Before putting on the spacesuits
medical sensors were attached to the body for a series of tests
devised by biologists and doctors.

Our pilot training programme included five flights one after
another every day. As you see all this was difficult and demanding work which depended on a lot of strength and knowledge.

The whole group worked well. One of us, Tatyana
Kuznetsova, left the team in 1962, because of illness. Four of us
remained for the final period of preparation. No-one knew
which two girls would be chosen as the pilot and back-up.

THE FLIGHT

A.L.   *Your own description of the first solo space
flight by a woman must be one of the most
dramatic pioneer stories ever told. Can you
give your personal account for the first time
now?*

V.T. I prefer short accurate accounts. I want to tell the truth
in a direct way about the time immediately before, during and
after the flight. This is what happened.

After a few days at home in Yaroslavl where I celebrated the
1st May holiday our group of four women – myself, Valentina
Ponomaryova, Irina Solovyova and Zhanna Erkina – flew to
the cosmodrome at Baikonur on 31st May. Other cosmonauts
and specialists taking part in the space preparation programme

flew with us. It was our second visit. We had been there in August 1962 to observe another launch. At Baikonur the State Commission headed by Georgy Tyulin, a well-known expert in space technology, met to nominate the pilots and back-ups for the two impending flights. Kamanin spoke of the equal preparedness of all four women cosmonauts. The Chief Designer Korolev confirmed the technical readiness of the launch vehicles. Finally, the State Commission nominated Valery Bikovsky to pilot *Vostok 5* and myself to pilot *Vostok 6*. Irina Solovyova was my back-up.

We spent the days before the flight in final preparations, and worked with the specialist engineers and doctors. It was necessary for all cosmonauts to spend the night before the flight under doctor's observation. I spent the final evening in the little house with my back-up, Irina, who was to stay with me up to the last moment. Korolev came to see us before we went to bed. We drank tea and talked about the imminent flight and the work to be done in space. It was his custom to do this before a flight.

The 16th June was the date of my flight. We got up at 7.00 and did 30 minutes of exercises. The evening before, and again on that morning of the flight, the doctors administered a cleansing enema. Then breakfast, but this was already space food, specially prepared for cosmonauts by nutritionists. After this we went to a special complex where there were rooms with the spacesuits and all the medical apparatus. The doctors continued their electrocardiograph tests and, before we put on the spacesuits, attached wires to measure breathing and heart-rate. Now we were ready to put on spacesuits and space boots. On top of the boots we put special protective covers which we took off when we got into the spaceship. We had to walk several metres to the bus which took me, Irina Solovyova, Yuri Gagarin and the other cosmonauts accompanying us to the launching pad. There was a joyful atmosphere in the bus, the end of months of preparation was in sight.

Near the launch vehicle I got out of the bus and reported to the Chairman of the Commission: 'Commander of the spaceship Lieutenant Tereshkova is ready for the flight.' The reply: 'Bon voyage. I wish you a successful flight and safe return to Earth.' A special lift took me to the top of the launch vehicle where the *Vostok* capsule was located. Removing the protective covers from the space boots, the specialists helped me into the seat of the capsule and closed the hatch. I switched on the communication link with Korolev and Gagarin. Then I was alone in the capsule. From embarkation to lift-off took two hours, which I used for checking the radio links, while the rocket carrier was being prepared for take off. Korolev, named *Zarya* (Dawn), was in constant link-up with me, named *Chaika* (Seagull), and Yuri Gagarin, named *Kyedr* (Cedar). For me there was no time to reflect on what was ahead, with so much work to be done at this stage, waiting impatiently for the final words 'lift-off'. Korolev's last words to me were, 'Seagull, we wish you a happy flight. We are waiting for your return to Earth. It's a pity I can't be with you now in the space ship.'

I replied, 'Thank you. I'll try to carry out all the programme. Don't be sad, Sergei Pavlovich, we will have a wonderful opportunity to fly together to Mars.'

I experienced the anticipated reactions at lift-off, which was seen from the ground in white hot flames. The launch vehicle took me further away from Earth into space. Through the porthole I was able to see my *Vostok* capsule separated from the last stage of the rocket as we reached the programmed orbit which brought me 183 km from Earth at its closest, 231 km away at the furthest point. I was constantly checking the equipment and the controls.

From space the beauty of Earth was overwhelming. The angle of the orbit enabled me to see the Earth's surface from the porthole. The blackness of the sky scattered with stars was impressive. From Earth we only see the blackness at night but from space the Earth was lit by the Sun, and the sky, although dark, was bright with stars. Instinctively the cosmonaut thinks that the dear, native home is not so far away.

*A.L.   Could you give details of what happened in-
side the space capsule?*

V.T.   It took me just 89 minutes to orbit the Earth and as I
saw the planet from space I realised how small Earth is, and
how fragile, and that it could be destroyed very quickly. I
established radio contact with Bikovsky. He was now in his
second day in space. It was the first of several conversations in
space between us.

It was time to work and begin the extensive set of tests that I
had to carry out as part of my contribution to the space programme. In addition to monitoring the controls and the equipment, I had to supervise biological experiments with seeds and
insects on board the spaceship. I also had to take a series of films
and photographs using a special *Konvass* camera to provide
footage and stills to study the Earth and its atmosphere.

*A.L.   What were the results of the photographs you
took in space?*

V.T.   The photographs which I took from *Vostok 6* depicted
the edge of the Earth in its twilight corona – the layers of the
atmosphere lit by the Sun. The shots were taken on the second
day of my space flight according to the programme of scientific
experiments assigned to me. One can see graphically from these
pictures that, as the spaceship got closer to the twilight corona,
both the size and brightness of this corona increased.

The part of the corona closest to the Earth is orange in
colour, the upper layers are white and gradually turn blue.
Using these pictures we were able to determine the vertical
structure of the layers of stratospheric aerosols. We found two
aerosol layers at heights of 11.5 ± 1 km and 19.5 ± 1 km. From
these, scientists were able to estimate the density and the size of
the particles in the upper layer and they were able to compare
the results obtained from my *Vostok* capsule with measurements
of aerosol concentrations made from balloons and aeroplanes.

In my archives I have kept a diagram which explains this. The aerosol particles are grains of microscopic dust from volcanoes and meteors, and help scientists to understand how the atmosphere circulates, and how changes take place.

A.L.   Were you the first to discover the changes in
the ozone layer?

V.T.   Everything said on this must be based on fact. The pictures I shot were only a beginning, the half-opened door into an unknown world. We formulated the problem and colleagues have been developing this area of research in the stratosphere since my flight. I can only claim that mine was a discovery whose results were developed later.

I certainly share concern about ozone holes. The thinning which damages the ozone layers which protect our planet from radiation is a very serious problem. These layers are becoming thinner and because they protect all life on Earth from destructive ultraviolet radiation from space, it is a real danger. We must encourage experts to co-operate and to focus the best brains of all countries to study this problem.

A.L.   Did you keep a log-book of your flight to record
various data?

V.T.   Naturally I kept a log-book of the flight. The data were as follows: cabin temperature, 23.6°C; heart rate and pulse, 64 beats a minute; breathing, 20.

I had to summarize my physiological reactions to various aspects of being in space and to record whether, apart from weightlessness, I felt as I normally did on Earth. Medical check-ups were part of my space programme and specific information on temperature, breathing, pulse and heart-rate were recorded in the space capsule. Telemetric data was simultaneously registered in the flight monitoring centre outside Moscow.

Having reached my programmed orbit I sent a radio report to the Kremlin announcing the progress of the flight. A short time later I received a telegram from Khrushchev. At 16.55 (Moscow time) this message was further reinforced by a direct radio link-up with Khrushchev in the Kremlin. He congratulated me and said that he was proud that a daughter of his country was the first woman in space. He wished me success and said, 'See you soon on Earth.' Then I prepared for sleep.

I informed Earth that I was going to rest. After a deep sleep I woke at 6.00 (Moscow time) and did 15 minutes' physical exercises. This was not easy in a confined space. I washed with an impregnated cloth. Then I had breakfast.

The flight had been due to be completed in 24 hours, but there was a prior agreement with Korolev that if it was going well I could extend the flight by another two days. The first 24 hours of my space activities were successful so I asked permission from the State Commission to extend the flight and land at the same time as the other *Vostok* capsule in orbit.

A.L.   *What did you see from your space capsule?*

V.T.   Looking out I could distinguish many geographical features: all the continents, the oceans, seas, rivers, fjords. The Suez Canal, Egypt and the yellow desert crossed by the dark blue ribbon of the Nile. The rivers were as easy to pick out as the oceans. I could see large cities and mountain ranges. I saw the blue ice-caps of Antarctica and the icebergs of Greenland.

A.L.   *Can you describe your return to Earth? Was this the most testing time?*

V.T.   I was in full control of the equipment of my *Vostok* capsule. This was particularly crucial in the final stages prior to descent and re-entry because in these early years of manned spaceflight it was necessary during the descent for the cosmonaut to be catapulted from the capsule at a height of 7 km and land by parachute.

During the descent and re-entry I saw bright yellow flames surround my capsule. When it reached 7 km an electric impulse caused the forced opening of the hatch which was ejected and fell to Earth. The chair was ejected with me in it. Then I separated from the chair and the parachute opened. It all happened very quickly.

After my parachute opened I looked below me and saw that I was approaching a lake. We had been trained to land in water. But, of course, I did not want an unpleasant landing. The gusts of wind helped me however and luckily I landed not far from the lake, in a nearby field where some farmers were working. Because there was a strong wind, blowing with a speed of about 17 metres per second, it was not a particularly soft landing. The metal rim of my space helmet gave me a beautiful bruise to commemorate my return to Earth. Despite the injuries to my face I was briefly able to enjoy the warmth of the summer's day, waiting for the rescue team, but there was work to be done. I had to take off my spacesuit, open up the container which had landed near me and change into a track suit. I had to collect everything together, the spacesuit, parachute and chair and take them to the capsule about 400 metres away. All the items were heavy. The people who had been working in the field came up to me later and helped me to carry the chair, since one person could not manage it single-handed. As you can see the final, descent stage of the flight was arduous, physically and mentally, and nobody helped me, I did it all myself. Obviously I could not have done it if I was not feeling strong enough.

I had landed in the Altai region. After I had communicated my location to the rescue team, I asked the farmers to drive me to the nearest village with a telephone, and there I asked to be connected with the Kremlin. That was my first short report to Khrushchev after the landing. I went back to the field to wait for the rescue aeroplane.

It took me to Pavlodar where I changed planes and flew by Ilyushin 14 to Karaganda. There I spent the night. On the morning of 20th June I went to Kuibishev where the doctors were waiting to begin medical tests. In Kuibishev I personally addressed the State Commission to report on the space flight. I was very happy to be reunited with Korolev and Gagarin. Everywhere I went there were oceans of flowers and goodwill. It was an overwhelming experience to find so much kindness, warmth and generosity as a response for my work.

On 22nd June 1963 Bikovsky and I arrived in Moscow to deliver our reports to the leaders of the USSR and I had to use make-up to cover my bruises.

A.L.   *You have said very little about the ordeal by fire on re-entry. One observer has written that the early cosmonauts had to be particularly disciplined so as not to panic when they realised they were flying in isolation at five miles per second above the atmosphere and then having to face the flames of re-entry. As he put it: 'It could drive the sanest person to mindless terror.' As one of the first cosmonauts and the only woman who has ever flown alone in space, would you say that re-entry was particularly testing?*

V.T.   Yes, certainly. This is the period of the flight when every second requires total concentration and attention from the cosmonaut, moment by moment. For the pioneers of the space programme that was especially testing since our re-entry capsules were spherical. A sphere has no aerodynamic qualities and follows a ballistic trajectory like a cricket ball. We suffered because of *g*-loads which reached between 8 and 9*g*. During this short time it was a strain to breathe and to speak. Even now when one listens to the recordings of my radio communications with Earth one can hear my voice at very high pitch under pressure. But I endured these conditions only for a short period of time. I cannot say that for later generations of cosmonauts it was easier to fly but these were the experiences of the early cosmonauts.

Each generation has its difficulties, and pioneers have their own destiny. For me, re-entry was closely connected with

Madagascar. Do you know why? The braking process of my spaceship was programmed to come on automatically over Madagascar. It was also programmed so that if something went wrong I had to operate it manually. This required me to be alert so as to watch the control panel. Each second counted. If the manual descent was delayed by one second the landing location would change dramatically; this was intense but interesting work. I was not afraid of the yellow and red tongues of flame beyond the porthole. Inside the capsule, because of the life-support system, there was normal Earth temperature. The capsule had its own heat shield. My landing went according to plan.

A.L.   *You have told the story of one of the most courageous human achievements as if it was a normal, ordinary, routine journey. The experts knew otherwise. They realised that you might die. But, after your safe return, was it from space into glory?*

V.T.   The welcome we received is still an unforgettable memory.

At Vnukovo airport we were met by Khrushchev and other important politicians and officials. There I was also reunited with my mother and a few close relatives. I delivered my report to Khrushchev: 'The commander of *Vostok 6*, Valentina Tereshkova, has returned to Earth and can report the successful completion of her space flight.' On hearing this my mother burst into tears. 'My daughter deceived me! My daughter deceived me!' she kept saying. Those who heard this probably did not know that I had told no-one of the real purpose of the supposed parachute work in Moscow.

From the airport the government officials accompanied us to Red Square where a huge crowd had gathered. Six Soviet cosmonauts flanked Khrushchev on the podium of the Mausoleum as the crowds passed by. Everywhere I looked I saw a sea of flowers and banners.

Two days later, in the Palace of Congresses in the Kremlin I attended the opening of the 1963 World Congress of Women. It was my first opportunity to address an important meeting of women and it was here that I made my first appeal for international understanding based on the fact that, seen from space, Earth is so small, so fragile, and in danger. My message was that we must protect Earth for future generations, and that I hoped *Vostok 6* would be a bridge to unite the hearts of women in the world to achieve this aim.

*A.L.   Do you think a woman's reaction to the fra-
gility of our planet and the beauty of space is
more sensitive than that of a man?*

V.T.   Certainly a woman does react to the beauty of space but no more than the men who have been in space even for long periods and who agree that the beauty continues to be striking. But in space there are other impressions shared equally by both men and women. I still remember how the powerful space capsule was docile in my hands. When the spaceship works well, there is a feeling of co-operation. If something goes wrong then there is a sense of competition, a need for quick reactions to control the capsule and get the sophisticated equipment to obey. Fortunately there were no emergencies in my flight. It was an exciting moment for me when I realized that I was actually, at long last, travelling so fast that in *Vostok 6* I could circle the Earth in only 89 minutes.

*A.L.   In space is there really no difference in perform-
ance when comparing women with men?*

V.T.   It was nothing to do with being a woman that some tests were difficult and complicated. I was young; this was my dream so I did not care about the discomforts. I had fitted into 5 cubic metres in the spaceship, mostly taken up with the equipment, seat and spacesuit. Difficulties did not hinder me. Everything worked well. This is the same for women as for men.

A.L.   This again is a genderless problem: did you get enough sleep?

V.T.   There was very little time to rest. The space work programme allowed six hours' sleep per day. Once I did sleep a little longer and I missed a call from Mission Control. This only happened once and when I replied to the call I admitted to having been asleep. A male colleague on a similar mission was more crafty and gave an excuse for oversleeping by saying he was working and missed the call, but they had seen him from Earth and laughed, asking, 'Which planet did you see in your sleep?'

A.L.   When I talked to your colleague Tatyana Kuznetsova she answered some of the questions I have asked you. She said the same thing about the equality in preparation for space for the men and women cosmonauts. I asked her if she felt confident or frightened at not knowing what was in store. This was her reply.

'We felt confident. It was a very exciting opportunity.

'We had seen the competition for space flights advertised in air clubs for skilled pilots and parachute jumpers, and we all hoped to take part.

'Candidates were interviewed by the Deputy Commander-in-Chief of the Air Force. There was a medical check-up in a Moscow hospital. Three of us first met at this time, and then gathered together later at the Cosmonaut Training Centre. I was 20 years old and a Komsomol secretary at the Institute of Scientific Research.

'We met in the Cosmonaut Training Centre. I arrived on a Monday. Irina from

Sverdlovsk, who had graduated from the same Polytechnic Institute, the other Valentina, and Zhanna arrived later. My first impression of Valentina, who was ahead of us, was that of a good communicator. I saw the "leader" in her.

'The tests were physically very demanding — the thermal chamber, the centrifuge vestibular tests, rotation and rocking. But they were identical for women and men. There were constant medical checks with a cardiogram, and taking pulse-rate, in the last stages of selection.

'When the physical exercises and tests became even more difficult doctors told us that women performed better in some tests than men, particularly centrifuge.

'There were continuous parachute jumps in spacesuits on land and water. We trained at sea for the first generation of space vehicles — that is why women were preferred who had parachute experience.

'We felt no fear except to fail. During the period of preparations no-one knew which of us would be chosen. This reaction was the same for women and men. I left the programme in the last stages because of illness.

'We all knew Korolev thought a woman could become a cosmonaut if she had the same physical and mental capabilities as a man, and the courage. The basic criteria were mental and physical fitness, knowledge of the spacecraft, and retaining all necessary information.'

V.T.   Tatyana's words are true. I too have to say that it was not easy for the first group of women to share in the difficulties of preparation for the flight and endure all the tests. Our female group had first of all to prove that we were experts, that we were not candidates for experiments or propaganda. We had to have the same knowledge of space technique as men, the same discipline by which to control planes, the same skill in parachute jumping. We had to prove that we were top professionals who could carry out scientific tests, experts who possessed the same skill in cosmonautics as our male colleagues. That was the challenge. On the other hand there was much to support us. First, we women supported each other and this solidarity helped us. Then we were encouraged by cosmonauts such as Yuri Gagarin and famous pilots like Nikolai Kamanin, and many other specialists who were training us for the space flight. Their attitude towards us was fair and helpful. For instance, if we needed extra training they were ready to spare the time and energy in the evenings, in the library, or for other training facilities like the simulators. Not once did any of the men say they would not find time to help us. They were happy in assisting us, and did more than was required by the flight's preparation programme. One of the finest aspects and traditions of the Cosmonaut Training Centre is that ever since it started in 1959 it has gathered together the top professionals, ground specialists and space pilots to work there. These people devote their heart and soul to what they are doing. It creates an outstanding team spirit.

Also there was a fraternal feeling in that we had been preparing for the flight in complete isolation from the ordinary earthly life of our country because the work was top secret. We were not allowed to communicate with our families or our friends. Each day was dedicated to the needs of preparation and training. We were under the strict control of those who trained us. This made us feel close to each other.

If we have to weigh up respective contributions, it is difficult to distinguish between men and women. Even my space vehicle was assembled by men and women together.

I must repeat that I never sensed antagonism between men and women during our preparation. The situation in the Cosmonaut Training Centre at that time put us in a privileged position. None of the women were qualified pilots while the men were already professional, licensed pilots. So we had to become pilots, and in order to master this profession, the men taught us how to do it. On the other hand we were all experienced parachute jumpers, and many of the men were not, so we taught them and shared this skill with the men. We taught them the best ways to jump and advised on the best or worst conditions.

A.L.   *It was said that women were only included for propaganda objectives.*

V.T.   There were many lies. I cannot understand the reasons for spreading fabrications. A typical lie was that a woman was only put on board the spaceship and launched as an experiment, like a robot without special scientific responsibilities, only to a see what a woman's reaction would be. That can be proved to be a lie. Preparation for the space flight took nearly two years' training. We started at the end of 1961 and were only ready in 1963. We were not spared any section of training. We were not given an easier time just because we were women. It was real sex equality, founded on the rigid expectation that work in space conditions was the same for men and women alike.

Another lie was about the physical effect on women on board a space vehicle. It was said that I did not feel well. I cannot understand why people denigrate and distort achievements in this way. I could not have completed my programme if I had been ill.

The third lie was that a woman's space flight was Soviet propaganda. Of course at that time there was rivalry between the USA and USSR in space exploration. We realised this was the case, it was never concealed, but my flight was not designed for propaganda purposes. It is not necessary to dedicate two years of preparation just to achieve a propaganda flight; that would have been achieved by including a woman as part of a space crew. My flight was a solo flight. I was alone on board the spaceship to pilot and carry out scientific research. It needed professional knowledge equal to that of a man.

A.L.   Were there lies about you personally?

V.T.   The lies repeated the same inaccuracy that a woman sent into space was only for propaganda purposes, and it was even said that I didn't go to space at all, but that it was 'all done by mirrors'. Also there was the lie that I nearly died during the flight and came back very ill. But you know me well, you know what my health is like now, sitting in front of you. You know my family and daughter. I especially suffered from these lies on account of my mother. Perhaps the lies were not meant to denigrate me personally, they were against my country, but it was difficult to explain that to my mother. She had been waiting for me all the time since I left home in 1961. She was very worried about me and about what I was doing. She did not have any accurate information. So the lies worried her even more.

A.L.   Did the Chief Designer Korolev doubt a
woman's ability for the flight?

V.T.   Korolev helped Gagarin and myself in a special way, perhaps because we were the first man and first woman in space, and had been his first concern.

He was not only a great scientist, a good manager and organizer, but also a man of high expectations. He was hard on undisciplined people who were not professional. He admired people who were committed to their work and he himself did everything to develop cosmonautics and in an unprecedentedly short time. I will always be grateful to Sergei Korolev because of his special contribution to prepare women to fly in space.

A.L.   There must have been other difficulties which
the group of female cosmonauts experienced. It
can't all have happened according to plan. Did
you all get on well together?

V.T.   Sometimes negative attitudes were expressed but not only within the women's group. It takes all sorts to make the world. Good people will always find good words, those who are envious or jealous will always find something ugly to say. That is true of both men and women.

A.L.   *Were there psychological ill effects following the*
       first man and the first woman space flights?

V.T.   There is a preliminary test of psychological strength as soon as a cosmonaut lands, and then from the first minute of his reappearance on Earth, he or she is placed under strict medical control and subjected to extensive medical check-ups.

A.L.   *Were there any alterations to your menstrual*
       cycle?

V.T.   Physicians checked on this aspect. I had been launched into space in the middle of my cycle, when menstrual bleeding would not start. After the landing this aspect of a woman's physiology came under medical observations. More recently again for Helen Sharman's flight there were no contra-indications for women cosmonauts.

A.L.   *Was your daughter Alyona's birth normal?*
       She was the first, and is still the only child of
       two cosmonauts.

V.T.   I gave birth to Alyona in an absolutely normal way, although it was by Caesarean section. She was born at seven months and I believe that was because I had been travelling and working exceptionally hard. But then my mother also gave birth at seven months, and not long before me she had premature twins and they died. So I might have been following my mother's genetic line. When Alyona was born she was normal in every way. She developed well and she is still very healthy. You know her and you know it is true. But I do now regret my exhaustion

244

before she was born. It was due to my endless trips abroad, my studies in the Zhukovsky Engineering Academy and the fact that my mother was paralysed at the time and couldn't help me. I had to do my own housekeeping and housework alone.

A.L.   *We know that your time in space was extended. Was this because you were exceptionally strong? Were you also exceptionally strong psychologically? It must have been a demanding challenge. Was the spacecraft properly prepared for the extra days?*

V.T.   Space vehicles have to be ready for emergency situations and the first space capsules had a reserve life-support system to last for up to 10 days. That was routine procedure.

Psychologically I was ready too, because I had Korolev's permission to stay longer in space if it proved possible. When we were training for the space flight we were taught to be ready for emergency situations, and I had an agreement with the State Commission and Korolev that I might be allowed to stay on. This permission was essential. Korolev knew I was fit physically and psychologically; it was nothing to do with being a woman when I was given permission to extend the flight from one to three days.

A.L.   *After your flight, when you first met the American astronauts, did you feel the same man-woman equality?*

V.T.   Our first meeting was in 1963, and it had a very special meaning for me. Cosmonauts and astronauts have met many times since and I can't put in words the feeling of having known each other for many, many years. It is like an inner certainty of brotherhood and sisterhood. We had seen the planet from space and this meant thinking differently. The first Planetary Congress of the Association of Space Explorers was held in Paris in 1985 and again we all felt like one family.

245

A.L. *You are smiling now.*

V.T.   That is because I am describing my profession – that of a cosmonaut and astronaut – and it is the best in the world. I genuinely suffer when, for many reasons, I have less opportunity to give to my profession the time and energy it deserves. I wish I had the possibility to give my entire life to this profession. Not to have enough time is my pain.

A.L. *How did you feel when you saw the American*
Space Shuttle Challenger *explode in the air*
in 1986?

V.T.   It was awful that it happened with relatives and friends watching. I cannot put what I felt into words. We Russian cosmonauts sent messages of condolence. The road to space is not decorated with flowers. I lived that tragedy. The death of the American astronauts was a terrible loss for cosmonautics and the world.

For relatives, friends, colleagues, parents and children to witness the death of the ones they loved was an unbearable drama. I watched the tragedy on TV and lived through the horror together with the people throughout the world who were watching. I have heard a very beautiful song by John Denver, an American singer and songwriter, dedicated to American and Soviet astronauts and cosmonauts, who have lost their lives. It is a song written with a lot of moral pain saying that they were young and beautiful and handsome and gave their lives to us ordinary earthly people. They didn't die but went away to the Infinity, Eternity.

A.L. *Which colleagues of yours died for space?*

V.T.   We suffered the great loss of cosmonaut Pavel Belyaev but my own deepest tragedy was the death of Yuri Gagarin in 1968. Four cosmonauts were killed in space: Volkov,

Dobrovolsky and Patsayev in 1971, and Komarov in 1967, who was killed when he was testing the new *Soyuz* space vehicle.

A.L.   *So whether in success or failure men and women are equal as space explorers?*

V.T.   Yes, and it was true of the first female group in the space programme. We were five women: two Valentinas, Irina, Tatyana and Zhanna. The main criterion at the final stage of preparation for the nomination of the captain of the spaceship was, first of all, to have full knowledge of space vehicles and the skill with which to pilot these. That was the evaluation of preparedness for the space flight. Obviously medical factors were important, that goes without saying. But in the final event the need was for knowledge of all applied disciplines so as to accomplish the major scientific programme, the space flight. It is not enough for a cosmonaut to be only a pilot or an engineer. The cosmonaut must also be a navigator, an astronomer, a physicist, a scientific researcher, to have the necessary control to programme the flight. That is the same for a man or a woman as a space explorer.

For me, a cosmonaut can be compared to the person who carries the last stone to the top of a pyramid built by a huge number of people. What are the criteria to enable this? How does that stone get to the top? One needs special skills, so that the stone is put in correctly. One must not stumble. One must have physical endurance to go through physical difficulties, and a sense of responsibility. Everybody will be looking at that person, watching carefully all his or her steps to the top. The pyramid is considered finished only after the last stone is properly put into place.

That might be an imaginary comparison but in reality the process is exactly like that. The space flight itself is the result of work and toil by many people but the final result, the overall success, depends on the skills and knowledge of the cosmonaut, man or woman.

A.L.   *As the first and only woman to fly a space vehicle solo, your story so calmly told for the first time will make a much-needed contribution not only to historic scientific records, but also to the balance of equality which should unite men and women.*

Valentina's father, Vladimir Tereshkov

Valentina with her mother in Yaroslavl, summer 1963

Valentina's mother, Elena Tereshkova

Valentina's grandparents' house in Maslennikovo, near Yaroslavl

Class group, Yaroslavl 1950. Valentina third row, third from right

Airclub near Yaroslavi, August 1959.
Valentina before her 22nd parachute jump

Valentina in the uniform of junior
lieutenant, her first military rank, 1962

The four women trainee cosmonauts, 1962. Left to right: Tatyana Kuznetsova, Irina
Solovyova, Valentina and Valentina Ponomaryova

Valentina with Yuri Gagarin, the first man in space, in 1962

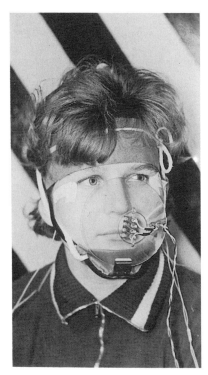

Valentina undergoes a medical test
during the training programme, 1962

Yuri Gagarin with Sergei Korolev,
the Chief Designer

'Cosmic food' in the training capsule, 1963

Valentina at the Space
Training Centre, 1962

The morning of 16th June 1963. Valentina is helped into her spacesuit by specialists

Baikonur cosmodrome, Kazakhstan. Final farewell before Valentina enters Vostok 6

19th June 1963, just after landing in the Altai region. Valentina waits for the rescue plane

20th June 1963, after the space flight Valentina leaves for medical tests in Kuibishev

22nd June 1963, Moscow. Valentina and Nikita Khrushchev and Valery Bikovsky, pilot of Vostok 5, on the podium of the Mausoleum, Red Square

Valentina attends the World Congress of Women in the Kremlin, Moscow, June 1963. Nina Khrushchev far right

The Fourth Conversation

Valentina Speaks

on

*Meeting World Leaders as a
World Heroine*

A.L. *Your achievement was more than just a demonstration that Soviet technology had the skill to
move humanity beyond Earth into space. It
was a signal to all nations that they could do
the same if they wanted to. Gagarin as the first
man, and you as the first woman in space,
attracted world-wide interest and admiration.
You met not only Russia's leaders, but the
world's leaders. Who impressed you most and
why?*

V.T. In Asia my strongest impression was of Prime Minister
Pandit Nehru, whom I met for the first time when he invited
me to visit India in 1963. I met Indira Gandhi there for the first
time also in 1963. She became a friend, very dear to my heart.
In 1973 I received her invitation as a Prime Minister to visit
India. I also met Indira when she came to the Soviet Union. I
admired her as a politician, a very wise, beautiful and strong-

249

spirited woman and also as a loving mother and grandmother. I had the opportunity to see her warm relationship with her son Rajiv, his wife Sonia and their children. I have many Indian friends, and I particularly love the very wise Aruna Assaf Ali. In Africa one of my most interesting meetings was with President Kwame Nkroumah in 1964 when he invited me to bring an official delegation to Ghana. He gave me the highest decoration in Ghana and asked a lot of questions about the space flight.

In Sweden I met King Karl Gustav in 1965. He appeared to me to be very discerning about world affairs. He was an expert archaeologist and we had a long discussion on how the mysteries and treasures of the Earth can be discovered through archaeology.

I vividly remember meeting your Queen Elizabeth, in 1964. Am I allowed to mention this? It was amusing as well as interesting. I was pregnant with Alyona and the Queen was pregnant too. Newspapers published articles speculating on the discussions we must have had, the two of us, about babies. As it happened we did not speak about babies but about cosmonautics, the preparation for space flights, and about women's participation in the space programme.

In Latin America I met Fidel Castro in Cuba and I value my good relations with this exceptional man. Castro invited me there for the first time in 1963 and I returned there in 1973 and 1982. I also met Castro several times in Moscow. I met Allende when he invited me to Chile in 1972. I fell in love with that country after I met the Chilean people and travelled widely there. From the United States President John Kennedy sent me a warm message of congratulation after my space flight.

A very memorable meeting for me was with General de Gaulle. In 1967 de Gaulle came to the USSR and there was a reception in the French Embassy. Yuri Gagarin and I were both invited. De Gaulle was a very interesting man to Russians – a colourful, patriotic and brave person, but also a great thinker. When Yuri and I were introduced to him as the first man and woman in space, he looked at me from his great height, turned me round, inspected all sides of me and said, 'Is that all? I thought you would be a huge woman.' He addressed me as Colonel Tereshkova.

I first met Olaf Palme, the then Swedish Prime Minister, in Mexico in 1975 during the United Nations Conference for the International Women's Year. His personal dedication to peace and justice impressed me greatly. In 1985 I met him in Sweden when he addressed the Constituent Conference of Women Parliamentarians for World Peace. Mme Maj Britt-Theorin, the Swedish parliamentarian, asked me to be the initiator of this organisation, which united women parliamentarians from all continents to work for peace. Olaf Palme was heartfelt in supporting this initiative.

When I went to the Philippines, heading our parliamentary delegation, I met Corazon Aquino. She is a very sincere and brave woman. Our delegation had interesting discussions with her on world problems and co-operation between our countries. Our delegation included the prominent politician Nursultan Nazarbayev, now president of Kazakhstan. I know him well. He is clever, sensible and intelligent. I wish him every success. Kazakhstan has been the 'Earth Harbour' for our space vehicles, with our space moorage in the Baikonur cosmodrome. It is the one from which manned space capsules have taken off. I was launched from there for my own space flight.

Yes, indeed, I have had the privilege and opportunity to meet many foreign leaders and prominent people when I went abroad. I was invited to Egypt by Anwar Sadat, who decorated me with the highest Egyptian honour, the Nile Necklace. I also met the King of Jordan, Hussein. He seemed to be very concerned for the plight of refugees.

A.L.   Did you meet Golda Meir or other Israeli leaders?

V.T.   I have not yet been to Israel, but when our countries had no diplomatic relations our organization was the only one which sent Soviet delegations to Israel, which welcomed our artistic groups. During the 1970s, when diplomatic relations between the Soviet Union and China were complicated, the Soviet Friendship Societies maintained cultural relations. I have been to China, which I first visited in 1990. It is an astounding country, and I have had many meetings with Chinese leaders and people. I admire this ancient civilization and the history and culture of its great people. In the city of Xiang I saw the archaeological excavations of a complete ancient city.

I have been to Japan several times, the first in 1965, and my last visit was in 1991. I have met almost every leader of nearly all the political parties, in government and parliament. Japanese people are industrious and talented. They know how to learn from the experience of other people. They have obtained remarkable results in electronics, technology and machine building.

A.L.   *You have often told me that you would never claim to know someone you had only met on official occasions, but was there something special you really respected in these leaders? You told me that Margaret Thatcher impressed you as a political leader.*

V.T.   I admire Margaret Thatcher and I believe she is an outstanding political figure. Leaders should have professional knowledge and not only popular appeal. A political leader should be wise and patriotic.

Recently I met the former President of the United States, Jimmy Carter, when he and his wife came to Moscow. We established good relations between the Friendship Societies of my country and the Friendship Force of the USA, of which he is the President. He sent a message to the non-governmental CSCE conference in Moscow on human rights in 1991. I was involved in this conference and I believe that we share many human rights ideals. I had several interesting meetings with the former UN Secretary-General Javier Perez de Cuellar. He brought an invaluable personal contribution to the success of the UN decade for women, 1975 – 1985. I was involved in these unprecedented UN activities as head of the Soviet governmental delegations at the Mexico, Copenhagen and Nairobi conferences. One of the positive results of these activities was the convention which ended many forms of discrimination against women.

I also respect the UN Secretary-General, Boutros Ghali, who was chairman of the Soviet-Egyptian Friendship Society and did much to establish co-operation between our two countries, finding time in his busy life to do so, and I admire the tireless efforts by the Norwegian Prime Minister Gro Harlem Brundtland defending the causes of global peace and sustainable development.

A.L.   Have you met Boris Yeltsin?

V.T.   Yes, several times. I first met him in 1984, when he was party leader of the Sverdlovsk region. I admire his purposefulness. I cannot say that I know him well. The several meetings I have had with him do not allow me to say that. But when I spoke to him about the work of the Friendship Societies and described what we have done and hope to do now, he was listening. I explained that our plans and work could be of use to Russia and the countries of the Commonwealth of Independent States in strengthening contacts with other nations. I could see that he was interested and afterwards he put questions to me. Then he said he found our organization important in helping to establish Russian international contacts, cultural co-operation, business co-operation and people-to-people diplomacy. He said that he would support the activities undertaken by the Friendship Societies and that he would consider inquiries into budgets for our activities. He knows that without Government support we cannot carry on the work of our Russian cultural centres abroad. The fact that despite his strenuous schedule he could find time to receive me, to listen to me, to give me his opinion, made me respect him as a leader. He is very hard-working.

A.L.   Was Yeltsin more attentive to your aims than Gorbachev?

V.T.   I never had any personal meetings with Gorbachev, so I can't say whether he was interested in our work or not. I asked to be received on several occasions but he didn't have time. Once, when at my request he received an important delegation of 400 representatives of the France-USSR Friendship Society, he said that he appreciated the friendship movement was important for our country.

A.L.   You have said your country is in a difficult situation. What will help the transition?

V.T.   The greatness of the Russian people, their wisdom, their unbending spirit. The history of my people has proved that they can rise from the ashes like a phoenix, overcoming all difficulties and becoming stronger and stronger. Do not forget that our country has everything it needs for recovery and prosperity: mineral resources, the genius of its scientists and the skill of its workers. There are leaders who are experienced and knowledgeable and who understand the Russian people's aspirations and potential. They will succeed.

A.L.   Historical evidence now proves that Khrushchev was the first Soviet Communist leader to try and restore some of Lenin's original ideals for Communism, which had been dangerously distorted by Stalin. Your flight happened just before he resigned. Did he die in disgrace? Did you regret this? How do you remember him?

V.T.   Yes, he died in disgrace in 1971. I value his support of the development of cosmonautics. That was his favourite child. In any case I would not want to speak badly about people who are dead. I believe that either one speaks well about the dead or

254

one doesn't speak at all. They cannot defend themselves. He had a wonderful wife, Nina Petrovna, a very Russian woman. She did many useful things on behalf of equal rights for women even before my involvement with the Soviet Women's Committee. She never refused anyone who asked her for help. She had a warm soul, a kind face, great tact, and she was a very intelligent woman. She knew how to help her husband and yet to remain in the background. She left with me the impression of a very reliable person, sincere in helping women.

A.L.   Have you known any other Soviet leaders personally? Brezhnev, Andropov?

V.T.   What do you mean by knowing personally? Khrushchev met us cosmonauts after the space flight, in Moscow. Brezhnev, being at that time president of the Supreme Soviet, gave us our decorations. Khrushchev spoke to me in space and I met him after the flight. But I have no right to say I know someone personally if I only met them on official occasions. I have never known politicians well.

A.L.   But when you were in Italy what did you think of the man from Poland, the Pope?

V.T.   I met the Pope in 1987 when I was invited to visit Italy by the Italy-USSR Society for Cultural Relations to celebrate the 70th anniversary of the October Revolution. I found him a man of goodwill. He was very kind, when he received me in the Vatican. I was interested to meet him. He showed genuine interest in scientific space research and he asked me questions about space.

A.L.   It is very interesting to hear of your meetings with famous men and women − particularly those in Russia. For too long in the West there was not enough known about Russian leaders.

V.T.   There are many outstanding Russians – artists, dancers, painters, singers, and brilliant engineers. But I do not only admire Russians. For instance I deeply respect Helen Sharman, the first British cosmonaut. She is a marvellous person and an expert in her field. She works very hard and she has stamina and courage. She is a good representative not only for Britain's women, but for all women.

A.L.   *Your impressions of world travel after the flight and meeting world leaders are as true and uncomplicated as I expected them to be. But there is another question I have not felt able to ask you until now that we can speak openly to each other.*

You have never told me of your personal impressions of the Western way of life. I have told you of my chronicle of discovery when I travelled from West to East and I met a Russia I never imagined existed because I had been cut off from it by a Black Wall of misinformation, ignorance and suspicion on both sides. Since then I have found it easy to record my impressions, even if I was the wife of a British government minister, because I was basically independent of official regulations. But I accepted that for you it was different. Your situation was parallel to that of Neil Armstrong, the first man on the moon, when he was serving at NASA as a member of his nation's space service and therefore unable to answer questions or give opinions without official permission.

So I have waited until now, when we can speak openly, to ask you about your journey from East to West. For a start, when you left the USSR were you suspicious? Did you find reasons to be critical?

V.T.   When I first left my country to travel abroad I was not suspicious. I was interested in meeting the other people and other cultures of which I had heard and read. From my space capsule I had seen all the continents and I looked forward to sharing my unique impression of the beauty and fragility of Earth with people living on our planet. As a cosmonaut one does not see any frontiers, only the planet as a whole.

So I would say that I was curious, not suspicious. You were right when you said that a wall of misinformation divided West and East. I wanted to travel beyond it and see the truth for myself. I never thought of the West as just another political system. I looked forward to knowing more about the centre of very rich and interesting cultures. As I have already said, my family loved music by Verdi and Beethoven, novels by Walter Scott and Victor Hugo, paintings by Raphael and sculptures by Rodin. I would say that I was preparing myself to meet the treasures of Western civilisation in all its glory.

Certainly, if unemployment and the alienation of individuals results from capitalism and the market economy, then I am critical. But I have never believed that Communist ideological differences with the capitalist system should separate East from West. One can always find positive aspects in every political and social structure, as well as dark sides. The positive factor between peoples and nations is that when we meet other social systems we enrich each other's experience. I have so often been happy to find similarities between Russian culture and the culture of other people. In Russia we cry and laugh, seeing films by Chaplin, exactly as people do all over the world.

So I did not travel throughout the world to judge other people unfavourably. I hoped to make new friends. But I admit I was always happy to come home again.

After the space flight I saw my future as giving me the opportunity to bring people closer together, and to help different cultures and civilizations to see one world, as I had seen it. For me the Western way of life you have described is part of Western culture, with its age-long traditions. The history of Western democracy includes great revolutions, major reforms

257

and cruel wars, but now we can all hope it moves forward to benefit humanity.

We are destined to exist together on our planet and I have appreciated many different Western achievements including Western-type democracy. But I have to conclude that I have not yet seen an ideal country with a faultless democratic system of justice and freedom. On our planet this does not exist so far.

Home to the Volga, 1963

Civic reception in Yaroslavl, 1963. 'A sea of flowers'. Valentina's mother sits on her right

Valentina with the president of the National Academy of Sciences, Mstislav Keldish, watched by Valery Bikovsky, Yuri Gagarin and other cosmonauts, 1963

Valentina with Yuri Gagarin in New York, 1963

Valentina with Fidel Castro and Wilma Espin, Havana, 1963

Valentina with Che Guevara, 1963

Valentina with the Indian Prime Minister, Jawaharlal Nehru and his daughter, Indira Gandhi, 1963

Yugoslavia, 1973. Valentina with President Tito

Left: Moscow, 1973. Valentina with Bussi de Allende, wife of the President of Chile

Below: Star City, 1975. Valentina with Soviet pilots including Ivan Kodzhedub, three times Hero of the Soviet Union

New York, June 1982. Valentina at the United Nations headquarters with the Secretary-General, Perez de Cuellar

Star City, 1985. Valentina with the Indian Prime Minister, Indira Gandhi and her son Rajiv Gandhi

Right: Washington, 1987. Valentina with the
American astronaut Mary Cleave

Below: Valentina with the American
Congressman Jesse Jackson, 1988

Valentina with the
American astronaut,
Congressman John Glenn,
1989

Valentina attends the Congress of Peoples' Deputies in the
Kremlin, Moscow with fellow deputy, Metropolitan
Pitirim, 1989

Baikonur cosmodrome, April 1991. Valentina with the French cosmonaut Patrick Baudry
on the 30th anniversary of Yuri Gagarin's space flight

The Fifth Conversation

Valentina Speaks
on
Personal Life, Interests and Friends

A.L.   *I need to ask you about yourself, so I suppose the first question must be: 'When were you born?' Some women do not give direct answers.*

V.T.   I was born on March 6th 1937. It is not correct to hide one's age.

A.L.   *A fine American author, Tom Wolfe, in his book* The Right Stuff *describes the experiences of the first American astronauts and asks this question: 'What makes a man willing to sit on top of an enormous Roman Candle and wait for someone to light the fuse?' Significantly, he writes 'man' even though a woman had accomplished her space flight at the time he was writing. Perhaps a woman in space strikes people as being different; particularly the first woman, the pioneer.*

> *Even now, thirty years after your achievement, when there have been many women space explorers, people still ask whether it is more difficult for a woman. What sort of woman can manage it? What does a woman cosmonaut do about her health, her hair, her clothes?*

V.T.   I have told you that cosmonauts in training prepare in the same way as men. We are equals and are assessed according to the standard of our work. Cosmonaut training requires the same from a woman as from a man. We work in the same conditions and are assessed on equal terms. Space is not gallant to women.

> A.L.   *I understand that equality does not favour women, but can you give me some personal details about how you manage always to look the way you do? There is no luxury, it is very simple – but it adds up to the Valentina who helps all women to be proud of being women, someone they know is capable of heroic achievements but also looks just as they would like to look.*
>
> *We would also like to know more about your personal interests, family and friends. But you never give interviews. You have been described as the Greta Garbo of space.*

V.T.   Garbo was a very beautiful woman and a wonderful actor. I am one of the admirers of her talent, but it is ridiculous to compare me to her. I am a straightforward aviation engineer. My expertise is in cosmonautics and I work professionally as a scientist. I also work voluntarily to achieve international cultural exchanges, women's rights and disarmament.

Yes, I have always avoided publicity in my personal life. There are so many details which cannot be important to those who do not know me; they are private details which should not become the property of people who are curious about me but not interested in wider problems. I am against personality cults, giving praise to one person when the achievement has been the result of teamwork. Also, more often than not, publicity exaggerates what is untrue while not reporting what is true. The modern tendency is to denigrate useful work and magnify sensational deeds. Nearly all my work has been with a team. When there is an achievement, many have contributed to it.

A.L.   Can you describe an average day in your life?

V.T.   If you insist I will try to tell you, but I warn you that it is an ordinary day of an ordinary woman.

Usually I wake up quickly when the alarm clock rings at 6.15 a.m. I feel it is important to develop self-discipline. For breakfast I usually have porridge, brown or white toast and jam, or sometimes cereals and scrambled eggs. I usually shop at the store in Star City close to my flat and often friends from my village bring me fresh cottage cheese, milk, honey and vegetables. Then I drive to my office for a long working day, returning late in the evening.

A.L.   What about housework?

V.T.   I must admit that I do not like cooking although I can cook most things. I find there is very little time for housework, but I can manage what is needed. Unlike my mother I do not knit or sew. I prefer to mend machinery. Sometimes, when I am in the mood, I like baking beautiful, aromatic bread. My grandmother showed me how. I like to share this bread with my friends drinking strong, hot tea or milk.

A.L.   How do you find time to bake bread?

V.T.   Not often. My working day is long and in the evenings I have to study official or scientific documents to prepare for the next day. Bedtime can be 2.00 a.m.

261

A.L.   *What strengths and weaknesses would you describe in your character if you were writing about yourself? You could start by saying that you are never boring. But if you were not yourself is there anyone else you would like to be: a man or woman from the past, or who is living today?*

V.T.   It is difficult to speak about oneself. I hope to be self-critical. I have a complicated character. When I love something I feel emotional but I always intend to stay calm in my reactions. I like helping people. I do not see this as work. From my office I can provide sick children with medicines, and help the elderly to receive their pensions. I get much pleasure from this. I never regret the time spent on these duties, or on helping people to find the work they need. I see kindness as most important for our modern times and it is often missing. I am delighted when I get letters from all over the world thanking me for the help given through my work.

Do you need to know any more personal details? I am satisfied with being myself. I am happy as a cosmonaut. If I was not a cosmonaut I would want to be an aviation engineer, as this is my greatest interest. After the space flight I worked hard to get a degree in engineering and could be happy working in an engineering factory. If you want me to answer more poetically I would like to be a spring, a spring of water, crystal clear, so that tired people who drink of this water would have strength again. Of course, my passion is the sky – the great ocean.

Truly I do not want to be anyone but myself and I try to make the best out of what I have in me.

I cannot think of just one man who was a star for me. I revere the great Russian designer and scientist, Konstantin Tsiolkovsky. He was the father of space travel and founded modern cosmonautics. He was a schoolmaster in a small village school and he was deaf. He was born in 1857 and he died in 1935, so he did not see his dream come true when *Sputnik I*, the world's first satellite, was successfully launched into space by the Soviet Union in 1957.

Or I think of our great Russian poet Alexander Pushkin, or Field Marshal Kutuzov, who defeated Napoleon. Then there are the great musicians. I cannot imagine my life without music.

A.L.   *During his flight Gagarin sang to Mission Control and he heard them play a popular song, 'Moscow Nights'. You also sang during your flight; can you remember the words?*

V.T.   They were something like this:

> I see the black Heaven close to me.
> Beneath me the Earth is full of poppies.
> You are awaiting me Earth
> I am flying, flying, flying.
> My Earth until you call me back.

Through song people can express their emotions. After my family, friends and work, music is my great love. It is my sound, as old as the world. I often listen to Chaliapin's interpretations. I think that he is not only the outstanding singer of our time, but also so genuinely Russian. He conveyed the love for his people and his country through his art. But I am not a chauvinist, I am inspired by both Russian and Western classical music. I am fond of Beethoven, his 14th 'Moonlight' Sonata, the 8th Sonata, 'Pathétique', and the 23rd, 'Appassionata'. However I must not pretend that I know more than I do or that I like everything. Tchaikovsky for me is the most Russian composer, but I also love the Italian composers who have made an enormous contribution to the world's civilization and cultural development. The same is true of many Italian painters and sculptors. I have met Luciano Pavarotti, and I can say that he is the combination of all the best Italian qualities, a great maestro who loves his country and his people, and when he is interpreting Italian songs, he does so with his heart. When I listen to him singing I appreciate not only his outstanding professional qualities, but also his human personality. His art speaks to us of Italy and the Italian nation. He symbolizes all that is best in the Italian character. That is what Fyodor Chaliapin did for Russia. He gave people the happiness to share in being part of our culture.

I also love the great painters, for example the late 19th century realists, the Russian *peredvizhniki,* and Sviatoslav Roerich. I have met Roerich several times in India and Russia. I treasure his gift to me, a painting of the Himalayas, which reminds me of sunset seen from space.

A.L.   Icons explain Russian spirituality to me. The
Italians painted the girl next door. Icon paint-
ers painted prayer.

V.T.   Russian painting started with icons. How could I not love them? These are the 'alma mater' of Russian art. I believe that painters have always taken their inspiration for art from nature or from women. Whatever the nationality may be, Italian, Russian or British, painters seem to me to reflect an inside world, inspired by nature. I value my friendship with the Ethiopian painter Efevork, who paints women's beauty, especially of mothers. He also shows us the beauty of his country and of African culture.

A.L.   Were you ever disappointed because of some
talent you wanted to develop, but it was not
possible to do so?

V.T.   In school I was an ordinary pupil. I was interested in some subjects more than others, particularly literature and physics. At first I underestimated mathematics, but afterwards I developed a passion for it. Love for a special subject in school depends so much on the teacher's personality, on his or her methods of teaching and personal interest in the subject. In my school we had very good teachers of Russian literature and history and they influenced me enormously. Growing up in Yaroslavl, steeped in the atmosphere of ancient Russian history and culture but not too far from Moscow and Leningrad, also influenced my interests.

May I say a few words about Yaroslavl? At the beginning of the eleventh century Grand Prince Yaroslav the Wise gave an order for the building of a fine city. Since then my city has been called Yaroslavl, and its coat of arms represents a bear holding a pole-axe. Yaroslavl is built on the Volga river, and because of this it had rich trading ties with many European and Asian countries. At the beginning of the seventeenth century, in 1612, when Moscow was invaded by Poles and Lithuanians, for a short time Yaroslavl became the capital of Russia. It was in the neighbourhood of the city that Russia's liberators Minin and Pozharsky conducted their struggle to free Russia from foreign invaders. I like the very Russian architecture of my city, the red brick churches and houses, the multi-coloured tiles, the carved wooden frames of the windows. The first Russian theatre, founded by the actor Fyodor Volkov, was in Yaroslavl and the history of the city has been inseparable from the Russian educator Konstantin Ushinsky, the great nine-teenth-century poet Nikolai Nekrasov and the outstanding op-era singer Leonid Sobinov. I love my city.

A.L.   Obviously you found much to love in your youth, but there must also have been disap-pointments.

V.T.   When I started parachute jumping my longing was to go to Moscow to enter the Aviation Technological Institute. I was fond of everything connected with metal, and the technology of metal. My dream was to pilot a plane. The city of Yaroslavl didn't have an aviation institute, and if I was serious about realising my ambitions I had to go to Moscow to study. How-ever, at that time my mother was seriously ill and I couldn't leave her. My dream came true only after my space flight, when I entered the Zhukovsky Air Force Engineering Academy in 1964. I graduated in 1969. After that I began my postgraduate studies which I finished in 1976. Earlier in my youth I had felt frustrated not to have this knowledge; that is why I applied to this prestigious higher educational establishment immediately after my flight. I wanted to acquire a thorough knowledge of aviation engineering and space technology. I was happy when I obtained my doctorate and could continue to work in the Cosmonaut Training Centre as an instructor, but I had to wait for this.

A.L.   *Was it more difficult for women to obtain technical degrees under Stalin than under Khrushchev?*

V.T.   Conditions were similar whether under Stalin or Khrushchev. There were no limitations, it depended on one's own desire and capabilities. This applied to both men and women. In technical education there were many women, since access was open and there were no difficulties in women applying. It was Soviet state policy under Stalin, even before the war, to involve more women in this field of work. After the war, women technicians became essential to replace the losses in the male population. That is why we now have such a high percentage of women engineers.

A.L.   *How were you elected to the Central Committee of the Communist Party?*

V.T.   At the 24th Party Congress in 1971 I was surprised to see my name on the list of some three hundred candidates for the Central Party Committee. Election was by secret ballot. Nobody had spoken to me before about this. I was not the only woman on the list; there were more than twenty other women's names. I was elected unanimously. For me this presented a great responsibility; the challenge to bring truthful information on women's matters to the notice of those at decision-making level.

A.L.   *When you became a member of the Central Committee did you have to find clothes to fit in with official occasions? Did you receive special privileges to obtain clothes which ordinary shops did not sell?*

V.T.   Why do you think that I had to dress better after my election to the Central Committee? Is that not ridiculous? I did not receive such special privileges. Like the other cosmonauts I bought clothes in our shop in Star City and some were made by dressmakers and tailors we knew. As you know my clothes are always simple.

Sometimes for special occasions a few outfits were made for me by my friend Slava Zaitsev, the famous Soviet fashion designer and his colleague, Olga Kolesnikova. Also when I am abroad and happen to like a dress in a shop, I buy it, as you will remember after taking me shopping in Edinburgh.

I don't like hats, I never wear hats. I don't like to wear anything on my head: hats, shawls, or scarves.

A.L.   *Your hair always looks attractive – and particularly the dark grey colour.*

V.T.   The colour was given to me by my parents and then, with the years, nature chooses what is most appropriate. I don't dye my hair. Perhaps it would be better if I did but I would find it very difficult to find a colour I would think was the right one. Nature takes care of my hair colour.

A.L.   *What about make-up and beauty treatments? Have you been to the Black Sea health centres? It was said in the West that privileged Soviet women often indulged in beauty treatments at such places.*

V.T.   I am one of thousands of people who have the opportunity to take family holidays in Black Sea resorts. I go there for my holidays with my daughter and sometimes to Karelia or Lake Baikal. I like water-skiing and horse riding even if there is never enough time. I also swim in the Cosmonaut Training Centre and in the Volga river. That is my health treatment. I do not like beauty treatments. I am allergic to all cosmetics, so I do not use any.

A.L.   *You are a soldier.*

V.T.   I am happy as a soldier – every person has their own destiny.

A.L.   *Do you remember the physical pain of having a baby? Did you have an anaesthetic? In the West some women prefer to have their babies naturally, at home.*

V.T.   I had a Caesarian. There were medical reasons for having a Caesarian, but not to avoid pain. On natural birth we have the same trends among young women here. Some even give birth in water. It depends on individual cases. But I believe many mothers need careful medical supervision. This safeguards the mothers' health and results in a lower mortality rate in babies.

A.L.   *What I remember most about your personal life is your love for animals. It has made my timetable with you difficult. The needs of your dog come before punctuality. What makes you love dogs so much?*

V.T.   I am fond of all animals. They are so defenceless and need our protection and help. They pay us back in love: disinterested love. The fidelity of dogs and horses is unique.
  I especially appreciate the beauty of horses. My first horse was a gift from a farm. When he sees me he puts his head on my

shoulder, we cannot speak but I read everything in his beautiful eyes.

I always have my dog near me. When I get home from work, often tense and tired, I open the door with my head still full of worries, and I hear my dear pug coming to meet me. I take her into my arms and I am sane and safe again. I am very sorry for people who don't love animals. Animals are so generous in paying us back for our attachment to them with honest, disinterested tenderness and faithful love. They love us to the end. They will never betray us. Their love is unique. The horse is the highest form of beauty and loyalty. It is sad that I cannot have a horse in my flat on the seventh floor! So I gave my horse, Mavrik, to a children's sports school. When I go to see my dear Mavrik he is so happy. If we respond to the fidelity of animals this makes us purer, kinder, more generous people.

A.L.   Do you love babies?

V.T.   How can you put this question to me? It goes without saying, they need our love and care. How can one not love them? Children are our great hope. We want our children to succeed where we have failed.

*A.L.   I have seen your flat in Moscow and also your
flat in Star City. Which one do you think of
as home?*

V.T.   As you know, Alyona and I have always thought of Star City as home, in our flat which is in a modern building to accommodate cosmonauts. The Moscow flat is useful and comfortable and, as Star City is some 50 km from Moscow, I often have to stay in Moscow because it is more convenient.

*A.L.   Don't answer if you don't want to, but how
did you fall in love with Alyona's father,
Andrian Nikolayev?*

269

V.T.   It was quite simple. He had been working with me in the cosmonaut team, preparing for the space flight. He was a cosmonaut and I saw him as a brave man. Like many girls in the same situation, I fell in love with him. I do not find it easy to speak about that period of my life. It is too sensitive. Our marriage came to an end in 1977.

Now I am quite happy to have my daughter and my other close friends. I have no regrets. Everything in my life, good or bad, has been part of experience and I am happy that my daughter has grown up as a decent person and a qualified practising surgeon. This is my greatest happiness.

Real life breaks many illusions about love. Perhaps women are too romantic, too emotional? But if we were not, life would be pale and dull.

A.L.   *You are telling the story of many women whose*
       hopes are eventually found to be illusions. It is
       a problem.

V.T.   For some it is a tragedy.

A.L.   *What were your feelings for Yuri Gagarin?*
       You have described him with the same words as
       you described your father.

V.T.   Yuri, like my father, was very kind and very pure. He was an expert in his work. After my space flight he was my most reliable friend on earth, a beloved brother. We helped each other. When he was alive we were sure we understood everything about each other.

A.L.   *Was Gagarin's wife worried when other*
       women loved Gagarin?

V.T.   She is very sensible. She knew that Yuri was in charge of the cosmonaut team. Cosmonauts have to work closely together and he had to work with the five women. There was the same feeling of trust between the women themselves. But of course there are different kinds of love. My special relationship with Yuri was that of two people sharing one profession. That is a very special feeling. My feelings were 'pure love' as we say in Russia – like a sister's love. Even now his death tears my heart. In our lives we all need someone who can give us moral support, disinterested advice and assistance. When he was alive he knew that in any difficult moment he could come to me for help. He was sure that I would understand him in everything. And he understood me. My mother loved him and we had a warm relationship with his wife and family.

In Star City our families lived next door to each other. When the world worshipped him I tried to help his wife to share him with the world. That was not easy for her. Now she has two grandchildren. I wish Yuri could have seen them.

A.L.   Do you believe Gagarin's death in the March 1968 plane crash was a natural accident? There have been rumours that he had become too popular and that people in power preferred him to be out of the way.

V.T.   I am sure it was a plane crash. Gagarin was killed when his plane, a MIG–15, crashed on March 27th 1968. I was personally involved in searching for his aeroplane after the crash and we collected all that remained at the site of the accident. Yuri Gagarin and Vladimir Seryogin were buried in the Kremlin Wall. The funeral took place on March 30th. It was an overcast day, as if Nature itself was in mourning. All members of the Soviet government, all cosmonauts, space scientists, relatives and friends attended the ceremony.

Just after his flight in 1961 Gagarin wrote a book entitled *The Road to Space*. I believe that if he were alive he would have written another book, a more detailed one, with the title *The Way It Really Was*. He had been collecting information for it. Knowing him well, I think he would have written a very serious book, not only on the preparation and the space flight

271

itself, but also on the history of the Soviet cosmonauts. He would also have given an analysis of the problems and difficulties of the Soviet space programme which we had to overcome and are still working on. He would have written about the great people we worked with. We were very lucky to know and to work with men like Korolev; Kamanin, the famous hero of the 1934 Polar expedition and air rescue operation; and Keldish, the then President of the Soviet Academy of Sciences. Unfortunately not enough has yet been written about the life and work of these great men. Korolev and Keldish were scientists, Academicians, and the story of their achievements is inspiring. There is still much to learn from them.

I am concerned by the tendency to denigrate much of what happened in that period. The criticisms levelled at past Soviet history encourage people writing about cosmonauts also to try and cast a shadow on the founders of Soviet cosmonautics, on those who were the pioneers of a new epoch for all humanity. Korolev was one of those pioneers – possibly the greatest of all. He had a special fondness for Yuri and me, as the first man and the first woman in space, but he understood the whole special fraternity of cosmonauts who have lived through an experience that cannot yet be fully shared with Earth-dwellers. I felt this fraternity when I met the American astronauts for the first time. We belong to one special family of explorers in outer space, all with the same experiences of having seen planet Earth shining like a fragile jewel in the darkness, so easy to destroy.

A.L.   *There was a time when the Americans feared they would be bombed from space as a result of Korolev's designs. These put the Soviets a long way ahead in the superpowers' space race. The Americans feared the Chief Designer who seemed to them to be a mysterious and dangerous figure. But I read that he had been victimized by Stalin because the Soviet military were jealous of him and that he was sent to a prison camp before the war.*

V.T. Someone denounced him by letter as being anti-Stalinist. That was a frequent occurrence during the time of Stalin's terror. A lot of people tried to help him, not only his colleagues but also one of our famous women pilots Valentina Grizodubova.

A.L. *In the West it was reported that Stalin released him because he knew that the Germans were drawing ahead in rocket research. It is known that when he was free again Korolev was not bitter, he immediately returned to serving the Soviet space programme.*

V.T. I believe it was our scientists' insistence that obliged Stalin to release him. Korolev was a leading designer of space launch vehicles and our country certainly needed his talent, knowledge and experience. This was equally the case concerning the Soviet aeroplane designer Andrei Tupolev, also imprisoned by Stalin.

A.L. *In America during the cold war Korolev was seen as the evil genius who wanted to enable a cosmonaut like you to bomb the USA from space.*

V.T. This is a huge exaggeration. It is an awful thought. Korolev was faithful to his own people but when you ask me about his feelings towards Americans I am sure he was not their enemy. Our scientists were working for our motherland. Their activities were not known in the West. But why did the West think of them as devils? Was it because they were discovering new advances in science? Their work did allow our country to achieve parity in deterrents and also to lead in space discoveries; was this the cause of jealousy?

A.L. *It was fear, not jealousy.*

V.T.   If Korolev had had the opportunity to meet scientists from the West they would have appreciated his qualities. He was not only a great scientist, but a genuine human being interested in music and the joys of life; a man of goodwill with total absence of malice. Of course there was rivalry between the USA and the Soviet Union in the field of space research and exploration. We were the first to launch *Sputnik* and a man into space and Korolev was responsible for this progress and we all respected him. Yuri Gagarin and I used to call on him at his home and he was very proud to show us the roses he was cultivating. When Alyona was born I received a message from Korolev saying: 'My beloved seagull, you have become grown up. You now have your own little seagull,' and he sent me some roses he had grown himself.

I also remember meeting him just before he died. He came in December 1965 to Star City to chair a meeting to discuss the Moon Programme. We all felt emotional and everyone wanted to prove that his point of view was the right one and wanted the others to hear it. Korolev was observing us and smiling a special smile with the corners of his eyes. He had a rare capacity to analyse and be very clear in his deliberations. And we suddenly realised he had his own vision of the programme but that he had patiently heard our views. He wanted to know what cosmonauts were thinking and saying and he took notice of our advice. Only two weeks after his visit to us in Star City he died of cancer. It was a great shock to us. He could have done so much more. He was very wise and combined many talents. He was particularly able to put problems in the right perspective. He was a brilliant scientist who saw far ahead. I will always remember his attentive eyes. Some of his colleagues tried to find negative sides. He was very strict when people would not work. But he made demands on himself as well as making demands on others. His death was a great loss for world cosmonautics. I am sure he would have been happy to meet American astronauts.

A.L. *Another great scientist, Oppenheimer, saw his creation dropped on Hiroshima so as to defend the West, especially America, the nation which employed him. But after it happened he retired to spend the last years of his life trying to unite scientists to work for peace. Would Korolev have felt the same if his designs had killed many people to defend Russia?*

V.T. Korolev never worked to develop atomic weapons. He was Chief Designer of space vehicles. Sakharov was one of those who worked on the Russian atomic bomb, and he eventually felt like Oppenheimer. Developing atomic weapons was the result of fear and mistrust between the superpowers.

A.L. *A whole century has been spent with East and West opposing each other because of fear. This is an extraordinary time we are talking in. The terror which dominated half a century and could have destroyed the world has now left us.*

V.T. We could not live permanently in fear. Resolve for change appeared in different countries and in all peoples. Do you remember the strong anti-war movement which swept practically the whole world? I am sure that the changes which enabled fear to disappear were obtained by ordinary people, both men and women. Politicians followed after them.

A.L. *You are capable of an important contribution to life, in that you genuinely love your friends and you do everything to help them. Have you loved many friends?*

V.T. You know that since our first meeting you and I have become not only friends but close in our aim to try and prevent human suffering. The road we embarked on in 1984 was not strewn with roses. It was difficult to remain loyal to our own

275

nations and at the same time open to each other's point of view. But we understood and trusted each other and now our understanding continues to develop even more deeply for the sake of peace. It is good that we have told each other the truth about so many historic developments from our own experience. It has been a challenging task for the two of us. Most of all I have wanted to tell the truth about my profession as a cosmonaut and about my country and its people as well as about my own personal experiences now in these *Conversations*.

In the teeth of international storms and confrontations you and I trusted and understood each other, and almost became two parts of one person as friends sometimes do. We have proved that people from contrasting cultures can meet and exchange genuine beliefs. This should encourage people to do the same and work together for peace. Our friendship provides evidence that this is possible in practice. I am happy that now so many more Russians and people from other countries have opportunities to meet, to know each better and to make friendly family ties as you and I have done. This is wonderful.

A.L.   *For me our friendship has been valuable be-*
       yond words. But tell me about your other
       friends.

V.T.   I had another friend who was very dear to me. She contributed greatly to East – West understanding. Her name was Lydia Schmidt. She was a deputy in the Luxembourg Parliament and one of Willy Brandt's deputies in the Socialist Internationale.

Lydia was very attached to Western values, to Western culture and politics, but she was one of the first to start East – West dialogue. I remember how difficult this dialogue was during the seventies. Our conferences and meetings at that time reminded me sometimes of the dialogue of death. We would not hear or listen to the other side and we did not want to know. Each side wanted to blame the other. My first discussions with Lydia were strained. But, like you, she highly valued truth and justice. That united us. In 1986 she organized a seminar in Luxembourg to discuss the dangers and benefits that outer space could bring to humanity. It was a difficult period in East – West relations and I had been asked to deliver a lecture together with the first American woman astronaut, Sally Ride. Something prevented Sally from coming, so I addressed the parliamentarians, scientists and students on my own. I spent four hours answering questions. Two things struck me. Firstly, Lydia's anxiety that the audience would not be prejudiced, and would believe my words were genuine. I had the impression that she was answering the questions with me, so compassionate was her face. Secondly, I remember the faces of the young people; students from the colleges and lycées who wanted to understand what would be the real future for them in space – Star Wars or star peace? Lydia died from cancer. I did not know she was seriously ill, she was so active and interested in life. For me her memory will always be in my mind.

A.L.   *When I met you I saw you as a leader on a road that travelled forward towards peace. We are now leaving ten dramatic years of change behind us, and we are moving towards disarmament after coming very near to nuclear war. I hope that the new space perspective seen by cosmonauts will draw humanity onwards to share solutions which will save the planet for our children and grandchildren and that they will enjoy the new opportunities for progress and prosperity in space.*

The peoples of the West and East have been prevented from knowing that the best way to avoid war is to learn that on the other side of any Iron Curtain there are men and women with similar hopes and fears to their own. Now Russia and the West are co-operating for a safe future and you have made a substantial contribution to this progress.

V.T.   What you say is like a poem about peace for me. Humanity must follow this road. It can happen. In Russia we say, '*vmyestye*' which means 'together'.

Valentina with the sculptor Grigory Postnikov preparing her statue for the Avenue of Heroes, Moscow 1963

Kirghizia, 1979. Valentina riding an Akhaltekhin horse

Valentina with a two-day-old pony
watched by Yuri Gagarin's daughters
Lena and Galya, 1979

Addis Ababa, 1981. Valentina with the Ethiopian painter, Efevork

Moscow, 1986. Valentina with Samantha Smith, the young American girl who wrote to the Kremlin and was invited to Moscow. She died in a plane crash one year later

Valentina with the Russian actor Alexei Batalov

Valentina with her pug Peppi, 1981

Valentina and her daughter, Dr Alyona
Tereshkova, with a model of the space capsule
Vostok 6, Moscow, 1991

La Scala, Milan, 1992. Valentina
with Luciano Pavarotti

The Sixth Conversation

Valentina Speaks
on
Women and Work

A.L.   *I remember how nearly three thousand women from all over the world looked to you as their leader during the 1987 World Congress of Women in Moscow. Your work for women's rights in the Soviet Union is well known and you represent one of the twentieth century's major achievements by a woman. Which do you see as the most important hopes and hazards for women as wives, mothers, daughters and workers now and in the new century?*

V.T.   The World Congress of Women called together women delegates from every nation. From the Soviet side we hoped for an open forum where all could exchange hopes and fears. You were there and you told me we succeeded. Unfortunately I attended only the opening of the Congress because my mother was dying at that time.

I have dedicated the best years of my life to working to help women achieve their potential. Women produce one third of the material value of humanity. This is the result of their hands, brains and energy. Their contribution to science and technology is increasing. We should let this be known. The role of women in the anti-war movement was crucial. Women could and should be an important political force.

But I see many problems which need to be solved before women can contribute their immense capabilities to furthering human progress. First of all, how can women best combine both a professional career and running a home? This is an eternal question. A number of thinkers have analysed this problem. As I see it, women have to determine for themselves which is the commitment they choose to give most time for. Is it to sustain a family or to build a professional career? It is a woman's right to decide her own priority. Many modern women choose a third version for the way they wish to live; this is to combine work and home. But for this it is necessary that the husband and other family members understand, assist and share in this decision. Husbands and wives should always be equal partners. Husbands who help their wives do exist and a few do not resent being outshone by their wives, but this is still too rare.

I believe that women come to this world mainly to be a kind of bright star to give birth, and to protect all who need protection. But this is an ideal not always possible to practise, and it should be more widely recognised that the protection of a family environment, which is essential for human harmony and peace, is a noble calling equal to fulfilling professional skills. It should be rewarded.

A.L.   *You were Chairman of the Soviet Women's Committee from 1968 to 1987. Can you tell me more about the work of the Committee. What did it try to achieve?*

V.T.   The Committee's main aim was to focus the attention of the government leaders on women's problems as there were too many declarations on paper and too few concrete deeds. Officially it was being claimed that Soviet women were well provided for, but I was receiving thousands of letters complaining about the hardships being experienced by Soviet women, for example difficult working conditions, long hours, low wages, housing problems, insufficient childcare facilities. I persevered, trying to make these and other problems which prevented women from combining their professional careers with work at home more widely known. It was essential for the decision–makers firstly to admit that these problems existed, and then to provide solutions.

To give you the history of the Soviet Women's Committee: my colleagues in the period before me were outstanding women such as the famous pilot Valentina Grizodubova and my predecessor Nina Popova. The Committee started in 1941 when Russian women made this appeal to all who opposed Hitler's tyranny and the Nazi invasion:

> We address all women the world over, regardless of political convictions, religious belief or social status. Our victory and the fate of our children, our brothers and our husbands, depend on us. In the face of danger threatening all of us here we call upon your emotions and your intellect to defeat the Nazis and join in our fight. Our unity is our strength and it is our guarantee of victory for the sake of a peaceful future.

In response, support was declared by Great Britain, the United States, India, Australia and many other countries.

When the war ended the Committee was faced with the difficult tasks of post-war recovery. The USSR had lost millions of men who left widows and orphans. Whole cities and villages had been devastated and industries destroyed when the Russian people halted Hitler's advance to Moscow and achieved victory for the sake of peace in the future.

I was proud to become Chairman of the Women's Committee so as to further develop its aims of progress for the welfare of women and families, not only in the USSR but also world-wide. I believe that through international contacts we did encourage women's solidarity all over the world and we also made known the wish of the world's women for peace.

When I was elected a member of the Central Committee in 1971 I did my best to bring women's problems to the notice of the Politburo whose responsibility was to formulate policy. The Women's Committee participated in drafting the constitution of 1977. We were constantly drawing attention to the fact that women's issues must be positively considered in the Soviet Union. We emphasized: 'We have proclaimed women's rights but we have a lot to do to make this reality.'

In 1977 our Committee made two important amendments to the Constitution, the main law of the country. One amendment was to Article 35 on the equality of men and women. Another amendment to Article 53 dealt with compulsory state assistance for the family. I was also able to persuade the government to adopt some important decrees, particularly the introduction of allowances for women with large families and for divorced women whose former husbands would not pay alimony. We founded an organization to support such cases. We realised that it was necessary to provide financial support for families which found themselves in need after a divorce or when the father had deserted them. So we arranged for regular alimony payments to be made by the State and then deducted these from the father's wages following legal proceedings initiated by the State.

We insisted on improved conditions of health and safety in the workplace. We set up a special Deputies' Commission to suggest safeguards for working women. Maternity benefits were introduced. There was special protection at work which needed to be obtained for women miners. After the war, women had to take up men's work which was hard and heavy, and we believed that working in mines or metallurgical factories with furnaces was harmful to women's health and their role as mothers.

In addition to working for these reforms the Women's Committee initiated measures to promote international relations and enable contacts so that Soviet women could increase international understanding and solidarity. I realised that this was also happening in the West and I know that you were like-minded, trying to develop genuine international sisterhood in and from the United Kingdom. To advance this aim I initiated a national commission for the UN Women's Year of 1975. This was headed by Mazurov, the then Deputy Prime Minister and member of the Politburo. I wanted to make certain that the Women's Year was given the importance it deserved by the Politburo. I wanted the government to take notice and respond. I kept saying, 'We must act – words are not enough,' and, being a member of the Central Committee of the Communist Party, I succeeded in initiating several measures to achieve action by using whatever contacts I could find to reach the Politburo.

I also raised questions on cosmonauts' welfare and tried to get more money for Star City's needs, especially for the widows and children of deceased cosmonauts. This and other aspects of women's welfare came within my official activities. I knew that there were many more who needed help because I received a mountain of letters and many women came to see me. I tried to meet them personally, to know more about their real troubles and difficulties. When they told me of their suffering I tried, by becoming their mouthpiece, to make their problems known to the government. Of course I was disappointed when I realised that politicians often do not respond to such appeals. That is why in 1986 I and my colleagues called for a National Congress of Women. I wanted the government to realise that problems concerning women's needs were an urgent area for action. The World Congress you attended in 1987 was also my initiative. I hoped it would draw attention to the views and expectations of women from all over the world.

A.L.　*The UK delegation was very impressed by the conclusions reached on so many world-wide issues following well-informed discussions in the workshops.*

The Congress struck us as the best evidence of the Soviet wish for peace. We all felt like one family of women trying to identify what should be done to make life safer in the developed nations as well as in the Third World.

V.T. I agree with you. Sitting on the podium of the Congress I looked around the hall. It was the same as in 1963 when after my flight I attended the World Congress of Women. It was then my first Congress.

In 1987 I saw the same enthusiastic and interested women's faces – black, white and yellow. It made me think about the road women had travelled on together since 1963 – a difficult and long one. But in 1987 at the World Congress of Women we understood each other better. Women now know that they are an important force in the world, and the majority are determined to protect the world together. I was genuinely happy that, both as a cosmonaut and as a woman, I had personally contributed a small part to this achievement and that working for women was part of my life. The only shadow on my joy was that just after my flight in 1963 I had seen my mother's happy, smiling face in the hall, but in 1987 she was not able to attend, because her life was ending.

A.L. *Do you think your daughter's life as a doctor is easier than your mother's? Is it happier?*

V.T. Yes certainly. Times are different now. My mother worked in a factory and at home. I do not know if she would have been happier to fulfil her talents in a professional capacity. She was proud of my expertise and my daughter's training and pleased that we enjoyed our work, but she was a wife and mother first and foremost.

A.L. *At this meeting of the World Congress of Women in 1987 I noticed how women from completely different cultures saw in you a symbol of equality and achievement. No matter whether from sophisticated or more primitive cultures, the women delegates shared the same feeling of satisfaction that a woman had flown in space. All human beings look up at the sky, and your achievement does not have to be explained through different languages.*

V.T.   Women often speak the same human language. When there is a tragedy or a disaster we see the universal language of protection, the pitiful but inspiring pictures of women of all ages saving the weak, the babies, the children and the wounded, as best they can and usually with resignation and dignity, as well as pain. This is the aspect of a woman's capacity for love and work which does not need to be explained through words.

The Seventh Conversation

Valentina Speaks

on

The Modern Family

A.L.　*You have many sides to your character – I have heard you sing, seen you dance, make lonely people feel welcome, speak to formidable scientific audiences, control vast meetings of delegates from all over the world and address international politicians and leaders. But what strikes me most about you is that above all you are a mother. There is this basic element in you to care for and want to protect others, and it enables you not only to understand but also to be understood by people everywhere. You often say that without families there would be a breakdown in our civilisation. What do you mean by 'family'?*

V.T.　Families are the most important workable units with which to hold the world together. The first cell of every community is the family, and the quality of family life in communities determines the world structure. The family is the furnace within which future citizens are forged. The citizens who help the world will have learnt, as children, to choose between good and evil. The stronger the small family community, the stronger the large world community. This is the model for living together.

A.L. *I do not believe that at any age it is natural to be good. After my parents divorced I rebelled without knowing that what I was doing was wrong. I enjoyed challenging regulations and feeling free. In the end I only changed because I found that my independence separated me from the friends I wanted to be with and who lived orderly lives. They were less lonely than I was and I decided that this was because they were part of a family.*

V.T. To belong to a family is an instinct in all human hearts. My family was very close but also friendly towards other families. It was natural for us to help each other, we felt involved in each other's lives and not just onlookers.

When I was Chairman of the Soviet Women's Committee my mother, for the first time, met people from other nations, from Africa, Asia, Latin America. They came to my flat in Star City and I was amazed at her inspiration in finding exactly the right gifts for each one, just as she did for her own family. She loved setting the table as she did in our home, beautifully, and baking cakes, Russian *pirogi* (pies) and *bliny* (pancakes). She always seemed to know which souvenir would please each guest. Sometimes it was a very Russian shawl from the Pavlovo Possad factory, or painted wooden craft-work from the Khokloma factory, or Russian faience figures, or cups from Gzhel, or Fedoskino boxes. To give guests gifts was part of my official duty, but she helped me with her mother's imagination. She would say to me, 'You youngsters on the Committee don't understand or care enough. Human memory cannot keep in mind every detail of a conference or visit. But even small things taken home will remind your guests of the people they met in a foreign country. That memory will live longer through this souvenir, no matter how small it is.' I noticed how happy my guests felt in my mother's company. She created a family of people who cared about each other wherever they came from. She was not pretending, she was genuinely interested.

It took my mother many sacrifices, above all of time, to bring up our family. Her example helped me to realise that I must also give time from my professional life to bring up my daughter and eventually give her the opportunity to train as a surgeon. This time was taken away from my own studies but I knew then, as I do now, that parents must dedicate time to give care and tenderness for their children. Without this there can be no family community, only lonely people. The deeds done by fathers and mothers to protect their families influence many generations. For me it is also important to see in a family a close relationship between youngest and oldest.

Obviously our children do not agree with us in everything but we should accept this. If they follow us without questions they will be robots and we do want them to go farther than we have gone. We should not make the mistake of expecting too much. Often when, as parents, we are not satisfied with our children, it is because we want them to be happy where we have been unhappy, to succeed where we failed. While we are alive we want to protect them. But we should remember that when they live on after us they will have to face all that happens to them on their own. That is how I see the family; a community which cares for each other and teaches us how to respond to whatever happens.

At my first press conference after the space flight in 1963 there were many journalists present from around the world. It was a huge audience. I was trembling as I looked into the hall. From the questions I realised that most of them were curious to know something personal about my life. Then one journalist asked me who was the person on this planet who was dearest to me. Spontaneously, even before I could think about the reply, I said, 'My mother is the dearest person to me.' The audience broke into applause. My mother was watching the press conference on her television at home. When I returned I saw from her kind and lovely dark eyes that she had been weeping, and I realised that she had been moved by my reply and was pleased.

Later, I received a long letter from the Soviet poet Rasul Gamzatov. He wrote that it was so good to hear that the dearest person to Valentina was her mother and that it had inspired him to write poems dedicated to mothers and their contribution to the safety and joy of the world. He saw mothers as not only a vital component in a family but possibly the ones who matter most for family security. I will read his poem 'To My Mother' for you. It is very Russian in sentiment.

> As a boy I was unruly,
> Many a rebuke I earned.
> With adult-like firmness, coolly,
> All remonstrances I spurned.

> Rating my own powers highly,
> Never have I run from fate.
> Yet I now approach you shyly,
> Like a child, and hesitate.

> Now we are alone together
> My heart's anguish I'll confess,
> And a head that's grey and weathered
> Into your soft palm I'll press.

> I have been a rash, ungracious
> Prisoner of vanity!
> Not enough consideration,
> Mother, have you had from me!

> As I whirl in dizzy circles
> I can hear a deep heart's groan:

Can I really be forgetting
My old mother, left alone?

Anxiously, but without censure,
Mother mine, you glance at me,
Heave a sigh and let a gentle
Tear fall surreptitiously.

As a star on the horizon
To its final goal has sped,
In your palm your boy contritely
Lays his weary, greying head.

I believe that many people would respond in the same way. Certainly the stronger the family the stronger the nation. When we are growing up we are not influenced directly by the leaders of our country. People usually live their own lives based on family traditions, even if they are outwardly obliged to live according to official legislation.

In our country there were not enough laws which protected the individual and the family but I found this to be the case in other countries as well as the Soviet Union. Is there any country in the world which gives complete protection to individuals?

In my childhood I was blessed by a loving family atmosphere which is the moral asset of every nation. Despite all difficulties my relatives instilled in us the best traditions of Russian culture, art and history. They taught us to appreciate such treasures and to make them part of our lives. I still try to work for this ideal and I believe much strength can be built in this way by families all over the world. Of course it is not enough for children to learn their parents' traditions. They must also learn to respect and to value the traditions of other peoples and nations, and to appreciate as many of the world's cultural treasures as possible.

A.L. *In the West we were told that Soviet children were taken from their families to be taught in institutions how to become soldiers of the State.*

V.T.   I feel sad that you think this happened in my country. Are you thinking of the pre-school nurseries for women who had full-time jobs or studies, so that they were able to fulfil these? A nursery helped me. My child attended a kindergarten when I was studying for my degree. I could not have worked in the Academy if my daughter had not been looked after. It gave pre-school help for mothers but this did not involve political propaganda. If child care is organized which ensures that children are well looked after, it gives women the chance to work. But children should never become the responsibility of the State.

Perhaps you are thinking of the Soviet system when school children belonged to the Pioneers from 9 – 14 and then, if they wished to join, they belonged to the *Komsomol* from 14 – 28? These were strict systems for education and training but the result was good.

At school I did read poems about Stalin and I learnt Soviet slogans, but I lived as I wanted to and most of all I enjoyed our school projects. All children should be provided with varied and interesting concepts to motivate them. As a student, I found that my most passionate interest was for parachute jumping, one of the projects which was available to me.

A.L.   *What helps family life to survive? Neither the philosophies of Communism nor of capitalist materialism have properly protected family life.*

V.T.   The Russian family pattern has always been three generations together. It is still a strong tradition unchanged by politicians. I see that as a good way to learn how to live. A child's education needs to be balanced by the experience of living with different ages and personalities and above all by the example of a mother and father, where the experience of one should balance the other. This balance does not happen if children are deprived of male vision, which is what happens if a marriage no longer exists and there is only one parent, usually the mother. When I was a child we looked to my mother's cousin Anatoly for the support which could be given by a man. We called him Uncle Anatoly.

A.L.   In our modern world so many marriages fail. What ingredients do you see as being most essential for a marriage to succeed?

V.T.   Love first. But different kinds of love: sex love, esteem love, sharing love. There must also be respect, infinite patience, and a willingness to work together to carry responsibilities and overcome difficulties. Tragedies should be shared.

The saddest element is when youngsters are unhappy. That is a blood-wound in a family. We must try to find out why. Is it because youth does not find challenging work to enjoy? Are they bored? We should provide them with ideals to overcome difficulties and teach them 'strength under pressure'. I am happy that the family ideal has always prevailed in Russia, and is stronger than any political philosophy. To value our family does not mean not taking pride in our homeland. Patriotism is important for every country. I admire how, from an early age, young Americans are taught to be proud of the USA. I think that, even with different ideological education, the overall aim should be to learn to love one's homeland first and then the homelands of other people, with deep respect for all people.

You say that one of the biggest problems now is establishing discipline so as to diminish violence, and that in Britain some parents pay for the discipline which is provided in private schools. But why should parents pay? In Russia parents are also worried that there is not enough discipline in schools. I am very concerned about the same problem in homes where parents are absent. Perhaps youth associations should be totally reorganized. Youth needs to be fully occupied.

A.L.   The young Communists we met in Moscow before the end of the Soviet Union were modest, well-informed and self-controlled. We admired them and the training they had

*benefited from. In Britain we have the Girl
Guides, the Boy Scouts and the Boys' Bri-
gade. These youth organizations are popular
with young people. But I fear that in the new
century, children will be deprived of their right
to security. Everywhere freedom is preached as
a right — but what sort of freedom? If young
people are bored by aimless freedom they prefer
the excitement of violence, and the solidarity of
belonging to a gang. With violence escalating
what will happen in Britain and in Russia in
the future? Where will order which is acceptable to youth come from?*

V.T.   I have met some of your youth workers. I know that the
Guides and Scouts are voluntary organizations and youngsters
join without feeling obliged to. I believe that the young will
look for order and find it, because many are very sensible and
know that anarchy brings suffering. But we cannot expect them
to live as we did. We treat young people as if they were our age
and have the experience to solve problems. We should be
providing what they need here and now, the opportunities
which they are too young to organize for themselves.

You have told me that the Duke of Edinburgh's Scheme is
popular in Britain and involves youngsters of all ages in exciting
tests, challenges and training. Perhaps we can organize something similar in Russia to motivate our young people? In my
country the Voluntary Association for Co-operation with the
Soviet Army, Air Force and Navy (DOSAAF) has achieved
something on the same line, particularly developing interest in
technical sports. I started my parachute jumping in one of these
clubs. It was an exciting challenge to get the chance of piloting
a plane and to skydive.

A.L.   *Young people certainly want home comforts.
Even the most rebellious enjoy being cooked for
at home and having their shirts washed.*

293

V.T.   A good family makes young people come home. A responsible mother is a harbour. This is very important work. If women are worried about the problems of youth they must be harbours at home. You have said to me that I am an example to one-parent families. If we decide the family is essential we must make sacrifices. I tried to be responsible. I always went on vacation with my child to give this time to her. Another important advantage in my own youth was the union of young people for and among themselves. But I had an argument with a teacher at school and so I did not join the Communist youth organisation.

My mother did not criticize, she knew that even if we were not all members of *Komsomol* we were all together working and training and sharing projects. My brother did not become a member of the *Komsomol*. But as I say there were other important components for a sound education which helped us children to become adults.

A.L.   *Is the mother the most important member of the*
family?

V.T.   I cannot say that. For me the combination of three generations in the same family – children, parents and grandparents – is the ideal. Small children love being with an old person. I still remember my grandmothers reading to their grandchildren. Children are enriched by growing up with a grandmother who has time for them. My grandmother Matryona taught me riding and swimming. My grandmother Sophia helped me to love nature, flowers and animals.

A.L.   *What is the right role for men? Women's roles*
have been discussed throughout this century.
But what about men?

V.T.   In our family Uncle Anatoly gave male support, but we did not often see him. For me the eternal male example will always be my father. As a father the man's role in the family is crucial as I think the educational process is unbalanced without a man's influence. The child's knowledge is taken from the reflection of the position of both parents in the world, and their attitudes. There is now the theory that there are no longer male and female roles, no more men and women – persons instead – but I think that this is impossible. Men and women are different. Children should learn from the marriage of their mother and father even when that is a hard lesson.

It is never easy to be married. It is difficult to live with a person who cannot be like oneself. But once the marriage decision is made the ideal should be to show children unselfishness. Every family needs to hold together through unselfishness and be determined to try and live together, even if this involves combining and accepting different attitudes.

A.L. *Should a husband and wife live as if in a space capsule, so that even if you don't like each other you have to remain inside? 'Heroic fidelity'?*

V.T. That is not always possible in a marriage, but children should be protected. Children who grow up having suffered in childhood often become a sad burden on society. That is why women who are harbours at home are so important.

Unselfishness also means changing our attitude to old people. We have to take care of our parents. If we don't care about them children will learn a sad experience from us. Children copy adult behaviour. I hope that when my daughter saw how I cared about her grandmother she learnt from this. She knew I was sad when I saw examples of indifference to old people. A friend told me recently that her children are not attentive to her. I remembered that she, in her turn, was not attentive to her old relatives. As I have already said, the three generations living together in one family is ideal. If there are no old people at home, children cannot learn from their life experience which is a great loss.

I believe that now, as we approach the new century, a concerted international research programme should be undertaken to work out the problems facing families, to identify them, and find solutions. I do not think the need for a family will disappear; because as you say, children want their shirts washed and their meals at home.

A.L.   *But what about the crisis of anger which ex-*
         plodes in adolescent rebellion? What can
         parents do?

V.T. This is a complex problem for modern society – a wound you want to cure but you cannot treat. What are the reasons? First of all adolescent rebellion seems to be a problem in difficult families, but then children from apparently secure families can also become violent and take drugs. We need to do fundamental research into the reasons for rebellion and deliquency. In this century women's problems have received attention and have been studied. But we do not yet know enough about why so many children are unhappy. We should draw public attention to the need for research into such an important subject.

Of course our generation has given a bad example on drugs. It has been the fashion that we could not live without alcohol, cigarettes and tranquillisers. It is urgent for us now to show youth that we ourselves can be happy without chemical help and that the message, 'instant happiness' is not a truthful answer. At the same time it is not enough for children to hear this from parents. We need experts, doctors, psychiatrists and educationalists to find ways to stop this self-destruction of human personalities. Youngsters must learn how to have strength under pressure. They should realise that 'be happy quick' often means 'die quick'.

A.L.   *So much money is made out of 'be happy*
         quick' advertisements.

V.T. But the anti-smoking campaign in the West is working. I believe people understand that it is important not to be deceived by money-makers and that they need to fight for what is true. This is how the public now look on the lies told in cigarette advertising. We need to educate people, especially children, to realise that advertising can sometimes deceive. They should be warned about this hidden danger.

A.L.   *Television can be an effective teacher as well as being a harmful influence.*

V.T.   I would like television to teach the arts, and to inspire love of beauty and moral strength to judge between good and bad. We have to admit that there is a force which works against the human wish for peace. People are attracted to pictures of violence – human beings enjoy loving but they also enjoy fighting. These are the two opposing forces which either help or harm. It is the beginning of a process we now face in Russia from the many violent films being brought in from the West, which children are excited to see. It is my great concern. These films don't teach children to choose wisely. Certainly, we have to show the bad and the good, but not to make violence seem exciting. Unfortunately this is a common problem for the whole world.

A.L.   *I am optimistic because young people today seem to be much less racist than when I was a child. Now all over the world they wear the same jeans and sing the same songs, and this unites them. The problem is that youth believes what it sees on television and the messages from television which unite youth are often created by materialistic sponsors, to sell their products.*

V.T.   I will always maintain that the most important need is for better programmes of education, including television programmes. This is the challenge we should be concerned with. All over the world we should be discussing what to teach our children. I am very anxious about this. For example I want children to be taught about the danger of the propaganda of hatred.

That is why if you ask me to speak seriously about problems for youth I must first call in question the quality of educational programmes in our schools. Fortunately there are already meetings and discussions between teachers, educational experts, writers and artists. To my mind, their efforts should be combined, first to work out problems together and then to provide new, internationally-approved textbooks for the generations of the twenty-first century. We also need to analyse the textbooks our children are being taught from now. We need to teach them to live in peace, to understand each other, to protect our planet. We need to teach children that our world is interconnected and that we are one family.

The Eighth Conversation

Valentina Speaks

on

Science and the Future

A.L. *What progress do you see for science in the future? You have recently returned from the Congress of Space Explorers which brought together cosmonauts and astronauts from all over the world. Your contribution was on the Russian programme for the exploration of Mars.*

Will a man landing on Mars ever become reality?

V.T. It is possible. If we combine our efforts then we can be there by the beginning of the next century. But before human beings can travel to Mars, our neighbouring planet and the one which most resembles the Earth, we must send automatic space vehicles, so that we can be sure that all equipment is working and that the life-support systems will guarantee the safety of the crew. Then we can send men to Mars.

This was one of the subjects we discussed at the Congress of Space Explorers this August in Washington, which brought together scientists, cosmonauts and astronauts. We exchanged information on what has been realized over the previous year, the scientific research and studies which were accomplished, and the practical steps made. We also discussed which future space programmes should be adopted. I spoke about the Russian programme for Mars exploration.

A.L.   *Will the children of the new century live on Mars? Would you encourage this hope?*

V.T.   There is a song in Russian about the dreamers who say that one day apple trees will blossom on Mars. It is not a dream. I want to encourage children to have faith in the future. The fullest experience for humanity is not only the experience which can be acquired on Earth; it needs to include the exploration and study of other planets in the universe. Among the planets of the solar system, Mars has always attracted attention; it and Venus are the two planets closest to the Earth. The formation of its surface and climate is very interesting. In the past it is possible that there were rivers and seas. I think Mars is the only planet in the solar system where there is a hope of finding life, and it is a planet on which the landing of astronauts is quite possible.

A.L.   *Can you explain more about the Mars Programme with which you are involved?*

V.T.   If you want me to, then I will have to give a long and accurate account.

The size and mass of Mars stand between those of Moon and Earth, and is the most important link in helping us understand the sequence of evolution which makes small bodies like the Moon different from larger ones like the Earth. Mars is the manuscript for the early history of our planet and to read this manuscript we cannot use only familiar earthly language. Mars is the key to understanding the past and future of the Earth. And a no less important reason for the exploration of Mars is the question of the existence of extra-terrestrial life in the Universe. Academician Vladimir Vernadsky considers life to be not an exclusive earthly phenomenon but a space phenomenon. In search of the traces of extra-terrestrial life, the biological researchers of earthly forms have considered earthly life a unique phenomenon. But if we find the manifestation of life or biological formations in other parts of the universe, this would allow us to consider life as a logical step in the evolution of organic matter, and not as a result of random circumstance.

The first stage of the Russian long-term programme of Mars research involves plans to carry out project *Mars 94*. The aim is to launch a space probe that will eventually become a satellite of Mars. This space probe will drop penetrators and small automatic stations on the surface of Mars, while the probe itself, which will contain a large complex of scientific research apparatus, will remain in orbit about the Red Planet. Its total mass will be about 250 kg. This satellite will photograph the surface of the planet for geological research, and it will search for a landing site for future expeditions. We need to determine how deep the Martian permafrost layer is, for Mars is currently in deep-freeze; to determine the chemical and mineral content of land in different areas; to monitor the movement of dust and dust-storms. Temperature maps of the Mars surface will also be necessary as well as investigations into the chemical composition, the physical characteristics and dynamics of atmosphere; and measurements of the magnetic field of the planet and surrounding space.

The new element in this project will be the use of penetrators. A penetrator is in fact a small autonomous space research tool which is able to penetrate into the landmass to different depths, depending on the physical and mechanical qualities of the soil, and the speed at which the penetrator meets with the surface. This apparatus has opened new possibilities in Mars research. The use of penetrators will allow us to obtain the maximum statistical data. The penetrators will provide us with a panoramic picture of the surface in areas that are difficult to reach, and geophysical and meteorological research and studies which will provide knowledge of the chemical composition and physical qualities of the land. We also need to know more about the organic matter in selected places; to research the composition of the interior of the planet; to measure the dynamics of the magnetic field; and to study the composition of atmosphere.

The penetrator is a new space research tool and designing it requires numerous engineering tasks, and the finding of solutions for problems as they arise. For example, we have to build accurately on the smallest scales, and the design has to survive penetrating the frozen soil on Mars. It also must have a very dependable line of communication during its lifetime.

A notable volume of work is connected with tests on penetrators. All new forms of space apparatus are subjected to engineering tests such as shock impact, vibration, temperature, electric and other types of impact. Penetrators also have to be subjected to a series of tests imitating real conditions. For example, they are thrown from helicopters and from other flying objects; shot from guns into the ground; and we even shoot them at high speed from special stands into simulated Martian rock. This enables us to check the correctness of our design, and to calculate the projected depth of penetration into Mars.

The designing and making of the scientific apparatus for the penetrator is also a difficult task. The penetrator is about 45 kg in weight and it contains ten scientific instruments, including a TV camera to obtain panoramic colour pictures of the surface, and a gamma-ray spectrometer to study the chemical composition of the surface matter. Then there are X-ray spectrometers and alpha particle spectrometers to determine the chemical composition of the interior of the planet at the depth of penetration. There is also a magnetometer to determine the magnetic field and magnetic qualities, an instrument to study heat transfer, and a seismometer to check the seismic activity of Mars. In addition, we have an accelerometer to study the process of penetration itself and the impact which occurs during this process, and a gauge to measure the angle at which penetration occurs. Finally the total mass of all these gauges should not exceed 4 kg, and the power consumption should not be more than 10 watts, even if all are switched on at the same time.

A.L. *It is very impressive to be sitting with someone who is actually working on a space flight to Mars. As a child I thought man would never reach the Moon, let alone Mars. Now there are many rumours about what man will find on Mars. There is speculation that photographs have shown one object with the face of an Egyptian sphinx and another in the shape of a pyramid.*

V.T. There is no evidence to support such speculation. Evidence can only be obtained by research which provides facts. Scientists who study Mars believe that these are rocks lit from unusual angles by the Sun – in fact, rocks lit in this way on Earth often look artificial.

Mars is the second world outside Earth which can be studied intensely, second only to the Moon. Its size (the equatorial radius is 3394 km) and its geological make-up place Mars between Venus and the Moon. On the Moon we find two major types of surface: very old continents with large numbers of craters that are found mostly in the southern hemisphere, and the volcano-type landscape located mostly in the northern hemisphere. Gamma-ray spectroscopic measurements have demonstrated that the content of uranium and thorium in the soil of Martian continental regions is very close to the composition of continental rock on the Moon, the so-called anorthosite-norite-troctolite rocks. We know that Mars had water flowing over its surface in the past, and must still have substantial amounts locked away. It is possible that the water is situated very close to the surface of the planet in a frozen form. It is even possible that liquid water may exist under a layer of ice if it is warm enough below the surface.

There is evidence that on Mars we can expect large, even vast, areas of permafrost. For example, on the borders of certain valleys we can see cavities, and in other areas we can see characteristic 'chaotic' relief due to the caving-in of surface layers of soil under the action of water. We can see telltale fan-like formations on the outer slopes of craters that remind us of snow avalanches. If we were able to obtain direct evidence that water is present on Mars and also evidence of the forms in which water can exist there, coupled with a detailed knowledge of the composition of the atmosphere and the isotopes in it, we could learn some very important things. We would gain an understanding of Mars's climate, which would lead us to the related question of the existence of living matter on Mars, and possible forms of life.

The main scientific problems that we have to study in connection with Mars are: the development of its structure and geology; the evolution of its chemical composition and magnetic field; the evolution of its atmosphere and climate; the history that water had to play in Mars's evolution; and the detailed interior structure of the planet. Then we have to search for biological and palaeobiological activity. We can perform these scientific tasks only if we carry out research on a systematic basis with the help of different technical means, such as spacecraft that can land on the Mars surface, vehicles of a 'moon rover' type, penetrators, and equipment like air balloons. For a detailed study of Mars's soil, we will need to arrange for samples to be returned to Earth.

We are convinced that the first stage of further study should achieve most of these aims. The main task of the second stage is to deliver Martian soil to Earth. The study of samples in the laboratory will guarantee a precision that is not obtainable through remote sensing methods. Samples will be analysed for mineral, chemical and isotopic composition. Then there will be geochemical studies to determine the absolute age of the matter, and further tests to see if organic matter is present. When we get this information we will be in a position to judge the character of the processes on Mars, the conditions of geological processes in the past, the possibility of the existence of life on Mars at present and in the past, and also the evolution of its atmosphere and climate, and the role of water – all questions so far unclear about Mars. We may also obtain an answer to the questions on the so-called 'monuments of Mars' which you have asked me to verify.

Meanwhile it is obvious that the time-effectiveness, complexity and results of this long-term programme depend to a great degree on what kind of technical means we shall use to launch the Mars probes. If we use in this Martian programme not only our launcher *Proton* but also the latest development, our heavy-lift vehicle *Energiya*, this will allow us to shorten the time of exploration and broaden the perspectives for the execution of this immensely important programme of Mars research.

A.L.   Do you hope that the Mars project can be
         shared internationally?

V.T.   Scientists from different countries already participate in the process of exploring Mars. They are from Russia, Germany, Britain, Bulgaria, Finland, Rumania, and the United States. Work on the penetrator is not finished yet but the results achieved so far justify hope that this new method of space research will be achieved very soon. Then we will be on the way to Mars. Penetrators will be the first research weapons for the future investigation of the Mars surface. They will be followed by the small Mars-rovers that NASA and the European Space Agency are planning. This should happen by the end of this decade.

The programme of project *Mars 94* will include the launch of the probe in October 1994. After eleven months it will come close to Mars and become its satellite. When it is close enough, two penetrators will be put on the surface of Mars and also two small landers. The satellite will be in orbit for not less than a year, and will follow a path with a minimum distance from the planet of 300 km, and a maximum distance of 8,000 km. In the course of two years it is planned that it will obtain pictures of the equatorial area. This is a band of the surface from 13 degrees south to 85 degrees north of the equator. The small landers put on the surface of the planet will have TV cameras, temperature, pressure, and wind velocity detectors, plus seismometers and gamma-ray spectrometers.

If we look back at research on Mars we can trace several periods. The first attempts were made at the beginning of the sixties; for example, *Mars 1* in 1962 and *Mariner 4, 6,* and 7 in 1964. These craft sent back to Earth the first photos of a very limited area of the southern hemisphere and indicated many craters. These appeared to be like very heavily damaged lunar craters, and that created a pessimistic image of Mars as being a world like the Moon: dead both geologically and biologically. Therefore, to some degree, scientific interest in Mars waned. Earlier ideas of seasonal change, of vegetation, of 'canals' and of the existence of life on the planet, seemed highly unlikely.

However, at the beginning of the seventies, when the first satellites were put into orbit around Mars (*Mars 3* and *Mariner 9* in 1971; *Mars 4, 5, 6* and 7 in 1973), interest in Mars re-emerged. The results of this research by the satellites significantly changed our ideas about Mars. The TV monitoring of the surface led us to understand what the dark and light areas on the planet were in reality: regions of rock regularly covered and uncovered by seasonal windblown dust. We could see the icy polar caps which grew and shrank with the seasons; and we could study the atmosphere and morphology of the surface.

Mars research was further advanced by *Viking 1* and 2 in 1976. These were the first probes to land on Mars and analyse its soil directly. Meanwhile, two *Viking* orbiters continued to circle Mars, sending back panoramic pictures of its surface, and helping us understand the complex development of its mighty volcanoes and vast canyons.

The *Viking 1* and 2 landing craft attempted to answer questions about the emergence and evolution of living substances. These two miniature laboratories were equipped to search for life in the Martian soil. The negative results of these biological experiments significantly reduced the possibility of finding life on Mars. These experiments also demonstrated not only a lack of life but also the difficulty in knowing exactly what to look for.

The *Vikings* were the last spacecraft to be sent to Mars because the interest in the planet diminished. What were the reasons for this lack of interest? There were several. To begin with, it was necessary to study and understand the information accumulated during earlier stages of research. Another reason was that one of the most important problems for the study of Mars is the possibility that it may, even yet, have life. *Viking 1* and *2* had carried out a number of delicate biological experiments, but it became clear that we would need to design more advanced technology for biological analysis, and to study the Martian soil in detail it would be necessary to return a sample to Earth. Possibly there is a third reason: with limited resources, we must address other problems, especially those that have relevance to Earth. One of the problems is the composition of, and the greenhouse effect on, the planet Venus. This also calls for research.

A.L.   *Do you believe there are other living beings on other planets? For example, 'little green men' provide inspiration for popular science fiction. Do you think there is any real substance in such apparent fantasies?*

V.T.   I cannot deny that there may be the possibility of intelligent life on other celestial bodies. To answer your question, we need more research and joint space exploration. When research has been developed further, then humankind can begin to answer such suppositions.

Modern concepts of the emergence of life are based on carbon and water, with proteins and nucleic acids possessing unique qualities. However, other systems of evolution have to be considered, such as other types of amino acids, nucleotides, macroergic and pigment compositions with other types of cells and their components, also membrane structures with different conditions and forms of development, reproduction and metabolism.

It is quite possible that extra-terrestrial organisms could use the resources of the environment and interact among themselves and with their planet in many different ways. But this kind of knowledge can only be obtained if we look for life beyond Earth, both on the surface of and inside the other planets and their satellites. The problem of searching for life beyond our own planet depends on the sciences of astronomy, physics, chemistry and geology developing the capacity to understand how evolution might proceed in the wide range of different environments in the Universe.

*A.L.   You have made me ask myself whether in
         future planet Earth will be only one of many
         human homes.*

V.T.   Yes, we are now living more in the life of the Universe and not only of the Earth; we are beginning to realise that space could be more important than Earth. I can already regard different forms of life as possible in the Universe. If science fiction wants to describe this as 'little green men', let that be. I call it 'different forms of life'.

*A.L.   Could space exploration provide new sources of
         clean energy?*

V.T.   One of the global tasks of the future is the use of solar energy on a larger scale. Solar energy can be transformed into electricity, warmth and light. Every day the Earth receives some 64×10^{16} kilowatt/hours of energy. But so far we use only a minimal part of this energy. There have been discussions recently by experts planning to create solar energy stations in high orbits, capable of generating electroenergy and of reflecting sunlight to Earth through mirrors. Such stations could become the basis for an absolutely new source of energy, which could assist industrial technology and agrotechnology.

Science and the future

*A.L.   There now seem to be many opportunities for
cosmonauts to carry out work in space so as to
benefit terrestrial life in peace and not war. I
have read that the space station Mir contains a
new concept for living and working in space.
Not only is there a laboratory but there are
tables and chairs in the living room, food supplies sent by launch vehicle from Baikonur,
individual sleeping compartments, music and
video facilities and even an exercise bicycle.
The only failure so far has been that quails
hatched in space did not adjust to weightlessness and died, and for human beings there are
minor strictures such as sleeping bags attached
to the bunks to prevent floating. Not only
Soviet cosmonauts but representatives of Germany, Great Britain, France and Austria have
worked on board this space station successfully.*

*Are those able to invest money sufficiently
informed about benefits which can result from
this space progress? This could provide the
necessary financial motivation to support such
work.*

V.T.   Yes, as cosmonauts we can now work on ecological
safeguards and other benefits for humanity in different fields,
and this also includes protection for animals. Space monitoring
is very important. It could prevent ecological calamities like
typhoons. It could help to fight pollution of soil and water.
My country has tabled a UN proposal for space monitoring.
The United Nations could co-ordinate the efforts of scientists
and experts of different countries for this, and the sooner the
better.

You have often asked me how best to obtain clean energy.
We know that the economic development of different countries, new technologies and industrial development all require
huge power resources. The campaign for clean energy is

309

encouraging, but this is only a tiny part of what humanity needs now. We must insist on safety in the field of nuclear plants, because there is no other way to develop nuclear energy. We cannot now renounce the use of nuclear energy.

I would rather focus our research on resolving the three main problems of nuclear energy: safety, protection and ecology. We can do that if we combine our best brains and efforts.

A.L. *Is there a possibility of producing a medical*
      preparation through space research which could
      cure Aids?

V.T. We should work for this. But the amount of work which will be done depends on how much money we are able to spend. The money challenge is two-sided. We need funding for scientific research, and then, if such research is successful, the sponsors will obtain maximum returns. You are right; we need publicity skills to describe the benefits space research could bring to people. We must persuade people with money that they will receive returns by investing in space programmes. But I have never been involved in publicity. It is not in my nature or part of my profession.

What I do believe is that new materials and technology developed in space could bring medical advances and economic growth. All branches of research look for new materials, such as gallium arsenide, which is used in computer microchips.

A.L. *You have quoted the man you call the Father*
      of Space, Tsiolkovsky, as saying: 'There will
      be mountains of bread and endless might for
      people to find in space.' Can you give me
      specific instances?

V.T. The great Russian physicist Konstantin Tsiolkovsky developed the theory of rocket power at the beginning of the twentieth century. The inscription on his tombstone reads: 'Mankind will not remain tied to Earth for ever.' He produced designs for multistage liquid-fuelled rockets decades before such vehicles were eventually built.

He was certain that man's exploration of space logically followed the earlier developments of our civilization, such as the resolve of human beings to investigate the mysteries of nature. The next step was to look for new spheres of habitation. There have always been fairy-tales dreamt and told about the nature of other planets. Now it could become reality as a result of the development of science and technology.

Tsiolkovsky made an enormous contribution. He formulated laws of rocket motion for a body with variable mass, he worked out the effectiveness of launch vehicles and researched the force of air resistance on the launch vehicle's motion. Tsiolkovsky's research shaped the modern aspect of launch vehicle building and cosmonautics.

Reading Tsiolkovsky's works I am always surprised by the scale of his scientific thinking, and the boldness of his scientific hypotheses. He foretold and foresaw not only artificial satellites and flights to other planets, but the creation of space settlements, of industrial complexes in space, and of new scientific laboratories in orbit. But the most inspiring aspect of all his scientific activities was that he was guided by a sincere and deep concern for the future good of humanity. He believed that this could only be guaranteed if different nations and people shared in joint projects to develop the potential of space.

The perfection of scientific thinking for me is the basic equation of rocket motion – 'Tsiolkovsky's formula' which he worked out in 1897:

$$V = V_1 \ln \left(1 + \frac{M^2}{M^1}\right)$$

$$V = V_1 \ln \left(1 + \frac{M_2}{M_1}\right)\left(\frac{p-g}{p}\right)$$

$$M_2 = M_1 \left[\sqrt[1]{\frac{T_1 P}{T_2 (p-g)}} - 1\right]$$

Transcribed by M. Luckins

You have mentioned him as saying 'There will be mountains of bread and endless might for people to find in space.' Do you know that his main dream was to live for people, not for himself? He wrote: 'I was working on plans which did not bring me bread and might. But I hope that in the future my work will bring humanity mountains of bread and endless might.'

He meant that with the development of cosmonautics, high technology and new materials would come much-needed knowledge of environment and nature. This would lead humanity towards co-operation with nature to achieve essential harmony.

By informed co-operation with nature Tsiolkovsky hoped humanity could co-ordinate favourable conditions for agricultural activities, so that people could always have enough food. When he said 'bread' in a metaphorical sense, he meant everything man needs to live by: bread, clothes, shelter, food.

When he said 'endless might' he meant new technologies. New sources of energy, high production levels, overcoming disease, a clean environment. Above all he wanted the creation of harmony in relation to nature and nations. For him, survival on Earth depended on establishing the harmony of man with his environment.

A.L. *Another great thinker, Fritz Schumacher, in his book* Small is Beautiful *said that human harmony depends on small self-supporting communities. So did Gandhi.*

V.T. I would begin with families to establish a network of co-operation and harmony. Harmony was seen as the essential ecological, scientific and interntional balance which could ensure human and planetary progress. This was Tsiolkovsky's vision from the small provincial Russian town of Kaluga, a rural area in Central Russia. He was the great pioneer for human advance in space.

*A.L.   Are you pointing mankind to an ocean of
        opportunity in space for the future, which will
        bring progress and prosperity?*

V.T. Yes.

*A.L.   Would the vast scale of such research justify the
        expense?*

V.T. This question is often asked. I have been involved in
discussions in my country and in different countries of the
world with scientists and parliamentarians, journalists and cosmonauts. I would say that the economic aspects of
cosmonautics have not yet been studied properly. It is difficult
to measure the financial and material advantages of space technology and space research before these have been specifically
analysed in detail. The United Nations has suggested three
general categories by which to measure the advantages of space
technology. First: tangible but not producing immediate results. Second: tangible but requiring evaluation. Third: intangi-
ble but with quantifiable value in the field of education, medicine, improved quality of life and other benefits.

We should study these benefits. For example, many artificial
satellites are used for international communications. The logic
of scientific and technological progress is to make us appreciate
the necessity of developing new technological systems to serve
numerous countries, and whole geographical regions of our
planet. Communications satellites have already contributed to
the improvement of educational and cultural links, assisting the
socioeconomic development of emerging states in Africa, Asia
and Latin America. Improved navigation and meteorology
maximises the use of natural resources, especially for agrarian
development. These are important advantages.

Another benefit will come from new materials. These will
result from the fact that the movement of a space vehicle
cancels out the effect of gravity, making astronauts and their
equipment weightless, and such conditions can be used for

313

manufacturing new materials such as perfect crystals, which can be used in advanced electronics.

Weather satellites have also been useful operating either in geostationary orbit or in polar orbit. Such satellites can survey the entire planet every 24 hours. Earth-resources satellites can be used to identify new mineral resources and to check the spread of disease in crops. Satellites can also monitor pollution.

A.L. *Could another and more frightening aspect of research involve genetic engineering? Could we end up creating a new type of human species able to work and to live in space – space slaves?*

V.T. It depends on the goals the scientists set themselves. I think genetic engineering might be beneficial. I do not foresee the fearful developments you are suggesting. Now scientists can influence cells and manufacture new cells. I am not enthusiastic about this, but I am certain that we need progress in science. The important point is that this science should be developed with clean hands and with the genuine intention of benefiting humanity. Scholars working in this field must be honest people. I think it is wonderful when a scholar succeeds in some new research, bringing a revolution to technological development. But the question should always be: 'What do we seek as the ultimate goal of this discovery?' Every deed must be considered as a choice between help or harm, depending on its ultimate effect.

Sometimes responsible scientists are frightened by the results of what they have done being different from what they intended them to be; for instance Einstein.

So we come back to the subject we have been discussing so often since we first met. The choice between right or wrong – in other words the need for moral choices. Morality should always prevail if human activity seeks to help and not harm.

The same refers to money. It can be used for good and for bad.

314

A.L.   *Do you think that an outside intelligence*
        might exist which would want to conquer the
        Earth and that this could be a great danger for
        earth–dwellers?

V.T.   It seems to me that our world has always asked this sort
of question. Perhaps one reason is that people do not want to
be alone in the Universe; they do not want their planet to be
the only one to be inhabited and they do not want to think that
they are as nothing in a limitless ocean. These possibilities are
said to encourage 'space pessimism' which even questions the
value of human existence. To my mind the opportunities to be
found in space bring humanity an infinity of possibilities for
extension and not for reduction.

My space optimism is based on fundamental scientific data
and research, which confirm that truly great new developments
for human civilization in space are now attainable.

Human beings want to be happy and they want to be eternal.
The history of science and technology gives us evidence that
scientific and technological progress has no limits. But we have
agreed, you and I, that this progress will have no real value if
there are no spiritual and moral improvements in the quality of
human life. These will depend on using the moral compass inside
each one of us, the compass of spiritual belief, because even if
humanity is equipped with extensive technical knowledge, if we
have no spiritual belief inside us, we are earth-bound, hesitant,
feeble and helpless. That is why the human intellect has always
asked and will always ask: 'What is the purpose of our life?'
'What is the basis for moral choices?' 'What is right and wrong?'
'What are the results of historical evolution for humanity?'
'What is the place of human beings in the Universe?'

We need to seek answers to these questions from within our
own moral compass in the raging ocean of man's life on Earth
and in space.

A.L.   *I can foresee worldwide 'Marsmania' if and*
        when man lands on Mars. It would be a real

315

advance if, with it, there could also be a new Mars mentality inspiring human beings to transcend their earthly quarrels and find human unity on another planet.

Your considerations have had to be mainly technical and professional. Can you give a spiritual vision for science in the future?

V.T. This is how Tsiolkovsky dreamt of science and the future: 'Humanity has acquired a universal ocean which was granted to unite peoples in one whole – in one family.' I believe that need not be a dream. It could be reality.

Valentina delivers a speech at the United Nations conference on Disarmament, 1982

Valentina attends the United Nations conference for the UN Decade for Women, Nairobi, 1985

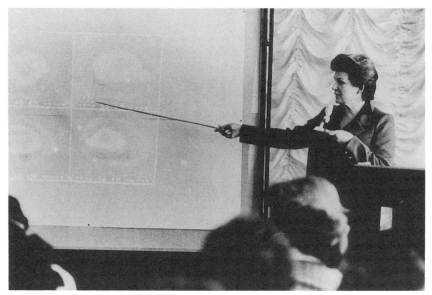

Valentina reports on the Halley's Comet project and the Soviet space programme,
Leningrad, 1986

Tbilisi, 1988. Valentina
addresses the
Soviet–American conference

Moscow, January 1990.
Valentina opens the
Helsinki Commission
conference on 'The Human
Dimension of the European
Process and the Role of the
Public'

Valentina at the United Nations speaking on the new international order, 1991

Berlin, 1991. The Association of Space Explorers at the 7th Planetary Congress. Valentina front row, fifth from right

Berlin, 1991. The Space Explorers Congress.
Valentina discusses the Mars programme

The Ninth Conversation

Valentina Speaks
on
The International Cultural Mission

A.L.   *In the last half of this century the two super-powers, the Soviet Union and the United States, seemed drawn towards atomic destruction in the name of self-defence. When you were awarded an honorary degree by Edinburgh University in November 1990 the Principal, Sir David Smith, described you as a person of incomparable courage who has not remained content to rest on her laurels but who has dedicated herself to building peace in East-West relations, which is bearing abundant fruit. He was referring to the joint work undertaken when you were Chairman of the Union of Soviet Friendship Societies which initiated the Edinburgh Conversations on Disarmament. Can you tell me more about your work for peace?*

317

V.T.   The aim of the Edinburgh Conversations was to build a bridge of understanding between Russian, British and American scientists and other international experts. This enabled responsible and influential groups to consider measures which would advance international co-operation for peace and progress in disarmament. The last meeting was in Volgograd in August 1991. The discussion was on 'Environmental Problems' to identify the global problems which threaten humanity.

A.L.   There have been many other international meetings which you have organized to promote co-operation. In 1990 you organized the Helsinki/CSCE conference in Moscow attended by the representatives of voluntary organizations from all over the world. Soviet dissidents spoke openly about their grievances. Do you believe such international meetings can inspire positive progress for disarmament?

V.T.   I organized the conference on the Helsinki process to achieve co-operation on human needs such as educational exchanges, human rights and disarmament because I knew that the Soviet people wished to travel on this road. For many years I have been personally involved in this process to bring people from all over the world together for peace.

I saw how, both from East and West, people realized that confrontation was not helping ordinary men and women. But the process of understanding had to develop on both national and international levels. Efforts had to be made by both sides. The process was understood to be urgent when it became clear that nuclear and ecological disasters could result from continued confrontation. Only people deprived of reason by God would seriously encourage nuclear war.

A.L.   Now we know how near the world was to World War III when in 1945 there might have been an invasion of Russia, and again in

1962 when there could have been a rocket attack on America. Obviously at the time of the first danger you were only a child. Were you aware of the later dangers? Living in the West at the time I knew nothing, probably because official reports deliberately provided misinformation in the so-called national interest.

V.T.   Unfortunately even now too much information is biased. You are right, we need an impartial history of the cold war period. It has to be written. A deep and objective analysis of critical situations is always important, both for the ordinary, middle-of-the-road citizen, and for politicians who are making decisions. To make a decision which will influence the life of millions, politicians should be well-informed on the historical reasons for the crisis and also understand the deep aspirations of the people involved in the conflict. Usually each side thinks it is defending the right cause. One of the purposes of objective analysis should be to clarify all the reasons which caused the injustice to happen. To my mind, desire for justice is one of the basic needs for every nation and every human being. To establish the truth there has to be negotiation which allows different points of view to be compared so that opponents can listen to the other side. But for human beings to be prepared to listen it is helpful if they have experienced mutual understanding and an increased enrichment through an awareness of different cultures. I have been working for this but it still seems to me that not nearly enough has been done to develop international cultural exchanges to bring people together. We have to do more. If we do not know each other we cannot begin to trust each other. This is the same for both international and human relations. It is a pity that politicians and statesmen do not yet seem to understand this.

For me human survival in the future depends on the development of international co-operation now. A main element is respect. For example, religious people need to respect

319

and appreciate each other's religions: Christians, Jews, Muslims, Buddhists. However idealistic it sounds, religious people should work together and tackle many problems that people suffer from today, such as hunger and disease. Humanity needs to unite to overcome dangerous problems such as those which involve the environment. If we can show tolerance and understanding towards each other because we know more about each other then this will build a future free from war.

A.L.   *The need to prevent a common catastrophe may still only be a cosmonaut's perspective. Have earth-dwellers really understood that they must unite to reduce the dramatic threats which cosmonauts have seen from above?*

V.T.   I believe that the fact that people have started to think about the smallness and fragility of the planet, about the possibility of man's devastating activities on earth, is partly due to the cosmonauts' vision from space. We were the first to see the dangers from an entirely new perspective. This entitled us to voice our concern so as to draw attention to global problems seen from space, such as the thinning of the ozone layer.

A.L.   *Our own exchange of understanding has proved that individual co-operation can develop from first meeting one another, then enjoying each other's cultural heritage. Nearly all my life's work has been inspired by the belief that human unity is possible. But to enable us to achieve this, barriers must first be broken down, whether the barriers concern women's rights, ethnic rights, religious rights, ecological rights or the pursuit of peace. People do feel safest in their own tribes but they should see that such security often proves to be a dangerous illusion.*

The international cultural mission

What is your view from the East now that
Russia, America and Europe are less tribal and
more committed to working together within a
renewed United Nations? Do you see progress
for international co-operation?

V.T.   To reduce armaments and to struggle together against global dangers has been a significant advance and we seem slowly to be learning to work together for this. We are also beginning to enjoy what is best in the world's varied cultures. Some ways of living may not be our own preference but it is always exciting and rewarding to share in other cultures and to be introduced to the many different sections of the world family. We should not aim to amalgamate cultures, but we should benefit from experiencing different cultures even if we still prefer our own as the one we want for ourselves.

A.L.   How does your organization achieve this aim?
It is an umbrella organization. What does it
work to protect? How many nations does your
collective include?

V.T.   We work at many levels to develop inter-cultural understanding. We arrange for representatives of the traditions of many regions and nations, small as well as large, to meet each other and it is exciting to see how, from throughout the world, people do enjoy finding out about each other's art, food, dance, dress, history and music. So many cultural treasures can be shared. In 1988 I was happy to receive a letter from President Ronald Reagan on the occasion of the Tbilisi conference – the fourth Annual Conference of American-Soviet Cooperation, He wrote:

'The Conferences, begun at Chatakoa, play an important part in developing our contacts. They serve as a forum for Soviet and American public affairs where we can discuss what divides us and what brings us closer together. These conferences have made it possible for thousands of Soviet and American citizens to communicate with each other and discuss topics of interest. I was pleased to know that many American participants are staying in Georgian homes just as many Soviets stayed in homes in New York State last year.

'I am convinced that such public discussions will help to remove our differences and find the sure way to co-opera- tion between our countries. I am grateful to the governing body of the Union of Soviet Friendship Societies and to the Chatakoa Institute and their many supporters from govern- ment and voluntary groups who took up this initiative four years ago. What you started then has become an important tradition.'

The President's encouragement strengthened our resolve to continue. But it is very difficult to establish cultural centres and pursue cultural activities without sufficient funds. The activities of our organization are similar to those of the British Council or Alliance Française, and the Goethe Institute. The Russian cultural centres provide information on the culture, language, history and traditions of Russia and also our scientific and technological achievements. In recent years the Friendship So- cieties have changed from being dependent on the State to becoming much more independent. I have tried to encourage them to choose their own forms of activity; now I have to find ways by which they can earn money themselves to finance their work.

It is not an easy task but it seems to me that we have begun to solve the problem. The Russian Agency for International Co- operation and Development, set up by presidential decree, supports the activities of friendship societies and their cultural and humanitarian programmes. Now in 1992 the chairperson of the Agency and Deputy Prime Minister of Russia, Alexander Shchokhin, understands our aims and activities.

A.L.   *You are the Deputy-Chair of this new Russian*
       Agency. What are its objectives?

V.T.   The Agency aims to provide information on the new democratic Russia, and we hope to enlist business, financial, cultural, scientific and humanitarian co-operation. It will be dealing with foreign investments to Russia and will co-ordinate foreign technical assistance. The Agency supports the traditional activities of the Friendship Societies.

At present our country faces enormous financial difficulties and our work cannot be carried out as before on only a small State budget. We must find new funds, including commercial sponsorship.

We will continue to co-operate as we have done for many years with the Friendship Societies of former Soviet republics which have now become independent states. For instance, we think it important to continue to give them the opportunity to organise their cultural events in our organization's Russian Cultural Centres abroad.

A.L.   *In the West voluntary work is sometimes sponsored by commercial companies. Could reliable foreign companies be asked to sponsor Russian cultural exchanges?*

V.T.   We have been working on many charity programmes, for example the one to assist the Chernobyl children, which have been helped by foreign businesses. I am thankful that today the attitudes of the people of the world have changed. There is an awareness of the interaction of our common earthly destiny, a growing understanding that the world is indivisible and interdependent. We now see that to achieve our common security there is the need to develop the exchange of people, ideas, information, and spiritual and material values. You and I have proved that international friendship can be achieved by understanding each other and that this can dispel prejudice and misinformation.

A.L.   *What were the achievements of your societies in the period when the world was moving towards nuclear war?*

V.T. We did our best to bring people closer together, to demolish the wall of enmity, to open channels for unbiased information through direct human contacts. Attitudes toward other people become more objective if we can see the facts on our own, and not through mass media. I do not want to minimize the role of radio, television and press, but as we say in Russian: 'It is better to see once than to hear about it one hundred times.'

As President Reagan wrote, it has been wonderful to see the result of personal exchanges. It is a really enjoyable experience accommodating foreigners in Russian families, as well as sending Soviets to foreign families. It is very interesting to learn about another culture, to compare it with your own, to identify what can be shared by different communities. It is a real school for the future community of human unity you believe in. It is a pity if we do not make the enjoyment more widely known.

A.L. *The contribution of your organization to the*
twinning of cities attracts increasing interest.
Can you tell me more about it?

V.T. The movement started in 1943 with twinning of Stalingrad and Coventry. This proved how people can unite and how, facing a common threat, they can move towards each other forgetting previous discord and disagreement. It showed that, in spite of the large distances separating people, they still want to meet. After the war the movement of twinned cities became international. More than 500 Russian cities and cities of the former Soviet Union participated in this movement. They have successfully shared learning different skills and traditions, setting up joint ventures, exchanging children, youth, students and artistic groups. This is a growing movement supported by ordinary citizens, as you say at 'grass roots level' and also by civic authorities. Our 'Twin Cities International Association' organizes the twinning of Russian sister cities through local government. This organization has deep roots in the history of our country. The Association is a member of the

324

Russian Agency of which I am now Deputy-Chairperson. There are more than one hundred affiliated organizations.

A.L. Do you include exchanges in religious culture? One aspect of Russian civilization which has enriched the world is its spiritual art, music, and literature. We should remember that half the Christian world shares the Orthodox faith.

V.T. Of course spiritual exchanges are important. I would like to see all religions contributing to this. Our organization co-operates with the Russian Orthodox Church and with representatives of other confessions.

A.L. Some time ago an article in The Times *implied that the Soviet friendship societies were dependent on the KGB, which gave money for their work.*

V.T. It is a pity that an authoritative paper such as *The Times* has published information about one of the oldest non-governmental organizations of my country in this way. Our organization, even in 1917, was contributing to the exchange of information and communication between Soviet Russia and the whole world. It was one of the first to build bridges of mutual understanding between West and East during the cold war.

Moreover, it was one of the first to support the Helsinki agreements and carry out citizens' exchanges and people's diplomacy. The Soviet Friendship Societies did not break relations with the people of China, Israel, Great Britain, even when official diplomatic relations had been suspended. As President Reagan has written, we initiated a project whereby thousands of Soviets and Americans were able to communicate with each other about the problems they were facing. I am sure that this kind of public discussion removes disagreements and establishes firm friendship between our peoples. I am grateful to the numerous assistants and activists in America, both from governmental and non-governmental circles, who started this movement. It has now become a very strong tradition.

*A.L.   Do you think of your work as an inter-cultural
        mission?*

V.T.   I feel a sense of privilege and responsibility to have been given an opportunity to work through our organization towards international friendship. For me it has been a task which has borne 'abundant fruit'.

The Tenth Conversation

Valentina Speaks
on
An Honest Exchange of Ideals

A.L. *We have agreed that human unity depends on respecting each other's ideals. But to be genuine such respect requires an honest exchange to explain why we are inspired by the philosophy for living that we believe to be best.*

For centuries sectarian enmity has been inflamed by uninformed antagonism, and the worst aspect has been that religious and philosophical groups often enjoy and gain strength from remaining isolated. Will it be possible for us to tell each other what we truly believe about capitalism and Communism, atheism and Christianity?

V.T. Tell me about your belief in Christianity.

A.L. *I have to start by saying that I think the teaching of Jesus Christ provides ideal guide-*

327

*lines for human justice, love and peace, but
that I know how many dreadful deeds, as well
as good deeds, have been done in the name of
Christianity.*

*When Mikki Doyle and I were in Moscow
together in 1987 for the World Congress of
Women – she the editor of a UK Communist
paper and me the wife of a UK Conservative
minister – Mikki told the other delegates, 'She
is a Christian. I am a Communist. We are
sisters. If we can do it, everyone can do it.'
There were many happy faces hearing this evidence of human harmony. But to be true sisters
means having real respect for each other's sometimes polarised philosophies. Also we may
have to answer uncomfortable questions. For
example how do you and I answer if we are
asked: 'In the next century can Christianity
and Communism survive?'*

V.T.   Women in particular have proved in these last decades
that it is possible to find the tolerance which ends enmity. We
can remain loyal to our own philosophies while trying to find a
bridge between the barriers which separate. So often having
become friends people realise that they are united by the same
hopes and fears. We can overcome the barriers of prejudice by
looking at other people as if we were looking at ourselves and
our own relatives. I see this as space-age spirituality. My main
spiritual ideal is the certainty that moral riches are more important than material ones. I think that we both believe this to be
true.

A.L.   *Do you think that Lenin's dream to make the
poor as powerful as the rich has now been
proved to be inspiring in theory but impossible
in practice? The same has often happened with
Christianity. Gandhi said he admired Jesus*

Christ but not Christians – because they were
not like Christ.

V.T. I would say that the ideals proposed by Communism,
and most of all those of social justice, have not died. The ideal
of sharing is so attractive from the humanistic point of view
that it cannot perish. Such beliefs are eternal. But a true Communist society was never achieved in our country. We cannot
evaluate the positive results of Communism in Russia because
we did not see genuine Communism, or even socialism, in
practice even if it was widely preached in theory. There is often
a great discrepancy between theory and reality.

I can only speak about practical evaluation. If our leaders did
not succeed in putting Communist beliefs into practice that
does not mean that the ideals of social justice our mothers and
fathers believed in were wrong.

To rewrite history to suit the changing wishes of politicians
is also wrong. In my opinion, Soviet history was made by all of
us together. In the West you suspected everything in our past,
especially our leaders, but when I speak about the Communist
hopes of our ordinary people I am thinking of their sincere and
strong beliefs when they tried to build a better life for everybody. This was believed at the grass roots of our society, even if
it was betrayed in practice.

My family is a good example. We were a mixture of Russian,
Byelorussian, Georgian, Ukrainian and Chuvash, and we all felt
part of a whole great continent. No one said that you were
different or despised you because, for example, you were
Ukrainian. You came from a different Soviet culture, yes, but
no one criticized or said you could not marry a man or a
woman because of nationality. I cannot forget that our union of
different nations defeated fascism and won the war. I think
that the best aspect of our Soviet system was evidenced by this
unity of people prepared to overcome hardship so as to restore
their devastated homeland after the war. We were not helped
by anyone abroad. The restoration was worked for by our
mothers, fathers, grandparents. How can we denigrate their

achievement? Our society was betrayed at higher levels by crimes and corruption, but at the grass roots our people lived by good human values.

A.L. *I have always admired your intelligence and now, more than ever, I see you are allowing history to pass through you, not trying to obstruct the truth. This is a special quality in you. I wish that the betrayals and failures caused by human hypocrisy and selfishness could be faced as honestly in the West, for example by extremists on both sides in Ireland and Ulster.*

So may I ask you another question about the Soviet system you served? When you became a member of the Party Central Committee were you worried about the fate of dissidents in prison? The West had proof that many dissidents were victimized.

V.T.   In a totally democratic state, which we have agreed has not existed so far, every citizen should certainly have the right to express independent individual opinions freely and not be afraid of punishment by the State for this right to freedom.

It was awful when in the USSR representatives of the intelligentsia, cultural leaders and workers had no opportunity to speak openly and some had to leave their country and also their relatives, because they did so. Personally I have known a number of dissidents and you were present when recently I encouraged many to participate in international conferences, including bringing them to Copenhagen, when the second CSCE conference took place in 1990. It was not easy for us to insist on free speech even then, but we did provide former dissidents with the opportunity to tell of their suffering. Our Association has very good relationships with these dissidents and now we are co-operating with them within the framework of the new Russian Association for International Co-operation in trying to achieve an Institute of Global Morality. Many former dissidents are writers, experts in different fields, and meeting them personally now I understand how little I knew about them before, or why they were dissidents. I am happy that now, with the new reforms, so many renew Russian citizenship and come back from abroad to live in Russia again.

A.L.   *But you will be asked: 'Did you not see the suffering at the time?' Martin Luther King said, 'Why do you not look and see?' when he met top US leaders who replied that what was happening to black people did not concern them.*

V.T.   When I was in the Central Committee and I was responsible for women's rights and the affairs of cosmonauts, this did not give me the opportunity to influence the leadership of the country on matters which were not my responsibility.

A.L.   *It is the same in the West. Seeking out injustice is not often an urgent priority for politicians. But may I put it another way to get a true perspective on the former levels of Soviet power and privilege? Both under Communism and capitalism people in power enjoy privileges. But Communism preached the ideal of equality, a difficult ideal to achieve. It is sometimes found in communes, as in Israel, or in monasteries, but probably nowhere else. Did you feel that from a position of power you practised this ideal? Did you receive special privileges?*

V.T.   I never lived at the top levels of influence. The fact that I was Chair of the Soviet Women's Committee only allowed me to sit with members of the Politburo for official events, not decision-making meetings.

Do understand that I have never been a member of the decision-making body. I truly do not know the precise privileges which they were given. In any case I have never been jealous of what other people acquired and I am sure that for people to carry responsibilities properly they must live under conditions which are helpful for their work, so that material hardships don't take up time and energy. Obviously no one should abuse their position, especially if they are responsible for top-level decision-making. It goes without saying that privileges must not extend to members of their families. If Politburo members earned some special facilities that would not worry me. For myself when I was a member of the Central Committee I was one of more than three hundred members. My life did not change drastically when I was elected. Members went on with the work they were doing before their election to the Central Committee and I continued to work in the Cosmonaut Training Centre where I earned my salary. My main preoccupation was working from morning to night. I did not receive extraordinary privileges as a member of the Central Committee. We each had our own work and only once or twice a year gathered for Central Committee plenums.

The contribution expected of the three hundred Central Committee members was to work hard and to set a good example of doing one's duty in good faith. When we met for the plenum we had to discuss decisions that had already been taken by the Politburo. The hierarchy was strict. However my position on the Central Committee did give me the opportunity to bring women's issues to the attention of the higher levels within the hierarchy, even if I was disappointed when the Soviet Women's Committee recommended provisions for women and children within the existing constitution of the country, and these were not implemented. There is a great difference between proclaiming equality and practising it.

A.L.   *It all sounds familiar. In Britain there are too few*
women in the Cabinet and Parliament and wom-
en's issues are often pushed under the carpet.

V.T.   When the new Constitution was discussed in 1977 I did achieve an advance for women thanks to my position in the Central Committee. I appealed to the Government to pay attention to the fact that, while they were proclaiming women's equality, women still faced a number of unresolved questions which presented inequality. I was determined to remind the decision-making bodies of women's needs. It was not easy for me but I managed to get the Government to take several important steps to improve the conditions of women. This influenced all levels of Soviet administration on behalf of women, not only the Supreme Soviet but also local councils. I know that I was able to use the mechanism for influencing the Government because of my position as a member of the Central Committee. I had the opportunity to ask for personal meetings with, and write information on the subjects I have described to members of the Government, to Secretaries for the Central Committee and to the General Secretary himself. This was true not only about women's issues but also for cosmonauts' issues.

There were other positive results for progress in women's welfare when I became Chair of the Soviet Women's Committee. Again this was voluntary work, which gave me opportunities to work for women and to meet women from all over the world.

A.L.   You are giving me a very honest picture of the Soviet system before the new reforms. But you speak mainly about your positive achievements on behalf of women. What about the negative aspects? Were there many failures in your work?

V.T.   When I started my work in the Soviet Women's Committee I realised that a number of problems were crying out to be urgently resolved. I spoke at Central Committee meetings and said, 'Look, this is the real situation, the true status of women. Let us convene a national women's congress so that you can be told the needs from every corner of the country. We must try and find a solution together.' I failed there. We could not succeed in convincing the Politburo that the congress was a necessity. I managed to do it only in January 1987. The initiative to gather women from all over the world to meet in Moscow was mine and I worked hard to implement it. You attended this World Congress in 1987 as a delegate from the UK and your participation was positive. It was of great importance for women of my country and of the whole world to meet each other.

But I had left the Soviet Women's Committee after the National Congress when I was elected Chairman of the Union of Soviet Friendship Societies. The work for the preparation of the World Congress of Women was continued by others.

A.L.   *As I believe you are one of the few world leaders prepared to be completely honest, can I ask you: How can justice become stronger than injustice in an autocracy when only a few have the power to influence decisions? In a democracy 'one man, one vote' at least gives individuals some influence.*

V.T.   I agree, but decision-making power nearly always lies only in the hands of a few. I never had that power. All I could do was to work well. I still work very hard. I live on the monthly salary from the Cosmonaut Training Centre where I act as an instructor. I work voluntarily for the Russian Friendship Societies Association and the Russian Agency for International Co-operation and Development. It takes a lot of my time, strength, energy, and gives me sleepless nights. I do not receive money for this. I do it because I feel that people need this work. If I did not believe that it helped people I would never do it. I know that all over the world there are people willing to work voluntarily. You work voluntarily too, so you can understand me. What does make it worthwhile and why I am happy is that I receive letters from people in different countries, from Russia and from other republics of the Commonwealth of Independent States and even from abroad, writing to me asking for help in different matters, particularly medical and social assistance. I always do all I can to help. My greatest happiness is then to receive a letter which says, 'Thank you for having helped my child. God bless you, Valentina,' or, 'We are grateful to you for having helped us to find a new flat.'

A.L. *I remember how you helped with the illness in our family by sending medicines from Moscow to London. But in your response to political decisions were you as free as you wanted to be to do as you thought right, or did your duty to obey official orders come first? I keep thinking about what I call the 'Oliver North versus Sakharov syndrome'. Oliver North, as an American serviceman, sincerely did his duty when he tried to save a few American lives by selling arms which could end the lives of many others. He said, 'Once you are a soldier what can you do except what you are told?' But in contrast, Sakharov, who was also patriotic, when he saw a question of right or wrong was prepared to sacrifice himself for what he thought was right. Would you do the same? It is the same moral challenge for servants of the State in both East and West.*

V.T. Perhaps you are right. There were some decisions which my Central Committee colleagues and I did not sufficiently question and understand. For instance, the invasion of Afghanistan in 1979. We were told that it was the demand of the Afghan people. But inside me I realised that it was wrong. Everything was controversial, the whole process was complex. Is it not the same in the West? Are Western motives always pure and disinterested? As you know my wish is to support and

335

work first for whatever is best for the people of my country and then for the world.

A.L. *Certainly the official requirements of Western democracy are often hypocritical, hiding intentions based on commercial interests. We also need truthful leaders.*

V.T.   Sakharov made his protest at the end of his life when he was over 50 and had had his life experience. This allowed him to see more clearly. His life experience and scientific experience led him to see what was right and wrong. I worked in the Brezhnev era long after Stalin's crimes had been exposed and our generation genuinely hoped that the development of socialism would bring a better life for everyone.

A.L. *When the British war hero, Leonard Cheshire, saw the atom bomb dropped on Hiroshima he did not think it wrong to act as an observer. He was a serving British airman, and he saw it as his duty. You might have faced the same dilemma if the USA and the USSR had become involved in nuclear war. You had seen from above the fragile planet in danger, you wanted to protect it but you might have been involved in its destruction after facing a personal conflict between your ideals and your obedience to superiors in command. Obviously it is impossible in both East and West for soldiers to disobey orders.*

V.T.   That is why I believed in a world movement to establish peace. Many Soviet women were involved in this. I always supported it and thought it essential to find peace before we found ourselves at war.

A.L.   *Were you disappointed that when the East called for peace, the West called it propaganda? I believed that myself. I had to meet you to learn that a Soviet cosmonaut could be so dedicated to save the planet.*

V.T.   We understood each other because we were prepared to trust each other. We were ready to listen and respond. The enemy image was built by fear on both sides – and people did not want to listen to each other. Now people are willing to listen, to understand, and to trust. This is a difficult process but different nations and individuals have started it.

A.L.   *Whatever happens in the future I will continue to believe that the Communist ideal at its best gave the oppressed and the poor all over the world the hope that exploitation could be opposed and overcome.*

   You have given me an honest picture of the advantages and disadvantages of life as a professional woman within the Soviet system. I hope I can be as honest with you about what is good and what is bad for professional women within the democratic system in the West.

V.T.   I have tried to answer your questions on Communism in theory and in practice truthfully. I have tried to describe how many of us worked as best we could to rebuild the USSR from the ruins after the war and how we tried to do so through the Communist ideal which we believed in even if we failed in the system. Now you will have truthfully to tell me about the advantages and disadvantages in your experience of the philosophy which means most to you – Christianity. You need also to tell me about capitalist and consumerist ideals in practice. In Russia today Western democracy is idealised. But as you have often told me, promises to help the poor in the West have often

337

not been carried out. There are still many examples of cruelty and hypocrisy.

A.L.   *The motivation for capitalism and particularly consumerism is usually financial profit. Christian ideals should be different. For me the Christian ideal was best lived by St Francis of Assisi. He was really in love with Jesus and he believed in what Jesus taught and tried to live like Him. St Francis was convinced that God, the creator of the Universe, had shown us how the Divine had become human in Jesus Christ so as to share in the poverty, persecution and suffering of God's creatures, as well as the joys.*

    For me it solved so many questions and problems in this world to hope to be certain that the world's Creator not only loves the sick and the poor, but that He teaches that this is where we must look for Him, and not among the rich and the strong. A famous Christian prayer says: 'By dying you have overcome our death, by rising from the dead you have restored eternal life to us.' This vision of resurrection inspired St Francis to love everything which was part of creation, all aspects of life, music, nature, the moon, the winds, the rain, the cosmos, trees and flowers, animals, birds, ants and even little worms. He was called the minstrel of Christ and he sang a great song, which is one of the most beautiful poems in the Italian language, called the 'Canticle of the Sun'. It is a hymn to harmony between man, God and nature. St Francis called everything created his brothers and sisters. Sister Water, Brother Fire, even Sister Death. He believed that anyone in need provided him with a special

338

reason for loving them. He built up joy, as well as compassion, but it was simple joy, no luxury. He sang that he was in love with the Lady Poverty, everything poor and sincere and simple was precious. He is now seen as a leader for ecology. Many Christians believe he did become like Jesus Christ.

That is why it shocks me that in our world today, in so many countries Christians identify with prosperity and power. They enjoy being comfortable minorities unaware of the vast majority of the desperately poor, homeless and starving which surround them. I believe that if Christian ideals are to be genuine they must be practised as St Francis practised them. Of course there are Christians all over the world, from all races, who do live like him, who nurse the sick and dedicate their lives to justice, and they are part of a vast number who do the same even if they are not Christians. But, as with Communism, the ideal of Christ's teaching has too often not been put into practice. Christians forget that Jesus died in pain and humiliation, nailed to two wooden planks to show the children of God the Father that all are one family whether rich or poor and that good is finally stronger than evil. Christ taught that God's love wants eternal happiness for all humanity, and if it does not happen in this world it will happen after the resurrection and last for eternity.

That is why St Francis is my ideal for Christianity even if I do not live up to the universal love he looked for. I read somewhere that Lenin said: 'Give me ten leaders like St Francis and I will win the world.'

V.T.   While listening to you I thought that the Christian ideals you have just spoken of – to love your neighbour, care for defenceless people, condemn of all forms of domination – all these are also socialist ideals. Trying to put these ideals in practice, I have seen several generations of my compatriots working hard, struggling against fascism, believing that they could build the most just society on Earth. Do you not think that Christianity is also a philosophical system? The founders of great religions were often thinkers and scholars as well.

A.L.   *The majority of Christ's first followers were poor and some were illiterate. They did not believe in philosophy. They believed they should do what the Maker of heaven and earth taught them to do.*

V.T.   I see it as a question of different philosophies. But we need to admit that philosophies either succeed or fail and we should look for the reason why. It will advance the process of understanding if we come back to the fact that we need to find unity through mutual respect and understanding. Certainly if we are to try and share the best in the different ideals we believe in, there first has to be a true exchange of our experiences of the ideals as we have known them in practice. You asked that we should admit to bad as well as good and I think we have attempted this. Perhaps if we can inspire more truthful exchanges like yours and mine it will lead to the human family agreeing on a new basic philosophy, even if not a new religion which all can practise and try to share in.

The time has come to try and change our world not only in words but in deeds and I believe that one of the first steps on this road is to look for new guidelines for living better, which could unite all people. Perhaps these could be called 'global morality'.

The Eleventh Conversation

Valentina Speaks
on
Ecological Harmony to Protect the Planet

A.L.   *Space explorers like yourself have warned that*
it is urgent to achieve ecological harmony to
prevent environmental catastrophes.

V.T.   We need to work for ecological harmony but it will depend on our agreeing and acting upon the measures necessary to achieve it. Human harmony with nature is essential in ecological terms, and as the space pioneer Tsiolkovsky foretold global harmony is possible, given the opportunities provided by progress in space science and technology.

A.L.   *Is there a crisis you could identify now as*
bringing humanity close to extinction? Using
'space science' is there one essential measure
you recommend so as to protect the environ-
ment from destruction?

V.T.   Our planet is ill: climatic changes, ozone holes – these are only the first small symptoms of that illness. What could be the remedy? To my mind, efficiency of treatment depends on the efficiency of diagnosis. For this we need reliable information.

To get this information we have to use space technology. So far, only seven satellites working for ecological purposes are operating. I am sure that all nations need to unite their efforts in taking care of their common home, after proper monitoring of the risks.

Certainly, we have to start the process gradually. First, the time of launching of space vehicles for monitoring has to be agreed, and also the characteristics of the orbits they need, so as to prevent duplication in programmes.

Our Russian experts have invited their foreign colleagues to place their equipment and devices on board Russian satellites. We have agreements in this field with the Goddard Centre (NASA) and National Centre for Space Research (France) that they will use the Russian satellite *Meteor 3* to carry their equipment for mapping the ozone layer, and for collecting data on the radiation balance of Earth. This is encouraging evidence of co-operation.

A.L.   *Throughout the world all human beings feel personally involved in environmental problems. Whether for rich or poor these are part of human living, the air we breathe, the sea we swim in, the water we drink, the fruit and vegetables, even the bread we eat, all can become harmful. It is a challenge for everyone of every age and country to choose actions which safeguard the environment. All feel part of this crisis.*

V.T.   Taxpayers have a right to ask the experts about the concrete results of environmental monitoring. It is urgent for the survival of our planet. For example, Earth-resource experts should report on what is being done to monitor dust storms, wind and water erosion, and the registration of pandemics which threaten flora and fauna because of pests.

Experts in the hydrosphere should give important information on the condition of world oceans, mountains, glaciers, and on the pollution of seas and rivers.

Researchers on the lithosphere should obtain and report essential information on the first signs and evolution of earthquake processes, volcanic activities, and landslides.

We need this global monitoring of the Earth's atmosphere; I would call it a 'World Ecological Service'.

We now have some experience in organizing world services from space, for instance COSPAS – SARSAT, the French/Russian satellite system which saves the lives of thousands of people by locating crashed aircraft and missing ships.

Regional and national information centres could bring together data from space to enable the matching of computer systems and mathematical analysis.

The programme for such an important world activity could be developed by a non-governmental organization such as the International Centre for Scientific Research. The headquarters for this world laboratory are in Italy. The UN should support such activities.

A.L.   *We are looking at the walls which form this room. They are made up of separate panels but all hold one room safely together. Could it not be the same for the nations and regions which agree that certain ecological dangers require urgent safeguards? Could they not remain separate within their cultures but all interact together on a world scale to obtain ecological harmony and security? In this way, with a central world authority as its foundation, the whole house would be safely maintained. Is that how you see a new world order in environmental terms?*

343

V.T. In 1991 I attended and spoke at the United Nations conference for non-governmental organizations. We studied 'Peace, Justice and Development; the ingredients for an emerging World Order.' I believe that such meetings and discussions have already begun to build a better future with positive measures to protect the environment. I hope the agreements achieved at the Earth Summit in Rio de Janeiro this year will also contribute to improvements in world justice and development. If so ecological harmony need no longer be a hope; it could become a reality with science used well to increase the world's resources. This would benefit all members of the United Nations.

We now have the experience of history to help us look at these problems in depth. But for the future I believe we must face the weak points. For myself I am anxious that when many communities act together to hold up a whole house, these communities should not lose their roots. I think it is not so much nationalism as traditions which people need, so as to strengthen the self-respect they rightly value. Human harmony depends on respecting each other's firm traditions.

For example we say, 'my history', 'my songs', 'my food', 'my language', 'my art', 'my poetry', 'my architecture', 'my sport', 'my way of dressing'. These are basic sources of individual identity and without these roots we wither as people or as human beings. Respect for each other's traditions can make ours stronger. That is why I believe in international meetings to learn about each other's individual identity and why I have worked for this. If we are to protect our planet from being destroyed we need human unity based on justice. Harmony depends on persuading people that the objectives are fair, helpful and advantageous for everyone. As you say, we need to achieve a better world for the South as well as the North, and here again harmony could develop in a world of cultures, representing large or small numbers but all prepared to value each other's traditions. For me the word *culture* also includes the most useful human deeds on earth, such as contributions to science, technological discoveries, systems of law and education and of course artistic achievements. It should be a union, not an amalgamation of achievements.

A.L.   *I am optimistic that the march of mankind away from nuclear war is finally unstoppable. It is my dream that for the new century the world will say 'NO' to the great dangers which could cause human extinction, including armed conflicts. When it is remembered that the planet we all inhabit together could be destroyed, this should inspire human unity to prevent, not create disasters. Perhaps worldwide control of harmful factors and the maintenance of ecological harmony could be coordinated by the United Nations? There was united world agreement during the Gulf War to oppose the invasion of Kuwait. World governments have shown that they can sometimes agree on upholding right against wrong. This should now be extended to protect ecological right and defeat ecological wrong.*

V.T.   You are putting forward a complicated proposal for the United Nations. It will not work unless people treat each other not from a political position but from one of human values. The challenge to choose between security or danger is a choice all individuals can experience and understand if accurate information can be obtained. Then, when such values are seen to be the priority, people will say 'no' to armed conflicts. To judge every problem on its moral merits based on sufficient information is the first step to the future. The second step is to treat other people just as you treat yourself, not to speak blindly according to political conceptions. That is very important. But in view of the ecological danger we all share, this may be the first time that such a new system will be welcomed by all people and nations because it is their only way to survive. Then they might call on the United Nations to be the central authority.

A.L. Is a world policeman needed to protect ecological balance and harmony?

V.T. Perhaps one single, centralised command could co-ordinate assistance during major catastrophes. The traditional purpose of an army or police force is to protect individuals and communities from attack. An army is not meant to be a peace corps. If we want to leave the idea of armies behind us, then the only alternative is to transform all armies into rescue services at an international and not a national level. Such protection would have to be global, and the peace corps should never be biased. The process now proposed to Russia, that we scrap nuclear weapons while other nations still have theirs, is not just. One nation must be sure that another nation will not use a reforming process to impose its interest and oppression on others, if humanity is to give up nuclear defences.

The ideal would be for all nations to feel safe to keep their doors open, just as in small villages, far from so-called civilized cities, people have the doors of their houses open because they do not fear an aggressor or burglar.

In the future, if we could establish a new epoch of trust and mutual confidence, we would only need a global rescue service or police force to guarantee global security in the case of aliens coming from other planets, or to give quick and trained assistance for natural or technological disasters such as typhoons, hurricanes, earthquakes and floods. This would not be called an army, as it would not need any arms to be used for warfare, and the word *army* comes from the word *armaments*. It would be a Special Rescue Service, able to undertake relief operations, and perhaps it could act as a world police force to control and prevent global wrongdoing. It should have at its disposal the best technical and medical equipment and highly trained personnel. This new body would also have to include administrators able to command operations with rescuers willing and able to act – doctors, experts in different fields. The same service could even protect the planet if there were dangers from space, such as asteroids off course.

346

I would like to see an international rescue service as part of the United Nations administration, a service which would have at its disposal advanced technological and medical facilities. These could be contributed through the combined efforts of different nations.

A.L.   *Can ecological catastrophes be prevented by monitoring from space? Can precautionary measures be taken in time, for example, to curb pollution? I believe that urgent reduction in the emission of greenhouse gases should be obligatory. I would like to see a world authority insisting that the rich countries should live less luxuriously.*

V.T.   Even now it is the most natural thing for me to live a modest life. My mother taught me to be content and it helped me to sustain the rigorous preparation for, and the conditions during, the space flight. However, I do not think it is advisable now to ask the rich to live like the poor, even if this would reduce pollution. In fact I would argue against this. Conditions of living because of the advance of science have made a gigantic leap forward during the post-war period. People are no longer ready to accept reductions in comforts: we have become used to the modern standards of life which have been provided by the technological revolution. What we need to do is to make the results of that revolution work for the good of humanity. We must use science well.

We should support every scientific advance when it benefits humanity. Now I regret to see that we make too many separate efforts and that by developing similar scientific programmes in different countries money and skill is wasted by duplication. Joint efforts by scientists of different countries working together would economize on resources. We already know that both bad and good ecological effects spread quickly throughout the planet and affect every country. This already calls for shared action by all people living on the globe. That is why scientists should be persuaded to solve global problems together, and combine their efforts to control serious ecological abuse. We already know that we are spoiling and poisoning the atmosphere and destroying ecological assets, not only for ourselves, but for our children, grandchildren and further descendants. We already see lifeless rivers, dead because of pollution not only in my country but also in yours and elsewhere. We see lifeless fields, entire rural areas killed by pesticides and fertilizers, the chemical substances used to over-cultivate soil. All these substances penetrate the earth, then rains bring them to the rivers, and the rivers bring them to the seas and oceans. Lands, seas and oceans have no nationalities, they are not Russian or British, they are planetary. The wind blows over all the world, and brings good and bad with it. There are no frontiers for these destructive forces. So I see the main task as being not a return to a more modest life, but to combine the efforts of different nations to prevent disasters, and act against the dangers which threaten our survival. In this way we can protect ourselves and others within one human family.

The United Nations leaders and the leaders of all countries should draw the attention of scientists to this aim, and support and encourage their combined work to achieve it. People should unite to allocate money and bring together scientific brains and resources.

A.L.   Your call is to use science well?

V.T.   Yes, certainly. We penetrated space with substantial space vehicles and have opened the way to other planets for purposes other than killing ourselves. Science can be used for the benefit of humanity. Having created nuclear energy we now face the problem of securing purity and not poison for our environment. This obliges us to search for new solutions. Our modern ecological problems are due to unconsciousness, disorder and carelessness and partly to the motive of profit. Greed and constant longing for money seem to be inherent in man, but now to save himself man must reject the incorrect use of resources and replace disorder by harmony between man and the environment.

To use science well we also need to direct our scientific efforts to study planet Earth, because we do not know enough about our own planet. We have no precise idea of what there is available and how we should use the resources inside our planet. We also do not know enough about dangers which could come from space and put our planet at risk.

I think that there should be a world scientific laboratory under United Nations auspices. This could promote and protect environmental priorities and in this way humanity could harmonize and make the best use of the resources available now, and also obtain new resources by scientific research.

If ecological harmony can be planned, worked for and established by the international community then our planet will be saved. It is an urgent matter. The hazards for human survival are increasing; we cannot afford delay in confronting them.

A.L. *We have agreed that democracy claims to allow the positive use of the 'one man, one vote' principle. This is the democratic process. It has many disadvantages but it is the only way to give influence to individuals, so that they can then in turn influence the decision-makers. Ecological harmony will depend on individuals being educated by reliable information to consider the options for action, and then voting to insist on the right choices being made to achieve environmental order instead of disorder.*

V.T. What exactly do you mean by democracy? When individuals vote for one or several candidates how can they know what kind of people they are, what they have achieved as well as what they promise to do? When they are ambitious for a mandate, candidates for high political posts promise 'gold mountains' as we say in Russia. Before we vote for candidates we should have reliable information on them and know much more about their skills, and after voting there should be control to monitor performance. You are right to say that 'one man, one vote' is the only way to give individuals influence and that this is the way by which they can change governments' decisions. But as you also say, for individuals to use their influence well, it is not only children who need to be educated. We ourselves should study and learn the lessons of world history so as not to repeat old mistakes. There is a Russian saying: 'One learns from one's mistakes.' Unfortunately we stubbornly repeat mistakes. We do not learn from the experience of the history of all nations, possibly because we have not studied world history sufficiently.

A.L.   *I see the current fragmentation instead of cohesion in the world as a terrible tragedy. For example we see deep divisions in the formerly integrated Yugoslavia and in other countries where people are willing to inflict pitiless cruelty and risk death to remain in separate tribes.*

V.T.   The unifying process is in the best interests of humanity, but it will only succeed if it never overpowers others. Those with power should not be in a position to discriminate against the weak. We need to establish real equality. You suggested that in a new world 'one family' structure, every country and culture could contribute its own sustaining panel with its own separate system and so uphold the whole house. But every system should be studied so as to be sure that we build only with what is safe. The level of development of states is so different that we have a lot of research to do before we offer a new world order in which all can share. It will need strenuous work and study before a just world structure which helps humanity and does not harm it can be realized, but we must continue to work for this, because without justice there can be no harmony, only suffering.

The road we have embarked on is difficult but it is not impossible. People need to understand that ecological harmony is essential for all and that the situation we have now is dangerous for all. People of one country should also understand that their lives would be safer if their efforts were shared and strengthened with the efforts of other countries. To reach this understanding, people also need to learn from mistakes. For example there are a number of positive and interesting experiences to learn from the European Community, but when we look closely, we also find weak points in this system. We need to proceed wisely on the road to protecting the planet.

A.L.   *Surely the planetary crisis is too urgent to*
       postpone efforts to establish ecological survival?
       Our children will be overtaken by catastrophe if
       we consider global problems too slowly and
       cautiously.

V.T.   I can only hope that our children will learn from our mistakes; if they do better than we did, go further than we went, I would be very happy. I pray to God they do. But also I hope our children will make progress without losing the finest feelings of patriotism, and so lose their roots. Progress towards harmony depends on developing what everyone can understand and appreciate, so as to enrich each other, not to merge totally. You say that in northern and southern Italy there are very different traditions, and also in Scotland, Ireland and England, but all can work together if the overall structure is just. We have so many different traditions in our country. Take the small mountainous republic of Daghestan. In its small territory there are thirty-three languages representing thirty-three minorities and ethnic groups, yet in one tiny piece of land they have co-operated and respected each other, because they believe that together they obtain a more comfortable way of life.

A.L.   *It is the same all over the world. I remember*
       how many regional dialects there are, for

351

example, in Italy; where there is one overall language but every region has its own idiom which the other cannot understand. It is unity in diversity.

V.T.   It is important for us all to understand that when we share in the attempt to protect ourselves and others by ensuring the survival of the planet, this not only achieves human unity but also strengthens national self-respect. You say Neapolitans become even more proud of their songs after they listen to the music of other nations. I also agree with you that enjoying different staple diets unites humanity. Personally I like both Italian pasta and Scottish porridge. I also greatly enjoy all kinds of international art and music.

But I am reminded of the man who travelled a lot, who saw different countries, and various nations, and became used to different traditions and languages, then finally he returned joyfully to his home, to his native land. One's own native land is one's cradle and to have everyone safe in their cradles but within one world family is my ideal of human harmony.

A.L.   *I will always remember your belief that humanity needs to live in harmony with itself and nature if we are to protect the planet from ecological catastrophe.*

V.T.   In the time I have left to live I want to work as much as I can for this intention. I will need to draw strength from the world's spiritual sources of inspiration, combined with scientific realism, to establish harmony and to save planet Earth.

The Twelfth Conversation

Valentina Speaks
on
Global Morality

A.L.   *You belong to the Association of Space Explorers, an international group of astronauts and cosmonauts.*

You work together to protect the planet you have seen differently from earth-dwellers. You have seen it as very vulnerable. Have you agreed on positive proposals to safeguard its survival?

V.T.   This is a question which is rightly asked but it needs careful consideration before an accurate answer can be given by the space explorers. First of all a change is needed in the attitude of all members of the human family. They should be prepared to take united action together. This must be supported by all nations and individuals.

You admit that you yourself ask many questions, hoping to obtain answers to secure human essentials such as peace and justice, but that you seldom find a completely satisfactory answer. I think the reason for this is that the most important questions have many aspects, and therefore need careful consideration because there are often different answers which are justifiable. In the same way, before space explorers can give specific warnings about global danger there has to be serious investigation into every aspect of that danger. Agreement must be reached at world level by experts, to confirm that it is a real and not an imaginary threat, and this requires in-depth scientific investigation and study.

The next step is how best to obtain world consensus to provide and support a global basis on which world co-operation can be built. This concerns me deeply. I have begun to try and work out a dependable conclusion and, for the time being, I see a new perspective on the co-operation which is so urgently needed to protect the planet. We need a new philosophy, and it could be called 'global morality'.

When the Association of Space Explorers met in Berlin in 1991 we drafted an appeal to world leaders based on the message 'Protect the planet'. For me this is the key to achieving global morality. Throughout the world now people speak about global problems, about a global community of peoples, about a global world order. That is why I believe that the time has come to try and agree on basic global rules for human beings to live by so as to avoid catastrophe. It will take time to achieve this, but today the threat of nuclear and environmental global destruction hangs over mankind. The creation of nuclear weapons and the rapacious exploitation of nature have made man technically capable of putting an end to his own existence. The old pre-nuclear thinking, which saw no need for the discipline of moral considerations, could now lead humanity to global suicide. So as I see it, today mankind has a choice; either human thought and action will establish a new civilisation, or life on Earth will disappear. A second Noah's Ark will not emerge from the universal, global flood.

Man has had to escape into space in order to understand how small, fragile and defenceless is his planet Earth. When you are in space, you think about Earth. She takes the form both of your nearest and dearest who, for each one of us, begins with our motherland and neighbours, but also of all humanity. In space one can see a different measure for the priorities of survival. These give value to each individual regardless of race, politics or religion, because all human beings now must unite within the common challenge to preserve their planet. We need a new framework of acceptable rules by which to live in order to safeguard mankind from catastrophe. Humanity is now obliged to identify the basic indispensable values which are essential for ecological survival, and then uphold these values, otherwise the planet will perish.

But the most necessary basis is to accept what divides us. We have to concede that we have different ideas about life, about happiness, about personal development. At the same time we must admit that to save the planet we must find new ways to work together despite these differences. We must find basic moral rules of behaviour necessary to protect the citizens of the twenty-first century who all face the same fate. 'Protect the planet or perish' is now an unavoidable challenge. The ways of protection need to be understandable and acceptable to all.

We have heard lately how the initiatives of public leaders who want to work together to eliminate nuclear and ecological threats have often failed. To my mind the main reason for this failure is that people continue not to understand or trust each other, and this is due to the fact that humanity has not yet established common ground for mutual understanding. Different nations have different concepts of what helps and what harms humanity, what is called by one nation violation of human rights is called by another interference in internal affairs. The same action can be considered by both sides differently. But now the imminent danger for the planet means that there has to be united support for actions which are ecologically indisputably necessary.

Logically humanity should have thought out earlier what the basics for survival should be. Now we are obliged to face this question urgently. We must ask what should the environmental code of behaviour be for people who want to still be living in the twenty-first century? We must remember the choice is an individual moral choice. Therefore we need discussions that first and foremost are free from prejudices, so that people can listen to and try to understand each other, while seeking the best ways to help everyone on Earth to survive together. This could be achieved if we all live by the laws of reason, but it is not happening now because individuals do not fear for the future. If we face the fact that survival for ourselves and our children depends on living as a World Family, the deep, divisive wish to be separate would radically alter. I am an aviation pilot-engineer and cannot contribute to a discussion on national administrative systems which I have not yet sufficiently studied. But I do know that already there are serious and obvious global problems which have no national frontiers, and for which there should be urgent solutions. I can readily identify two of them.

First, there is the need for Third World development and socio-economic progress. Secondly, for the health of man and society, an environment is necessary which does not cause disease and can sustain all its inhabitants within an agreed degree of sufficiency.

Fortunately these problems are already being studied by the supra-national non-governmental organizations, and their active help to develop international relations has already improved many negative traditional situations. But the basic ethical and spiritual aspirations of mankind have not yet been sufficiently strengthened or given the importance they merit. Their influence is great because as, increasingly, we live in a mutually dependent world, one of the main problems facing us all is to find spiritual and intellectual values which can inspire us and which all can respect. You say a cause in which all people on Earth feel they can become involved is unity to protect the environment. I would say that this can only develop from world awareness of the influence of individuals, and that the motivation for personal action depends on their spiritual strength.

We know that the United Nations has contributed much to global co-operation, and this is a time when through shared international effort we can together strive to preserve our common home, to guarantee a common future, and common security by sharing a new purpose which I see as 'Global Morality'. That is why I hope that the United Nations will make global morality an urgent concern, perhaps by calling a special meeting for the year 1995 when it will be celebrating its golden jubilee, fifty years after it was first formed in 1945. This time also marks twenty years after the Helsinki Declaration of 1975, which proposed realizable measures for co-operation by the USA, Europe and the USSR. I would like to see a Global Morality Charter proclaimed for the year 2000. I think this would be a wise way to begin the new century.

To agree on the main objectives, leaders of all world religions could first be asked, 'What positive measures would your beliefs inspire and your fellow believers act on to prevent our planet perishing?' I think we would be surprised to find how many of the same aims are shared by all religions, and that there could be agreement on basic proposals. That would be a beginning for the new shared aims.

Further study and wider consensus would be needed to identify the positive actions which could be accepted as important internationally. Of course they would have first to be formulated carefully, agreed on and proved to be viable in practical terms. For example scientific experts would need to be involved to ensure that the scientific proposals were practicable. Then I would hope that a Global Morality Charter could incorporate these agreed basic aims to save the planet.

Non-governmental organizations could start now to discuss and agree on the priorities for such a charter. There are already programmes to enable youth exchanges, professional meetings for engineers and doctors, lawyers and economists, journalists and entrepreneurs. We could take a new step forward by asking these to formulate a few fundamental and indispensable requirements which will protect environmental survival. This would begin to establish mutual understanding and agreement not only between governments, but also on a human level. This would be an important beginning for action to follow.

I see this new picture of morality not making everyone good, not making everyone idealistic, but making everyone realistic about survival. But I myself would propose as a basic priority for the charter that we should respect each other's different moral attitudes and beliefs as an inalienable human right, and so end dangerous religious discord.

A.L.   *Could there be a new language which all world communities would speak and understand? Language barriers encourage tribal thinking, particularly in the writing of prejudiced national histories. But I admit that you and I have been able to exchange our thoughts through an interpreter, so speaking the same language is not necessary for understanding.*

V.T.   The language I prefer is that of global morality; that people living on our planet should be prepared to assess problems and solutions, choosing between what helps or what harms the planet. This attitude would not depend on language. I think that languages are good in that they reflect the mentality of people. The idioms that we Europeans have in our languages are not understandable to Africans or Chinese, and vice versa. This is true also of Latin America. We all feel comfortable with our own language even if many now speak and read languages from all over the world. Humanity could create a new language, like Esperanto, or something like the basic language which science uses now for computers, in order to communicate solutions. It might be possible, but I hope that we can continue to value all that is creative in our own language and share this also. There is so much good to share, not destroy. I am very lazy; I have not learnt other languages except for scientific purposes, but have communicated through interpreters. Whatever happens, I will always continue to take pride in the language of my own nation even while I work for worldwide harmony. Russia is my homeland and I am proud of it. I remember the Russian poet Nekrasov said: 'The Russian people will survive, withstand all hardships and pave their road.' He also said: 'What a pity we will not be alive for this marvellous time.'

A.L.   *It is good that you are alive for this road now,*
       and not only for Russia.

V.T.   Am I a road? I would rather be a spring of fresh water for people who are tired, and, if it is a difficult road, a spring that will invigorate them. Certainly I hope you and I will be together at the end of the road, and not so anxious about difficult problems any more. At the same time I hope that what we are trying to work out now produces some practicable ideas for advancing human progress. This would mean that our meeting in this world was not just a chance happening. We have heard ours called a destined friendship. That will be true if we can continue as an example of human unity. I hope that we have a mission for peace to achieve together.

Meanwhile, we should be encouraged by the progress already made in human understanding. Now in Russia we are pleased that people can speak freely to each other and can communicate. We also understand other nations better. I am happy that we no longer say that American ways do not suit us and I hope it is the same in America. We are willing to learn from each other now. We believe that Americans have many good experiences to show us and Americans seem to find the same positive experiences in our Russian lives. This is a promising outlook on which to build agreements for a new world order which will achieve environmental balance and harmony.

A.L.   *At the same time many human beings still*
       enjoy divisions and prejudices, believing that
       these reinforce their defences against an un-
       known, hostile world.

V.T.   It is difficult to answer that. First of all, communities of people are needed to protect the history, culture and traditions which have been created by several generations. There may be minor differences but they do unite genuine communities. We should be careful before we cut roots.

A.L.   *I have seen two supra-national social philoso-phies inspiring humanity. The Communist ideal of sharing equally. The capitalist ideal that if you want money you must work for it and then you can share it if you want to. Now you have suggested another powerful human consideration: 'If the world does not live as one family then we must expect the destruction of the world.' Could this be the lodestone to pull the other ideals together? If all are faced with extinction, the rich nations are as much at risk as the poor nations.*

V.T.   Yes, I see it as a strong moral argument and a realistic one to formulate an acceptable set of basic rules for survival, if as a starting point, we prove how urgent this is, and that the dangers facing humanity demand united action. We need to use our brains and hands to work, not only talk and think. We must be active if we are to find agreement as to how best to over-come global dangers.

Progress towards living as a World Family is a necessary objective, but it is complicated. Everyone understands it differ-ently. We will all have our own notion of what is most impor-tant to unite the family. For me it starts with the best for my country, my people and the planet. But for others there are many different attitudes, standards of expectation and behav-iour. That is why scientific and moral leaders should first meet to study and submit proposals and then enlist the co-operation of the majority to agree on what is desirable to uphold right and oppose wrong.

A.L.   I have always resented it as discrimination against women that it is mainly only men who are expected to be influential philosophers and thinkers, and not women. You certainly disprove this.

V.T.   I saw the planet from space; a very rare privilege. My first feeling was, 'How beautiful.' The second feeling was, 'How awful. We would lose everything if were to lose the planet. We must help people not to harm Earth itself.' It is with this in mind that I ask what criteria would be acceptable to all humanity to save the planet? The planet is waiting for urgent action to be taken, but action needs to be thought out.

I believe that the United Nations could bring this discussion into the lives of people all over the world, and also teach the world's children to ask themselves, 'What helps and what hurts the planet?' The next generation is already instinctively interested. It is an important goal for the United Nations to prepare people for the new century by asking questions and providing answers on defence against destruction. There are many such subjects which already unite people everywhere in the world: environmental problems, protection of the seas, cures for disease, control of food production and water supplies to avoid contamination, homes for the homeless and international security for the stateless.

A.L.   I see one major obstacle to prevent immediate shared action. Many people are rightly suspicious of ideals which sound good in theory but are not then put into practice. This has been a century of great deceptions. There is the valid criticism that the West insists on human rights in countries whose policies they oppose but not in countries whose support they need. Britain retains nuclear weapons while insisting on Russia dismantling hers. Some nations in the Western alliance have invaded other countries.

361

Many of us have become suspicious of talk in theory and different action in practice. Self-interest seems stronger than moral responsibility. Would this equally apply to environmental proposals?

V.T.   If what you say is true you speak about double morality. Global morality in human relations means that if we want others to be honest with us we must ourselves be honest with them. Justice and equality are eternal aspirations. Everyone has the right to expect that a better balance between rich and poor must ultimately be attained. The Soviets did a lot of harm practising Leninist ideals in the wrong way; only a few tried to share equally. But civilization has now moved into a different epoch: 'Unite to protect the planet or perish.' The need to choose is urgent, and it will not become a deception if it is based on true human safeguards which are so urgently needed by all mankind.

We have seen that there has been genuine enthusiasm about the end of the cold war with its former political and psychological dangers. But we also see that there is continuing violation of human rights and a frightening situation of division, violence, disintegration and lawlessness for millions of people. This is another reason for individuals to insist on solutions for survival.

That is why I believe we need to start moving urgently towards establishing the rules for global morality. I do not mean that we should worship the same icons, but to realize that we are one family, suffering the same dramas and enjoying the same joys. The first drama for us all is the possible destruction of our global home. We need to start the process of elaborating and developing a new spiritual code to prevent this. We cannot postpone this under the pretext that there are more important or more immediate problems: starvation, ethnic wars, underdevelopment. Historical experience demonstrates that if we cannot develop spiritual strength and moral responsibility we will not have the strength to confront global dangers. The reality of our common home in the next century depends on the reality of its inhabitants today. That is why I hope for the realization of global morality which all can support and share.

A.L.   *I respect your call for more spiritual strength to choose right and not wrong in ecological matters. But human beings are material as well as spiritual and they are attracted by ideals of material security for everyone. What do you see as the material minimum humans need. Four walls for shelter – locally grown food – medical care?*

V.T.   I do not think it is possible to assess or impose minimums. People must build these for themselves. No organization can provide the whole world with minimum levels. People of the world must earn these. Sometimes people need special help, and through the organizations I worked for, I was happy to help people to work, and work better, to achieve something for themselves. But for example, how can we measure a minimum for the great artists who created the masterpieces of music, of painting, of architecture?

My deep conviction is that moral riches and material riches are different and should be seen in this way. I am thinking of the centuries of the Italian Renaissance and the great masters. These painters were not rich. The same is true of other great artists. They created invaluable treasures for humanity but they were not rich materially. A number of them died in poverty and misery. What was it that inspired them to create all these riches? Take the example of the Russian icon painter, Andrei Rublev. He worked in the fifteenth century, a difficult period of Russian history. He was very poor. What gave him strength to continue his work, to paint icons and to decorate churches? When he painted he did not draw his inspiration from material sources. Of course it is important to have sufficient food, clothes and a roof. But human strength and satisfaction also comes from the beauty of nature and from the best talents of man which have been the source of inward inspiration for every artist. There are too many materialistic aspirations now. Humanity needs to find the right balance again and value spiritual achievements as they deserve to be valued.

A.L.   *I see morality as behaviour. Spirituality for me*
       is in a different dimension. It cannot be re-
       stricted to moral rules. It is something like
       music — fulfilling a very great component inside
       us which otherwise remains empty. It also al-
       lows some of us to hope that there is eternal life
       after we die. This brings in an important added
       perspective of human equality.

V.T.   People do not die. Life continues in the good deeds one did before death and we go on living in the memory and deeds of our children. After death, people leave this world physically but they go on living in what they have left behind.

To have lost my mother means I suffer enormously. I would walk the whole world just to see her again, at least once. But I realize that is impossible, so she remains to me my moral criterion; the star which gives me light. And perhaps this is more important than staying alive. I have a great respect for religious people. If their belief helps them in their lives to be more moral and more pure then they are right. When people go to church, when they are praying, they are being guided by something good inside themselves. This also is part of global morality. I also agree that people want to believe in eternity, but can anyone prove it is true?

A.L.   *I see faith as believing in what we can neither*
       prove nor disprove, but I realise that for many
       that answer is too uncertain.

V.T.   I still maintain that global morality and spirituality are interconnected, since behaviour is controlled by consciousness, which is spiritual. When people are spiritually rich they are unlikely to harm others. They have an inner threshold of spiritual awareness which results in moral behaviour. This is the spirituality I believe in. The questions we are discussing now, which we have talked about since our very first meeting, are complex. We know that we cannot find easy solutions, but at least we agree and continue to maintain that the spiritual element in human life deserves deep respect.

A.L.   *On the dangerously negative side there is the*
       constant abuse of genuine morality by hypoc-
       risy.

V.T.   That is why global morality should expect integrity in political leaders. However, political integrity is only one aspect of the multifaceted problem of hypocrisy.

Certainly to achieve a better human life there are still more questions than answers. We have to think about this. Insisting on integrity is a challenge for all humanity.

A.L.   *Certainly you have extraordinary integrity.*

V.T.   It can be a source of suffering. I suffer because of this. For example I value respect for facts in community life as well as in science, and I value order.

It would lead to disaster if we had no order in our cosmonautic work. The minutest imprecision, the tiniest neglect or disregard for proper and necessary order, the smallest violation of essential regulations, would lead to catastrophe. The regulations are dictated by the inherent laws of science, indeed by life itself.

As I see it, order is also necessary in earthly life, dictated by human necessity. But it must be combined with freedom, and respect for the life of others. A main principle for the new global morality should be to establish order which helps all people to live equally well, always set against the background of avoiding global destruction.

A.L. *I see a major advance towards global morality
in that among so many people now there is an
acceptance of the need to respect each other's
spiritual beliefs so that the Creator can be
worshipped in love and peace instead of divisive religious enmity. This respect should be
developed by all religions instead of the political fundamentalism which is not real religion.*

V.T. We have agreed that it is in the unprejudiced exchange
of individual beliefs and religions and in the context of planetary survival that shared global morality will develop. If it
does, the planet will be saved for the new century. At the same
time we need to encourage experts to study and give ordinary
people truly objective information on scientific subjects such as
economics and health. Any exchange of opinions needs to be
based on facts. That is the cosmonauts' perspective.

We also need common sense so as to agree that to ensure
survival in the twenty-first century, people must come together
and support rules of behaviour which are ecologically sound,
because otherwise space catastrophe will overtake humanity.
This is what I mean by the urgent need for new thinking and
behaviour based on agreed essential moral principles which can
protect planet and people.

Those of us who have worked for peace hope that it is
possible in this last decade of the century for humanity to use
scientific progress to increase freedom and prosperity for individuals and nations. The fearful tragedy could be that there are
still so many divisions, so many rivalries, so much killing
among nations that we will not achieve this aim. We need to
strive more than ever to raise awareness of the dangers faced
by all mankind as a whole if the world perseveres in the paths of
war.

A.L. *New century children want to survive and they
deserve to survive.*

Global morality

V.T.   Shared global morality could build bridges of education among all children, and teach them to ask themselves what will help and what will harm the planet. Taking guidance from the basic principles of global morality, together they could open up a golden road for the future equipped with advances of science, the best traditions of human civilization, culture and spirituality. We must not fail the children. The children will follow us on the golden road if the objectives are sincere, simple, necessary and reasonable.

As the Conversations ended there was a long silence. Valentina had answered my questions on three levels: as a very private person, as an expert in cosmonautics, and as a philosopher for today and tomorrow. It seemed necessary to give time and thought to what had been said.

Throughout our Conversations my opinion of Valentina as an outstanding leader for human unity had been confirmed. Her answers had reflected her wisdom and integrity as well as the capacity for love in a woman who values being a woman, and who delights in the art, literature, music and treasures not only of her own land, but also of the world.

That is why her views on the great events of the past as she has experienced them, and of the future as she assesses them, are increasingly important not only to promote progress for the human species but also for the continued existence of planet Earth.

As she spoke, Valentina never failed to maintain the self-discipline and ordered thinking which had enabled her to become one of the first human beings to pioneer space exploration. She was only disturbed if she sensed any attempt to alter facts. She wanted to give a completely honest, practicable assessment of the positive measures needed for planet and for people to survive. Valentina was always true to herself.

Moscow 1992

Epilogue

The New Century — What Next?

This is the thirtieth anniversary of Valentina Tereshkova's flight into space and it is ten years since she and I first began a West-East journey travelling from misunderstanding to understanding and away from nuclear war.

In the time span 1983-1993 prospects for peace have changed beyond recognition with the turning inside-out of Soviet, European, American and Japanese power. Change was certainly needed. Not only had Communism developed practices resulting in corruption and suppression, not only had capitalism developed a First World of unequal wealth often promoting irresponsible commercial expansion through deceptive advertising, not only had the needs of the Third World remained largely disregarded, but scientific invention had provided two opposing superpowers with atomic armaments which could destroy every man, woman and child on Earth several times over.

Now in 1993 the new century is fast approaching with increasing dangers for mankind, and as I see it the space explorers' call for international action to protect the planet is the best hope for global ecological survival.

In the early eighties I heard three world leaders warning that the end of the world was not only possible, it could be imminent, and with it the extinction of our human species and the planet which is our home in the Universe. I heard Margaret Gowing, Professor of the History of Science at Oxford University and an expert on atomic power and weapons, appealing for the Earth to be preserved from a nuclear holocaust. At the same time I heard Barbara Ward, foremost economist and environmentalist, predict the destruction of 'Spaceship Earth' if mankind did not unite to save it. She ended her appeal with five prophetic words: 'We either love or die.' Then I heard Valentina Tereshkova, Soviet cosmonaut and first woman in space, giving a similar warning in London. 'Unless it is prevented the merciless fire of nuclear war will not spare a single nation or a single continent. Our planet is big enough for us to live in peace on it but it is far too small to be exposed to nuclear menace.'

From West and East these thinkers had crossed a deep and dangerous political divide with the same message: mankind must either find a way forward to understanding and co-operation or take the consequences of atomic annihilation. It was a serious challenge.

When Valentina and I met and became friends, some called it destiny. I believe that if our friendship was destined it was because it proved that two patriots who worked first and foremost for their own homeland could at the same time work for what was best and safest for the world. Valentina and I did overcome apparently invincible barriers of prejudice to exchange different and sincerely-held points of view, but it was made possible because we trusted each other to support measures which would advance peace.

We also knew that our journey from misunderstanding to understanding reflected the hopes and fears of a vast number of people throughout the world who did not want war. There were some who were sceptical but the present transformation in East-West relations proves that seeking co-operation was justified.

Many factors contributed to the new international understanding, but the major cause was undoubtedly the resolve of Soviet people in the East and of democratic people in the West to travel on a new road towards peace. I believe that history will confirm one fact when the political and moral developments which first created and then healed superpower hostility are analysed: the opposing forces which seemed immovable from 1917 to 1987 only collapsed because the Soviet people undertook first the new openness of glasnost, followed by perestroika with its philosophy of reconstructed Communism and then democratic reform. After that, having heard of the Soviet peoples' revolution, in all the nations of the world ordinary people were inspired to find freedom. Even if those who hoped to achieve lasting peace had started on a long road inevitably obstructed by human weakness as Valentina and I found on our journey, the objective remains worthwhile.

Valentina is optimistic about the new century. Her belief in the genius of the people of Russia remains undiminished, and she also has confidence in the United Nations as the most powerful force for international safety.

Her vision is of one world family, made up of independent homelands and cultures together protecting each other and the small fragile globe she saw from space. She believes that the planet can be saved through this new 'global morality'.

Valentina also believes that space offers an ocean of opportunity for mankind in the future. Speaking on space programmes to the Faculty of Engineering at the University of Valencia in 1991 she advised: 'Man's presence in space is the logical extension of his earthly presence and an irreversible historical process. Space opens up limitless possibilities for the scientific, economic, ecological questions of energy and resources. Space can save mankind by uniting all countries on one aim – peaceful collaboration.' This is Valentina's dream and I share it.

However, in the last years of the twentieth century, the absence of Soviet superpower has left a void which has not yet been filled in a way which strengthens international stability. There is disagreement among philosophers and disarmament experts on whether planet and people will survive in the future. From the USA Francis Fukuyama is hopeful. His faith is that human fulfilment can be provided by American home-town sufficiency and basic liberal democratic ideals. For him the new century is about the happy, satisfied 'last man' and 'the end of history'. But in Europe, Pierre Leluche and William Rees-Mogg warn against the spread of nuclear and chemical weapons. They foresee North-South confrontations following the removal of the former world balance of power established at Yalta in 1945 by Stalin, Roosevelt and Churchill. They also fear ecological disasters.

The last man and the end of history? Dangerous world disorder? Or is the solution to be found by following the space explorers' advice to the global family?

One more century – one more try? The French call it '*le malaise du fin du siècle*' when a century draws near to its end and society is full of fear.

I often sit by the sea and I observe how storms alter the beach, with only a few rocks standing firm. In the context of human survival the previously familiar international seascape has become almost unrecognisable except for some reassuring unchanging rocks. In the next century, which of these will stand strong enough to protect the planet from being destroyed and humanity with it? I believe the frontierless sharing of 'one world – one family' ideals will still provide the only reliable safeguard.

Like a seagull in a stormy sea the friendship between Valentina and myself transcended many weather changes because it was upheld by our shared anxiety to avoid atomic war. In his novel *1984* George Orwell foretold that this was the year which would bring the culmination of Communist brainwashing. It was actually the year when the Soviet people supported a breakthrough which resolved East-West confrontation.

It was at this time that I found everything that was best in the USSR exemplified by Valentina Tereshkova and her fellow cosmonauts. Until then, for me, there had been a black wall of fear about Soviet policies and intentions. My friendship with Valentina provided the light for me to see the other side. It is essential for the human family to see the other side.

In the chronicle of the journey Valentina and I shared, I have given my personal impressions as seen from the West of the momentous events which happened during the ten years which have been described as having changed the world.

In the *Conversations* Valentina gives her view from the East not only about the past, but also about the future.

Obviously hers is the most important section of the book and after readers have heard what Valentina has to say I hope they will want to know more about an unprecedented decade in human history and about an unprecedented human achiever. But above all I hope that none of us will take lightly the advice on what is most necessary for global survival as it is given by the first woman in space.

A. Lothian, New Year 1993.

Appendices

Appendices

1. Speech given at the Women of the Year Lunch in London, Monday 20th October 1980, by Professor Margaret Gowing, CBE, FBA, FRS, Professor of the History of Science, Oxford University.

2. Guests of Honour attending the Women of the Year Lunch October 1984. Royal Guest of Honour – H.R.H. The Duchess of Kent. International Guest of Honour – Valentina Tereshkova.

3. World Congress of Women, Moscow, June 1987. Report to the Women of the Year Association by their representative A. Lothian.

4. The Blue Planet. This photograph was presented by the Astronaut Corps to Valentina Tereshkova. It was published in Soviet Woman Magazine No. 7, July 1988, to mark the occasion of the twenty-fifth anniversary of the flight of the first woman in space.

5. CSCE Conference in Moscow, January 1990, on the human dimension of the European process and the role of the public. International delegates attending.

6. 'The Yaroslavl Factory Girl.' Poem written in honour of Valentina Tereshkova in June 1963.

Appendix 1

Speech given at the Women of the Year Lunch in London,
Monday 20th October 1980,
By Professor Margaret Gowing, CBE., FBA., FRS.,
Professor of the History of Science, Oxford University

Science in the last 25 years – I suppose if non-scientists ask:
'What difference has it made in our everyday lives?' the answer,
surprisingly, must be not all that much. We have had a wide
diffusion of inventions made earlier, and, more recently, small
cumulative advances, but few completely new revolutionary
science-based inventions. The pill, yes and the laser. But what
else? 1980 is very like 1955 although – to go back in 25 year
leaps – 1955 was vastly different from 1930 and 1930 even
more different from 1905. However, now microchips, and
biotechnology, herald a new era of dramatic change.

Let us lift our eyes from everyday life to the heavens – as
men and women have done ever since they walked on two legs
instead of four. The stars and heavens have been their source of
wonder, their fount of religions, philosophic, scientific and
mathematical speculation and also their means of navigation by
land and sea. In the last 25 years the heavens have been the
most exciting realm of science. Scientific theory and experiment, aided by extraordinary science-based technology, have
found a distant universe inconceivably vaster than we supposed
and have told us how and when it probably began, and what it
is made of. Nearer home in the solar system man has acquired a
new dimension – space – has travelled in it and made direct
contact not only with the Moon but with some of the planets –
something unimaginable 25 years ago except in science fiction.
This, too, heralds revolutionary change and as astronomers
observe light that began its journey towards us millions of years
ago, so the very concepts of time – carving it up into the past,
the present and the future – seem meaningless.

So back to earth. Television pictures of astronauts circling the globe succeeded – where generations of cosmologists had failed – in convincing the layman that the Earth is but a small planet, finite and vulnerable. But space exploration has also shown the Earth to be infinitely precious and unique in the solar system, teeming with life among the wastelands of its neighbours. The supreme challenge for the next 25 years and beyond is to keep the Earth uniquely living, to preserve it from a holocaust which would leave much, most, all of it – who knows? – as desolate as it was thousands or millions of years ago. The threat is the arms race and it is science-based.

Nuclear physics – one of the finest fruits of the human intellect – had led to the atomic bombs which ended the Second World War. For a brief decade these primitive bombs, carried in aeroplanes, did preserve a balance of terror. But then came terrifying escalation: hydrogen bombs with no theoretical limits to their size: missiles, chemical and biological weapons. The sublime atomic irony of which Churchill spoke, with survival as the twin brother of annihilation, was true no longer. Ever since, any brief balance of equilibrium of arms has been swiftly upset by the inventiveness of scientists and technologists, futile for security when existing weapons could destroy every man, woman and child on earth several times over. Yet defence claims a large proportion of research and development in many countries, and in this inventive fever the multilateral arms control, let alone disarmament, that we need so desperately can scarcely begin. The scientists have a leading role in arms control alongside the politicians, the military and, increasingly we hope, public opinion. They have been pioneers, but should they go further? Scientists in every country have their powerful established institutions, close to governments and in communication with each other.

Proud of their internationalism, can they take a major rather than a minor lead in urging mutual restraint on ever more scientific development of weaponry? This restraint of science is more important than any conceivable advance of science in the next 25 years. Science could take the lead in mankind's race to survive.

GOWING, Prof. Margaret Mary, CBE 1981; FRS 1988; FBA 1975; FRHistS; Professor of the History of Science, University of Oxford, and Fellow of Linacre College, 1973-86: *b* 26 April 1921: *d* of Ronald and Mabel Elliott; *m* 1944, Donald J. G. Gowing (*d* 1969): two *s*. *Educ*: Christ's Hospital; London Sch. of Economics (BSc(Econ); Hon. Fellow, 1988). Bd of Trade, 1941-45; Historical Section, Cabinet Office, 1945-59; Historian and Archivist, UK Atomic Energy Authority, 1959-66; Reader in Contemporary History, Univ. of Kent, 1966-72. Member: Cttee on Deptl Records (Grigg Cttee), 1952-54; Adv. Council on Public Records, 1974-82; BBC Archives Adv. Cttee, 1976-79; Public Records Inquiry (Wilson Cttee), 1978-80; Trustee: Nat. Portrait Gall. 1978-92; Imperial War Mus., 1986-87. Hon. Dir. Contemporary Scientific Archives Centre, 1973-86. Foundation Mem., Academia Europaea, 1988. Royal Society Wilkins Lectr, 1976; Enid Muir Lectr, Newcastle, 1976; Bernal Lectr, Birkbeck, 1977; Rede Lectr, Cambridge, 1978; Herbert Spencer Lectr, Oxford, 1982; CEGB Lectr, Southampton, 1987. Hon. DLitt: Leeds, 1976; Leicester, 1982; Hon. DSc: Manchester, 1985; Bath, 1987. *Publications:* (with Sir K. Hancock) British War Economy, 1949: (with E. L. Hargreaves). Civil Industry and Trade, 1952; Britain and Atomic Energy, 1964; Dossier Secret des Relations Atomiques, 1965; Independence and Deterrence: vol. 1. Policy Making, vol. ii. Policy Execution, 1974; Reflections on Atomic Energy History, 1978; (with Lorna Arnold) The Atomic Bomb, 1979; various articles and reviews. *Address:* Linacre College, Oxford.

Appendix 2

WOMEN OF THE YEAR LUNCHEON 1984

Founder President: The Marchioness of Lothian
Founder Vice Presidents: Lady Georgina Coleridge, Mrs. Odette Hallowes, G.C., M.B.E.,
Legion d'Honneur
Vice-Presidents: The Countess of Airlie, Mrs Edna Healey, Miss Virginia Wade, M.B.E.
Luncheon Committee Chairman: Miss Anne Dickinson
Organiser: Mrs Joanna Forrester
Assistant Organiser: Miss Jennifer Buhaenko
Presiding: The Marchioness of Lothian

The Theme:
"HOW TO BE FIRST"

THE SPEAKERS

Madame Valentina Tereshkova, *Chairman USSR Women's Council*
The Right Honourable The Lord Mayor of London, Dame Mary Donaldson, D.B.E.
Ms. Brenda Dean, *President – General Secretary-Elect SOGAT*
Lady Antonia Fraser, F.R.S., *Author*

THE GUESTS OF HONOUR

(at the time of going to print)
IN THE PRESENCE OF H.R.H. THE DUCHESS OF KENT

Mrs Jennifer Adams, F.I.L.A.M. Dip.P.R.A.,
Superintendant of Royal Parks
Ms. Margaret Alexander, *Social Editor, The Times*
Ms. Joan Armatrading, *Singer, Song-writer*
Mrs. Anne Ballard, M.A., *National Federation of Women's Institutes*
Dr. Ann Barrett, M.D., F.R.C.R., *Consultant Radiotherapist*
Miss J.A. Beak, *Royal College of Midwives*
Dr. Tessa Bleckstone, B. Sc., Ph.D., *Deputy Education Officer/ILEA Resources*
Mrs. Lynda Chalker, *Minister of State for Transport*

Ms. Caroline Charles, *Dress Designer*
Miss Heather Couper, B.Sc (Hons),
President-Elect of British Astronomical Association
Dr. Anita Davies, M.R.C.P., F.F., *Hom., Physician*
Miss Anne Diamond. *TV-AM Presenter*
Dr. Elizabeth Evans, B.S.C., Ph.D., *Research Fellow in Nutrition*
Mrs. Anne Gibson, Dip. Arch. R.I.B.A.,
Architect
Professor Margaret Gowing. C.B.E., F.B.A.,
D.Litt., *Professor of History of Science, Oxford University*

378

Appendices

Mrs. Tricia Guild, *Interior Designer*
Miss Audrey Head, *Chairman, Unit Trust Association*
Miss Virginia Holgate, *Horse-rider, Olympic Medallist*
Mrs Jennifer Jenkins, M.A., Hon F.R.I.B.A., Hon R.I.C.S., *Chairman, Historic Buildings Advisory Committee*
Ms. Marle Jennings, *Director, Public Relations Consultants Association*
Miss Joy Kinsley, *Governor, Holloway Prison*
Miss Maureen Laker, *Social Editor/Daily Telegraph*
Ms. Prue Leith, *Restaurateur, Journalist*
Dr. Oonagh McDonald, M.P., Ph. D., *Opposition Front Bench Spokesman on Treasury and Economic Affairs*
Ms. Beatrix Miller, *Editor in Chief, Vogue*
Mrs. Francis Morrell, *Leader, I.L.E.A.*
Ms. Debbie Moore, *Business Woman of the Year, 1984*
Ms. Anne Mueller, *Deputy Secretary, Department of Trade and Industry*

Ms. Molly Parkin, *Writer, Performer*
Her Excellency Madame Popova
Ms. Laurie Purden, M.B.E., *Editor, Woman's Journal*
Miss Bridget Riley, *D. Lit., C.B.E., Artist*
Ms. Deborah Rix, *Presenter, BBC TV*
Ms. Joan Ruddock, B.S.C., A.R.C.S., *Chairperson, CND*
Miss Tessa Sanderson, *Olympic Gold Medallist*
Miss Monica Sims, O.B.E., M.A., L.R.A.M., *Director of Programmes, BBC Radio 4*
Siouxsie, *Singer*
Mrs. Barbara Switzer, *Deputy General Secretary, AUEW-TASS*
Mrs. Jean Viall, *President National Council of Women*
Ms. Julie Walters, *Actress*
Colonel Violet Williams, *Salvation Army Officer*
Mrs. Andrea Wonfor, B.A., *Director of Programmes, Tyne Tees TV*
Ms. E. C. Zolina, *Interpreter*

Appendix 3

World Congress of Women, Moscow, June 1987
Report to the Women of the Year Association
by their representative A. Lothian

Representing the Association, I attended the Moscow World Congress of Women as an official delegate from June 21st to June 29th. It impressed me as a triumph of generous hospitality and genuine international friendship with a welcome from the USSR Women's Committee. The organisation was of the highest standard, resulting in constructive free discussion of shared problems by women from all over the world, resulting in identifying solutions – above all for peace – but also to narrow the vast division between developed and under-developed nations.

We saw new towns – art exhibitions – architectural achievements – sports stadiums – and schools.

Everywhere Gorbachev's call to peace was expressed particularly in the education of young children.

For me the greatest glory of the USSR is the children – happy – healthy – self confident – appealing for peace. This was particularly evident at the closing concert where children from all over Russia danced and sang almost as well as the Bolshoi.

In her opening speech Freda Brown from Australia, the Vice- President of the Congress, identified genetic engineering among the many problems which worry women. The Soviet Women's Committee leader Zoya Pukhova stated that 150 countries were represented at the Congress and 100 international organisations.

The work of the Congress was divided up into 9 commissions and 3 centres. The commissions inquired into – 1. Women and problems of development – 2. Women and national liberation, independence and self-determination – 3. Women and mass media. – 4. Women, children and the family

– 5. Women in society – 6. Implementing the long-term strategies approved in Nairobi for improving the status of women – 7. Women for peace and disarmament – 8. Women and the Trade Union movement – 9. The problems of young women and violation of women's rights.

Three centres enquired into – 1. Environment protection – 2. The influence of new technologies – 3. Religious women and the struggle for peace.

Also available were meetings to express solidarity with women from Southern Africa, the Middle East, Central and Latin America and also Soviet-American dialogue.

I heard particularly relevant statements made by delegates from Ireland, Chile, Senegal, Finland, West Germany, Ghana and USSR.

In the workshops the best use of scientific advance was scrutinised. As one delegate stated – "Freedom means having the right to prohibit what hurts humanity". Drug dependency, including alcohol poisoning was carefully considered. Other subjects of particular concern: pollution – irrigation – assistance for women at work – opportunities for developed countries to aid under-developed countries – problems of women working at home – and disarmament.

Throughout the week I remembered Valentina Tereshkova's words in London 1984 to Britain's Women of the Year:

Unless it is prevented, the merciless fire of nuclear war will not spare a single nation or a single continent. Our planet is big enough for us to live in peace on it, but it is far too small to be exposed to nuclear menace.

The Congress certainly did not need convincing.

Appendix 4

THE BLUE PLANET

Inscription

To Valentina Tereshkova
with admiration
and warm personal best wishes
From the Astronaut Corps

This picture was published in Soviet Woman Magazine No. 7, July 1988

Appendix 5

CSCE Conference in Moscow, January 1990,
The Human Dimension of the European Process
and the role of the public.
International delegates attending,
taken from the conference list

Austria	H. Erlinger – "Grune Alternative", Parlament – Gruner Klub
Bulgaria	D. Filippov – All-nation Bulgarian-Soviet Friendship Society
Belgium	H. Hoornaert – Parti socialiste (secteur jeunesse), Secretaire General
DDR	S. Dernberg – Praesident des Komitees fuer europaeische Sicherheit und Zusammenarbeit in der DDR
Ireland	M. Brown – writer
Great Britain	M. C. Harper – UN Association – U.K. Director
	A. Lothian – National Council of Women, Patron
	G. Radice – House of Commons, MP
	J. Morgan – Standing Conference of Local and Regional Authorities of Europe, President
Denmark	E. Hunderwadt – Danish UN Association, Secretary General
	G.V. Jensen – Danish Center (CSLEa), pastor
	O. Richter – Steering Committee of CSLE parallel Activities, Coordinator
Italia	C.B. Tarantelli – Parlamento italiano, deputato

	G.E. Viola – Societe Europeenne de Culture, Secretario General
Canada	P.Roberts – ex-Ambassador of Canada in the USSR
	B.Wood – Canadian Institute for International Peace and Security, Director
Czechoslovakia	L. Shmid – Czechoslovakian Society for Foreign Relations
Norway	A. Eide – Norwegian Institute of Human Rights, Director
Poland	W. Loranc – TPRP (PR). Czlonec Prezydium ZG
	J. Symonides – UNESCO, Director of the Division of Human Rights and Peace
Romania	F. Ichim – *Romania libera* newspaper
	G. Vasilescu – CLSFRJ, Member of Central Leadership
USA	M. Mendelsohn – Dilworth Paxon Kalisht Kauffman, Attorney
	R. Neuheisel – Sister Cities International, President
	P. Shifter – Deputy Secretary of State
	W. Smith – "Friendship Force", President
	H. Mars – TC of Atlanta, President
	S. Eisenhouwer – International Fund "Survive and development", member of Council
France	D. Mitterand – "France-Liberte", Presidente
	R. Doueb – "France-Liberte", Secretaire General
	T. Collar – "France-Liberte", Secretaire
	M. Lesage – Institute des Recherches Comparatives, Professeur
	C. Latil – France – URSS, President delegue adjoint
	J. Battut – France-URSS, membere de la Presidence nationale

	N. Nogueres – France-URSS, membere de la Presidence nationale
BRD	W. Torsten - Bundestagsfraktion der F.D.P. Parlamentarischer Geschaeftsfuehrer
	G. Haemmerle – Bundestag, Mitglid des Bundestages
	O. Hahn – Minister, bevollmaechtigter Vertreter der Regierung Saarlandes in Bonn
	G. Schumacher – SDP, Leiter der staendigen Vertretung der F. Ebert – Stiftung in Moskau
Finland	R. Klaerich – Rotary International, Past President
	H. Olander – Finland-USSR Society, Vice-chairman
	M. Touminen
Switzerland	P. Jolles – Former State Secretary for Economic Affairs, now Chairman, Nestle SA
Sweden	D. Magnusson – Royal Acad. of Science, Academia Europea, member of exec. – committee, Vice-president
	B. Getberg – "Sweden-USSR" Society, President
United Nations	T. Zoupanos – Centre for Human Rights, Director

Appendix 6

'The Yaroslavl Factory Girl'
Poem Written in Honour of Valentina Tereshkova
in June 1963

The morning clouds sail across the Volga
And a seagull circles in the sky,
A Yaroslavl girl stood here for a while
And waved to the seagull.

She wandered along the banks of the Volga
A lock of hair falling on her clear brow —
This Yaroslavl factory girl
From 'Red Perekop'.

She has flown far into the Cosmos
And raced around this Earth
Her countrymen waved to her
Fondly called 'Seagull'.

She sings of her journey
By the distant star-strewn banks
This Yaroslavl factory girl
From 'Red Perekop'.

The sky illumines Earth's beauty
Bathed with light and warmth
Moscow presented her with all its flowers
And spoke in words of love.

Once more she wanders the banks of the Volga
A lock of hair falling on her clear brow —
This Yaroslavl factory girl
From 'Red Perekop'.

M. Lisyansky

Index

Index

388

Index

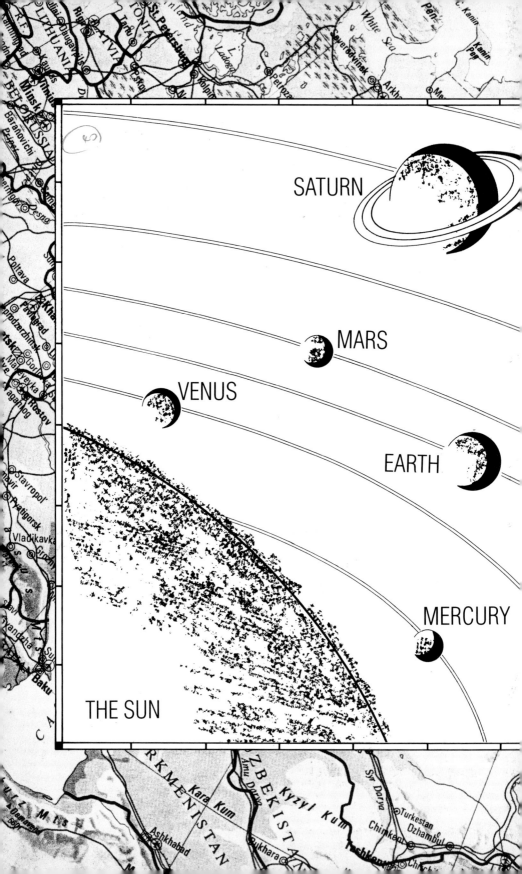

SATURN

MARS

VENUS

EARTH

MERCURY

THE SUN